The Modern Horseman's
Countdown to Broke

The Modern Horseman's Countdown to Broke

Real Do-It-Yourself Horse Training
in 33 Comprehensive Steps

Sean Patrick

Foreword by Dr. Robert M. Miller
Photographs by Charles Hilton

TRAFALGAR
SQUARE

First published in 2009 by
Trafalgar Square Books
North Pomfret, Vermont 05053

New edition published in 2022

Disclaimer of Liability
The author and publisher shall have neither liability nor responsibility to any person or entity with
respect to any loss or damage caused or alleged to be caused directly or indirectly by the information contained
in this book. While the book is as accurate as the author can make it, there may be errors, omissions, and
inaccuracies.

Trafalgar Square Books encourages the use of approved safety helmets in all equestrian sports and activities.

Library of Congress Cataloging-in-Publication Data

Patrick, Sean, 1973-
  The modern horseman's countdown to broke : real do-it-yourself horse training in 33 comprehensive steps /
Sean Patrick.
      p. cm.
  Includes index.
  ISBN 978-1-64601-168-1
  1. Horses--Training. I. Title. II. Title: Real do-it-yourself horse training
in 33 comprehensive steps.
  SF287.P38 2009
  636.1'0835--dc22
          2009002359

Photographs by Charles Hilton
Book design by Carrie Fradkin
Cover design by RM Didier
Typefaces: Century Expanded, Avenir
Printed in China
10 9 8 7 6 5 4 3 2 1

For Madilyn

Contents

PART TWO: THE COUNTDOWN 27

Foreword

IN 1987 I RETIRED FROM PRACTICING veterinary medicine—I had done so for 31 years and in that time my experiences with people and animals had run the gamut, from heart-warming to heart-breaking. But I had a new calling that I was determined to devote my hours to: what I have termed the "revolution" in horsemanship that began in the late twentieth century and is now a worldwide phenomenon.

"Natural horsemanship" and its premise that horses can be trained *without* the use of force—thus breaking free of age-old traditions that at best lacked empathy and were at worst brutal—grew increasingly popular beginning in the 1970s. Now the techniques of the great horsemen responsible for the early proliferation of "think like a horse" philosophy are widely recognized, and many—if not most—of today's horse owners use bits and pieces of their methods in all of their daily riding and horse handling practices. In fact, natural horsemanship has come to define the "Modern Horseman."

Well, now a real Modern Horseman and student of the first generation of clinicians espousing natural horsemanship techniques has written *the most* comprehensive how-to training manual I've seen for today's horse-owning public. Sean Patrick's intent is to provide the reader practical instruction in preparing *any* horse for a successful career—whatever the discipline—and to do so in ways that best serve the horse and his physical and emotional stability. Central to his work is the careful balance of being both a leader and a trusted friend to one's horse, and his sensible, progressive exercises are certain to build the horse's confidence, physical strength, and common understanding of what's expected of him.

Truth be told, I have *never seen* a book this meticulous in providing step-by-step instruction. Sean is incredibly specific in his descriptions—he doesn't say "Practice this move a bunch of times," he says, "Practice this move 32 times." He doesn't write, "Hold the reins above the mane," he writes, "Hold the reins 2 inches above the mane." This is of indescribable benefit to the average horse owner who may be training his own horse. In fact, I highly recommend that readers take this book to the round pen or arena with them—or better yet, photocopy each lesson and tack it up on the arena fence where they can ride over and take a look during rest breaks. They may not get beyond a paragraph or two during a training session, but having Sean's guidance on-hand will be invaluable.

Sean is so sure in his writing and specific in his lessons, I worried some that he believes that there is only one way to train a horse—a kind of "my way or the highway" mentality. However, I was reassured to find that he actively encourages his readers to be open-minded. "There are many styles and methods of horsemanship that work," he writes. "Each variation can teach you something new and is worth investigating. Be open to new ideas and different disciplines, and try to see how their 'style' can help you with yours."

You'll find that Sean writes in an interesting manner. The book is a fascinating conglomeration of rather technical scientific terminology, classical riding vocabulary, and cowboy slang. It is unusual—and for today's horse-loving audience accustomed to masses of information gleaned from radically different sources, including television and the Internet—entirely appropriate.

You can't go wrong with this training program. It's a top-down, all-inclusive trip to the ultimate working, performance, or pleasure ride. All the while nurturing a promising horse-human relationship through the use of appropriate pressures and reinforcements, light hands, and a fundamental desire to stand beside or sit upon your horse in a state of mutual equilibrium, respect, and understanding. If you follow the Countdown as it is laid out, and do exactly as Sean recommends, you cannot mess this up—you are going to end up with a sane, well-trained horse.

The forefathers of the revolution in horsemanship would be proud to call Sean one of their own.

Dr. Robert M. Miller
Father of Imprint Training
Author of *Imprint Training of the Newborn Foal;*
A Revolution in Horsemanship (with Rick Lamb); and *Natural Horsemanship Explained*

Introduction

IN THIS BOOK, I have put together a complete "beginning to end" training program. The lesson objectives are clear and the steps easy to follow. I look to eliminate the guesswork from training a horse. This book counts down the steps it takes to get your horse "broke." I use the term "broke" to mean one that has perfect respect, perfect trust, and an endless skill set; a lofty goal that you should always work toward.

This is a true *foundation program;* it is ideal for any horse. In a natural sequence you can take either a range colt, backyard pet, or performance prospect through these steps and give him the start that he deserves. This program isn't about being fast or slow, hard or soft, it's about the horse and what's best for him.

Each lesson presented explains *what* the goal is, *why* it is important, and *how* to teach it. I hear the case that "every horse is different" and that no one plan can suit all of them. This idea is only half accurate. It is true that your pressure levels (you can read about my use of "pressure" in training on p. 17) may have to vary from horse to horse, and that each one will test you in ways you never imagined, but your objectives remain exactly the same: gain respect, build trust, and develop a skill set. This is not a "cookie cutter" program by any means—in fact, by understanding the objectives and steps, you will be able to complete each one in a variety of ways. Since I like to be told exactly how to do something when I am first learning, so I have written this book to you. I will give you clear instruction in order for you to concentrate on your horse and his progress.

Modern horsemanship is a result of lessons learned throughout history, with the distinct advantage of information-sharing. I have had the benefit of personal instruction, books, articles, videos, Internet communication, clinics, and formal schooling. I am also able to draw from various fields of study ranging from agricultural sciences to equine psychology. Horsemanship still requires large amounts of time on the horse, but you no longer have to limit your learning to the saddle.

Through a deeper understanding of how horses learn, what their natural instincts are, and how to keep them

healthier, the Modern Horseman is able to be more effective. I emphasize the *fair* application of pressure and small progressive learning steps. As you find success through these lessons, you will learn how to gauge pressure and pace your teaching.

The Countdown to Broke will guide you on your path to training a respectful, trusting, safe mount that has all the necessary skills to perform. You are checking off and zeroing in on getting him "broke." You will have much reason to celebrate at the conclusion of the Countdown as you can then combine all of the skills taught and reach an even higher level of horsemanship and performance.

You will transform as a horseman. Your ability to recognize behaviors—good and bad—will improve. You will understand the root of the issue and know how to work on it. You don't have to "forget everything you know," but be ready to see your horse in a new light. As you work through this program you will be amazed at how efficient and effective these lessons are.

Part One
Getting Started

Where Do You Begin?

Evaluating Your Horse

Prior to embarking on this journey with your horse it is helpful to evaluate what your starting point is. If you objectively assess what both you and your horse's capabilities are at the present time, you can then easily gauge your successes as you progress through this training program.

I look at three things when evaluating a horse: respect for the handler, overall confidence, and skill level. When you work with a horse that has limited handling and is just being started, he will score low on all three of these attributes. If your horse has had ground and/or saddle training, you will be in a better position to determine what areas need work.

I believe that every horse, regardless of attributes, has room for improvement. My training program, the Countdown to Broke®, is not only ideal for the young horse but will greatly improve one with more experience, too. Regardless of the discipline that you ultimately intend your horse to pursue, he will be much more enjoyable when he is respectful, confident, and skillful.

If you are new to this style of horsemanship, I recommend first working through the 33 lessons in the Countdown with a horse that you are comfortable riding. This will help you learn unfamiliar exercises and ideas without being overwhelmed by a young horse, that by virtue of age, presents additional challenges.

How the Horse's Age Affects the Countdown

Horses are started at varying ages. Those destined for futurity classes, for example, are often worked as long yearlings and are already being ridden as they turn two years old. With short, light workouts and ample turnout time, these young horses are then ready for longer, more strenuous sessions as they mature. In these early stages, establishing respect and building confidence should be the main objective.

Many ranch and outfitter horses are not asked to work until their bodies are more developed and they are able to handle longer days and more physical stress. This is because handling a lot of horses each day, for short periods of time, is not usually an option for working outfits. Therefore, many three- and four-year-olds are started when time allows, and then they are put to work right away. Many of these horses come off the range and have had limited prior handling. They can pose some real challenges, such as an abundance of "fear issues," as humans have not been a part of their life up to this point.

Of course, there are numerous disciplines and hundreds of breeds, and those who specialize in them wait for differing milestones in the horse's life before they begin any type of structured teaching sessions. Without detailing each and every one, here's the gist of it: when your horse is old enough to sustain movement and carry weight, he is ready for my program. (It is best to consult your veterinarian as to whether your particular horse is developed enough.) Since I start with the very basics, it is ideal for *all* horses. Each training step builds on the last, and despite your horse's previous experiences and age, you will ultimately find success.

How Long Will the Countdown Take?

Only you and your horse can answer this question, and usually not until the work is already done! The amount of time spent, the effort put forth, the willingness of your horse, and your experience level are just some of the factors that affect the time needed to complete each training step. If you are able to work your horse five or six times a week, my program should take about one year to complete. Your horse's education will be far from over at that point—in many ways, it will have just begun in terms of pursuing a specific discipline or area of specialization—but working through all 33 of my lessons in a year is a good, reasonable goal.

Your objective should always be to remain safe while setting high goals. What will help you in the process is experience, which cannot be obtained quickly. Here are just some of the things that you will learn, attain, and appreciate over time:

▸ How to time every release (see p. 14) at exactly the right moment

▸ Recognition of the horse's level of acceptance and his demeanor

▸ "Feel" for the horse's movement under saddle

▸ Ability to pick up on the horse's thoughts

▸ Knowledge of how to stay safe and recognize danger before it happens

▸ Excellent balance and a good riding seat

▸ Anticipation of a problem and how to solve it

▸ Knowledge of what you desire in your horse's performance

▸ Understanding of the time it takes to build your horse's confidence and skill set

▸ How the horse's age and breeding affects the lesson plan

Equipment Needed

Quality equipment is important to me. I use the best quality I can afford and have it ready when I need it. Below is the list of items that I use regularly.

▸ Round pen 55 feet (plus/minus 10 feet) in diameter

▸ Riding area, preferably enclosed by a sturdy fence

▸ Protective boots for all four of your horse's legs (I like SMB Elite Sports Medicine Boots by Professional's Choice®)

▸ High-quality saddle pad (again, the SMX Air-Ride Show Pad by Professional's Choice® is a good one)

▸ Rope halter

▸ Lead line, 12 to 15 feet long and ¾-inch thick

▸ Extra-soft lariat, 32 to 60 feet in length

▸ Dressage whip, 36 inches long

▸ Favorite saddle—whether Western or English, it must fit both you and your horse properly

▸ Snaffle-bit bridle with one continuous rope rein (I discuss this in detail—see below)

This list is a good place to start. There are a number of other items you will want to acquire in time, but if you begin here, you are well on your way.

The Horse's Bit

The bit has little or no significance if the trainer does not properly employ it. *How you use* your training aids is far more important than *what you use* as training aids.

My typical setup includes an O-Ring snaffle bit, rawhide bit hobble, and a leather headstall with a browband. My headstall is constructed out of top-quality leather and secured with leather lacing. I use a continuous rope rein about ¾-inches thick, fastened to a pair of leather slobber straps.

Countdown to Broke is designed to be started and completed in the snaffle-bit bridle. A snaffle bit works on the corners of the horse's mouth and does not apply any *leveraged* pressure on the bars of the mouth, chin, or poll. This is ideal for your horse's early education. My goal is to fully teach my horse in a snaffle bit before I even *think* of graduating to an advanced bit—a bit with "leverage."

In Western horsemanship, the natural progression is to begin using an advanced bit after the snaffle-bit training stage. Many performance horses are required to show in an advanced bit, while trainers and riders often look for the improved *feel* and *signaling* that can be attained with it.

Photos 1 A & B   Here is a great snaffle-bit setup. The headstall is 5/8-harness leather with leather lace, instead of Chicago screws. The slobber straps can be removed from the bit by undoing the laces, without having to undo the reins. The bit hobble is made of rawhide, which softens in time. The bit is a sweet-iron O-ring. The rope reins are 10 feet long, attached to the slobber straps with waxed string.

Photo 2   This is a correctional bit with split reins, a leather curb strap, and a high-quality browband headstall with leather lacing. reins are rolled-leather, roman style.

The Cavesson Option

If your horse consistently opens his mouth when bit pressure is applied, you can supplement your setup with a leather cavesson, such as this one made of adjustable rolled-leather. This will discourage him from opening his mouth and prevent formation of a bad habit.

Photo 3   Here is a fixed leverage bit bridle. The headstall is a split ear with leather lacing, the curb strap is a wide chain, the bit is a medium-port solid bit, and the reins are rolled-leather, roman style.

While snaffle bits at higher levels of competition are more common in English disciplines, there, too, is the tendency to turn to a stronger mouthpiece after the early stages of training are completed.

Even though this book does not go into detail regarding types and use of advanced bits, it is important to know where you are headed in terms of bitting and what the related training timeframe might look like. To that end, here are the three "main" bits used today and where they tend to appear in the horse's training schedule.

1　As I mentioned, my training program is designed with a *snaffle-bit bridle* in mind (photos 1 A & B). Plan to spend at least one year in this setup, or however long it takes for the horse to successfully complete all the training steps, from Lesson 33 to 1.

2　Upon completion of the snaffle-bit stage, introduce leverage with a *correctional bit* (photo 2). Allow your horse time to grow accustomed to the new feel of this type of bit. The design creates leveraged pressure on your horse's jaw, chin, and poll while still allowing you to teach your horse rein aids with both hands. (The "break" in the correctional bit's mouthpiece means you can signal the corners of the mouth individually, as you do with a snaffle bit.) Use split leather reins with this setup. You can spend anywhere from several months on up with this variation of bit.

3　Once your horse is properly introduced to a correctional bit, you may want to move to a *fixed leverage bit (*photo 3). This type of bit has no moving parts and lies quietly in your horse's mouth. This is a true *one-handed* bit—because it is a solid mouthpiece, it is not meant to be used for two-handed rein cues. Split leather or romal reins can be used. Start with a medium port in a normal grazer style.

This is a vast topic and there are many views on how and when to "bit up." There is also a very wide range of bits available. In any case, it is most important to remember that when teaching your horse to respond to a bit there is *pressure* and there is *lack of pressure*. If *pressure is released* when a horse responds correctly, he will learn from the experience—as long as the pressure does not come in an aggressive, unexpected, inconsistent, or painful way (see more about the concept of "release" on p. 14). Increasing bit severity to solve a training problem is almost always wrong. (I only say "almost" as there seems to be an exception to every rule!)

A Special Note on Safety

Even though a well-mannered, highly trained animal is far safer to be around than one that is not, you can never completely eliminate the risk of injury to either you or the horse. Take *all* available safety precautions.

As a rider you can wear a proper riding helmet to minimize head injury. You should only wear narrow-profile riding boots with a heel to avoid the chance of being "hung-up" in the stirrup. Your tack should be made of high quality material and in good repair.

Your horse should wear protective boots on all four legs and never be asked to work in an unsafe environment—only use well made, quality round-pen panels, fencing, and stalls. Safe riding!

"Jargon-Busters"

Throughout this book, I use a number of terms and phrases that are probably somewhat familiar to most of you, while others will be reading them for the first time. Either way, it seems to me the modern evolution of horsemanship has given rise to a whole new type of "language," one that is spoken and traded so often and in so many different sorts of environments, that the true meaning of the words within it have either been lost or were perhaps never really understood to begin with. So, with the intent to clarify much of what we hear in the clinician's presentation, the training arena, and the show pen today, I've pulled together a list of "jargon-busters," which you can refer to at any point as you move through the Countdown—or any time you're feeling a little "behind the lingo"!

Angle of Rein Pressure Since the bit is a source of many cues (see *Cue*), the angle at which the bit pressure is applied is important. Your hand position will dictate what you are communicating to your horse.

Avoidance Behavior The actions a horse shows when he is agitated or has lost confidence.

"Back off the Pressure" During the teaching process, a handler or rider may add too much pressure (see *Pressure*) and negatively affect the horse's confidence or learning curve. In these situations, he or she needs to "back off" and settle for less at the time in question.

Balling Up When a horse rounds out his back (see *Rounding Out*), positions his face inside the vertical, and brings his hind end low and underneath his body. This term usually applies to an exaggerated form of the position ideal for training purposes.

Bit Pressure Cues (see *Cue*) that come from the movement of the bit in the horse's mouth and the application of the reins.

Body Pressure Cues (see *Cue*) that come from the handler's physical position and posture during groundwork sessions.

"Bounce off the Bit Pressure" A horse that is developing a strong reflex (see *Reflex*) to a bit request will "come off" bit pressure very quickly in order to avoid it. This is very desirable.

Break Down When the horse changes to a slower gait.

"Breaking at the Poll" When a horse overflexes with his chin pulled inward toward his chest, resulting in a tight throatlatch.

Bridle Pressure Any pressure and/or cue (see *Pressure* and *Cue*) that comes from the bridle. This includes bit, curb, poll, and rein pressure.

Bridle Work Training that involves the horse's response to bridle pressures and cues (see *Bridle Pressure* and *Cue*).

"Broke to Ropes" Literally, a horse that is confident with ropes around his legs, dragged behind him, rubbed all over his body, and swung over his head. This kind of horse has usually had ample experience roping and/or staking out on grass.

Busy Mouth This can mean two very different things: a horse that is relaxed will have a loose jaw and often lick his lips, chew, yawn, or sigh; a horse that is nervous, playful, or unaccustomed to a bit can also demonstrate these characteristics when a bit is in place.

Catch Corral A small pen used to "catch" or contain a horse that is particularly hard to get a hand on.

Colt As many of you know, a colt is technically a young male horse, but it is common amongst horsemen to refer to *all* young horses as "colts." Therefore, "colt-starting" does not exclude fillies! If someone wants to be more specific they may use "stud colt" for a young male horse and "filly colt" for a young female. Once a colt is gelded, he is a "gelding."

"Come-To" Cue A cue (see *Cue*) that asks for the horse's attention and for him to approach you.

Control Point There are five points on the horse that the rider/handler needs to have "control" of in order to accomplish *any* maneuver: the right hip, left hip, right shoulder, left shoulder, and nose (see more on this, p. 14).

Cross-Firing When the horse's front end and hind end are on different leads during the lope—an extremely unbalanced and undesirable state. Also known as a "disunited canter" or "cross-cantering." (Note: "cross-firing" is also used by some to describe when the diagonal fore and hind feet strike.)

Cue A signal to your horse to perform an action, provided via a training aid, legs, hands, or voice.

Direction The line or course that the trainer desires the *spot* (see also *Spot*) to follow: forward, backward, left, right, up, or down (for further discussion, see p. 14).

Directional Control The ability to choose where the horse's feet move.

Disengage the Hind End (Hips) Taking away the horse's means of propulsion by requesting lateral movement in his hip or hind end area.

"Drilling Hips" Spending a lot of time guiding the horse through hip movement. Since our goal is for the horse to work off his hind end (see *"Work off His Hind End"*), this overloading of the front end can become a practiced mistake.

Emergency Stop A term used by some for a hip disengagement cued by a direct rein, which will many times bring a horse's unwanted forward movement (see *Forward Movement*) to a halt.

Engage the Hind End (Hips) Asking for movement and propulsion that begins in the hind end, such as in a turn on the forehand or a lope departure.

Exposure A situation where your horse is experiencing something new. This can be a new item, such as a saddle pad, or a new environment, such as a ride in the horse trailer.

Face Pressure The pressure (see *Pressure*) from a halter, bridle, or hand that is applied to the face of the horse.

"Falling Apart" When the horse's learning curve "heads south," or his confidence is blown. Essentially, this is an equine mental breakdown and a good indicator that you need to slow down, take several steps back, and gradually rebuild your horse's comfort level.

Flat Head Elevation A good topline on a horse, with a straight back and neck and a relaxed, natural-looking headset.

Forward Motion Movement that involves lateral motion (forward-and-sideways), such as in shoulder movement to the left (the front right leg must pass ahead of the front left leg); shoulder movement to the right (the front left leg must pass ahead of the front right leg); hip movement to the left (the hind right leg must pass ahead of the hind left leg); and hip movement to the right (the hind left leg must pass ahead of the hind right leg). Read more about this on p. 116.

Forward Movement Straight movement—the horse's hind feet are tracking in or in front of the path of the front feet.

Frame The ideal headset (flexed at the poll, "soft nose"), round back, and engaged hindquarters.

Front End Movement The horse's shoulder action.

"Further, Faster, Softer" The trainer first asks the horse to complete a movement in response to a specific cue (see *Cue*), then to perform repetitions of the movement in succession (*further*). Next the trainer asks the horse to execute the movement more quickly, or with speed (*faster*). Finally, the trainer asks the horse to perform the same movement correctly and quickly in response to progressively lighter, more subtle cues (*softer*). I discuss this concept in detail on p. 20.

"Get off Pressure" The inclination to "move away" from pressure (see *Pressure*). Some horses are natural at "getting off pressure" while others need to be taught.

Give A horse is said to "give" when he acknowledges a cue (see *Cue*) and responds correctly. A "great give" is when the horse recognizes the lightest of cues; responds correctly, quickly, and accurately; and rider control is both gained and maintained.

"Give to Bit Pressure" The horse's ability to recognize and respond to pressure from the bit.

"Give the Reins Back" To release all rein/bridle pressure, giving the horse back his head.

"Go Forward" Cue A cue (see *Cue*) that asks your horse to move his feet forward.

"Good Hand" Someone who is "handy" with horses and not only experienced, but effective.

Halter Pressure The stimuli that comes from pressure being applied to a halter, including chin, cheek, nose, and poll pressure.

"Head Down" Cue A cue (see *Cue*) that asks your horse to drop his head.

Hip Cues Signals that a rider or handler uses to cue (see *Cue*) the left and/or right hip to move in a specific direction.

"Hips In" Cue A cue (see *Cue*) that requests the horse push his hips to the inside of the bend while remaining straight in his front end and traveling forward.

"Hips Locked Down" When the horse's front end is light, free, and ready to maneuver, while his hind end is balanced and bearing much of his body weight.

Hump Up When a horse rounds out his back with the intention of bucking, or is actually performing small bucks.

Indirect Pressure A signaling force that does not come directly from the handler's position—for example, a lead rope that is passed around a post, where the horse is asked to give to the direction of the post, rather than the position of the handler.

Joined-Up The now common term recognizing when a horse has come to you and accepted your leadership.

"Keeping the Horse between Your Legs" The goal of teaching your horse to "get off" leg pressure, so he has no alternative but to stay straight between them. This allows you to ride using your seat alone.

Leg Pressure Cues (see *Cue*) that come from the rider's thighs, knees, calves, toes, heels, and spurs.

Locked On When the horse looks attentively to the handler and awaits instruction as to his next task. (Usually, a horse that is "locked on" you is waiting for you to "let him in" for a rest!)

Locking Up When a horse stops moving his legs, often due to fear, defiance, uncertainty, or discomfort.

"Love On" the Horse Giving the horse positive affirmations and pleasing stimuli.

Motivator The trainer's tool for creating an unpleasant stimulus (see discussion of negative reinforcement, p. 12)—for example the *legs squeezing* or *the dressage whip tapping* (see also p. 17).

Moved Out Going forward under saddle.

"Muscle" the Horse When the rider or handler uses too much pressure (see *Pressure*) to make a maneuver happen.

Negative Reinforcement The removal of an unpleasant stimulus—for example, the cessation of bit pressure (see further discussion, p. 12).

"No" Response Usually this is "positive punishment" (the addition of an unpleasant stimulus) when the horse acts aggressive or rude. This may be a response in kind or body posturing to reassume authority.

One-Rein Exercise An action that only allows the use of one rein at a time.

Operant Process The teaching method that employs the use of reinforcements in order to achieve conditioned responses (see further discussion on p. 12).

"Outfitter" Horses Used by guides/outfitters for packing, high-country hunting, trail riding, and a large number of ranch functions.

"Performance" Horses Used for showing in "performance" classes, such events as cutting, jumping, reining, racing, dressage, barrel racing, team roping, team penning, Western pleasure, or driving.

Poll Pressure The pressure (see *Pressure*) from a halter, bridle, rope, or hand that is applied to the poll (the area behind the ears) of the horse.

Positive Reinforcement The addition of a pleasing stimulus. This can be a head or body rub, kind words, or treats (see also p. 12).

Practiced Mistake Every rider or trainer has an "ultimate goal" for his or her horse—his master plan of "desirable behavior." Any poor movement, imbalance, or clumsy cue that does not serve to further the pursuit of this ultimate goal may be a "practiced mistake." One example: a horse is asked to travel in tight circles, and while doing so, he leans in and drops his inside shoulder, forming a bad habit. Another example: a Western pleasure horse's forward movement is improperly "blocked" with bit pressure, so he learns to shorten his front legs' stride to compensate.

Pressure A signaling force that comes from the handler. Pressure can come from our hands, legs, body posture, or a training/signaling aid, such as a bit or halter (see further discussion on p. 17).

"Pull with Body Pressure" When the entire horse, or just one part of him, moves toward you through a conditioned response to your body position or posture. (Note: a horse may also be "pulled" toward you due to natural aggression, the desire to socialize, or curiosity.)

Push The addition of pressure in the form of a motivator or an exposure (see *Motivator* and *Exposure*). A push that is too strong may negatively affect the learning process.

"Push with Body Pressure" Posturing with poise and acting assertive toward the horse—for example, squaring up and walking toward the horse in an authoritative manner with accompanied voice commands—in order to gain your horse's respect for your position and/or make him move off.

"Quit" Riding When the rider allows his or her body and mind to relax and doesn't "think forward" any longer. This change in the rider's body is transmitted to the horse and tells him to stop moving.

"Quitting On the Cue" When the rider or handler removes the cue or motivator (see *Cue* and *Motivator*) before the release point is reached (see *Release Point*). For example, when a rider uses leg bumping to teach forward movement, but before the desired movement is attained, stops using leg and allows the horse to avoid his request, he has "quit on the cue."

"Recreational" Horses A term for horses that are not used for working, showing, or breeding, but instead are simply enjoyed by people who are looking to build their own horsemanship skills and a relationship with their equine partner. Although these horses may do many of the same things as "working" or "performance" horses, it is at the discretion of their owner.

Reflex A habitual response to a stimulus or cue (see *Cue*). In training a horse, we attempt to condition reflexes to reflect our wishes. In this book and in many discussions regarding horse training theory and philosophy, *reflex* can be used interchangeably with *response*.

Release The action of *removing* any unpleasant stimulus (see *Motivator*), such as leg pressure or the tapping of a dressage whip, at the moment that the spot (see *Spot*) has moved in the desired direction (see *Direction* and further discussion, p. 14).

Release Point The moment of success where the removal of any unpleasant stimulus (see *Release*) should occur. Because of an appropriate response, the horse is rewarded with *negative reinforcement* (removal of the unpleasant stimulus) and sometimes a *positive reinforcement* (the addition of a pleasing stimulus), as well (see further discussion, p. 14).

Response Any behavior resulting from the application of a stimulus. Through the training process, we are attempting to condition the horse's responses. In this book and in many discussions regarding horse training theory and philosophy, *response* can be used interchangeably with *reflex*.

Retreat The action of taking pressure away from the horse (see *Pressure*). This term is usually reserved for the "sacking out" process, where new items are being introduced (see Lesson 29, p. 50). This can also refer to the total release of all pressure if and when your horse appears stressed or unsure.

Rounding Out When the horse's back has an upward flex to it, or is convex. The opposite is a "hollowed out" back, which sags and is concave.

Sacking-Out The term used to describe desensitizing a horse to fearful objects, historically in the form of an empty grain bag or "sack" (see Lesson 29, p. 000).

Self-Carriage When a horse is balanced, collected, cadenced, confident, and traveling without the help of bit, leg, or harness pressures.

Shaping The teaching of a nonexistent or complex action.

Shoulder Cues Signals that a rider or handler uses to cue (see *Cue*) the left and/or right shoulder to move in a specific direction.

Snubbing The removal of any slack in the reins or lead rope, where the horse's nose is tightly held toward a fixed object, such as a tie post, or a rider on a pony horse.

Softening The process of conditioning your horse to perform great "gives" (see *Give*). A "soft" horse gives his face and body to your light cues, whereas a stiff horse requires more pressure or is unable to respond at all.

Softening the Nose Conditioning the horse to "get off" bit pressure and come back to you, bringing his nose toward your hands. With well-executed rehearsal, the horse learns to come back off the bit after only a very small amount of pressure is applied.

"Speeding the Feet Up" Asking for a requested movement to be performed more quickly, whether forward, backward, or laterally. Usually, a "cluck" or "kiss" is the vocal cue (see *Cue*) for this request.

Spot A small, distinct part of the horse that serves as the trainer's focal point and barometer (standard to measure success) during an exercise (see also p. 14).

Startle Reflex The natural reaction that comes from a sudden or unexpected stimulus.

Success Anytime a release point is reached (see *Release Point*).

Successive Approximations Small steps that build toward an ultimate goal.

"Switching of the Eyes" When a rider or handler shows the horse's eye on one side an item or movement and then changes sides.

"Teaching Hips" Conditioning a response to a cue (see *Cue*) for hip motion.

Threaten When a rider or handler shows intentions of using a motivator (see *Motivator*)—for example, moving the hand holding the lariat without actually throwing it.

Three-Tracking When a horse is moving forward while his hip is moved to the inside or outside of the bend, he travels on "three tracks." For example, when a horse is walking forward on the left rein and his inside hip is shifted to the left, both the front right and the hind left feet are traveling in their own track, but the front left foot is treading directly in front of (in the same track) as the hind right.

Trapping the Horse Constricting the horse's freedom to move.

Turnaround Also known as a "spin," this is a reining and cowhorse maneuver that requires the shoulders to move around a stationary hind end.

Two-Handed Stop A stop/backup cue (see *Cue*) that involves the use of both reins simultaneously.

"Working" Horses These horses have a "job," which usually involves much more time on their back. They are used by ranchers, guides/outfitters, law enforcement, range riders, and other individuals who perform repetitive, necessary daily tasks with their mount.

"Working off His Hind End" When a horse has shifted much of his weight (which naturally falls on his forehand) to his hindquarters and is using his back end for balance and power. His front end is then light, maneuverable, and ready for change. Examples of a horse "working off his hind end" can be seen in a reiner's rollback or a dressage rider's canter pirouette.

"Yes" Response Your actions (or reinforcements) at the release point (see *Release Point*) or once desirable behavior has been exhibited.

The Teaching Process

Horse Psychology 101

Depending on environmental conditions, a herd of horses will graze one-third of the time, travel another third, and rest for the remainder. By understanding some of the social patterns that govern a "natural" herd as well as its tendencies, you can "domesticate" your horse with greater success. As in the example of the herd, think of proper horse care in thirds: First, give your horse what he wants most, which is to be fed in a way that is natural to him. Ample roughage in the form of hay or pasture satisfies his grazing instinct. A well-designed feed program also gives him vitamins, minerals, and added calories, but *only* in addition to the necessary roughage. Second, give him a substantial amount of free movement and exercise. This allows the horse's body to function as it should, while keeping his mind relaxed. Many conditions that ail domestic horses are due to lack of movement. And finally, allow time for rest.

During their normal day, the horses in the natural herd would be on the lookout for predators and when spotted, either respond with *fight* or *flight*. Since the horse is naturally a "prey animal," he will most likely choose to flee a frightening situation and only fight if he feels he absolutely has to. If you wish to be a part of the horse's life, you'll need to establish respect (see below), but also build and maintain trust. This can be a delicate balancing act in the beginning as your horse figures out what his role is in his new relationship with you.

Since there is a hierarchical "pecking order" in a natural herd, you must be the leader in your domestic herd (even when your herd only contains one horse and you!) When you do not command respect, you will be moved around, threatened, bitten, and kicked. It is normal for horses to test their place in the herd ranking, but with consistent leadership, you can maintain your integral role as "the boss."

Photo 5 Alisha uses a treat to teach Clash to bend her neck while keeping her feet stationary, in order to stretch her neck muscles. This is an example of positive reinforcement, as she is adding a pleasing stimulus.

Conditioned Response

Horses conduct themselves on two very different levels: *innate behavior* and *conditioned behavior.* Innate behavior—or instinct—comes from natural brain processes that horses inherit from their predecessors. Conditioned behavior is a result of learning from the environment around them. Horses learn how to respond to different situations, based on their previous experiences.

As a trainer, your aim is to condition a horse to behave in a way that is appealing to you. This translates into a horse ceasing to act instinctually while under your guidance, and instead only acting in response to your requests—for example, when your horse doesn't whirl and bolt when confronted by a strange, fearful object and instead remains steady under your control, keeping you safe.

Positive and Negative Reinforcement

Operant conditioning is a teaching process that uses reinforcement in order to "condition a response"—create such desirable behaviors as the one described above. Both *positive* and *negative* reinforcement strengthens behavior, making a desired response more likely to happen in the future.

Positive reinforcement is the *addition of* and use of a pleasing stimulus. A horse that is brought in from the pasture for his daily grain ration is far more likely to be caught easily than one who receives nothing. And, you can easily teach a horse such tricks as bowing down on one knee with the enticement of sugar cubes. The horse learns that certain behaviors guarantee a reward (photo 5).

Positive reinforcement (although powerful when used with people), is not a practical primary teaching tool with horses. You are obstructed by the horse's inability to communicate through reason and language. You can, however, use a type of positive reinforcement, such as kind rubs, in combination with the next approach—negative reinforcement—to further strengthen a response from your horse.

Negative reinforcement strengthens behavior with the *removal of* an aversive stimulus (something that the horse wants to avoid). Because this stimulus is physical, it allows you to communicate to the horse how you would like him to respond—for example, bumping your legs to encourage your horse to move forward more quickly, and once he does, discontinuing the use of your legs (photos 6 A & B).

I realize the term "negative reinforcement" sounds, well, *negative.* It is not! It is simply a term from the field of psychology that refers to the *removal of the stimulus;* so, in fact, it is a *positive* experience for the horse, and consequently, a wonderful teaching method.

Shaping

Shaping brings about a nonexistent or complex behavior through an operant process. It is achieved in small steps known as *successive approximations,* which pro-

Photos 6 A & B Teaching your horse to move his feet faster requires a fair application of increasing leg pressure, as Alisha demonstrates in A. At the moment she achieves the desired response, she removes her leg pressure as a reward, shown in

B. It is at this release point Clash learns to respond to the leg cue. The cessation of leg pressure is an example of negative reinforcement, as Alisha is removing an unpleasant stimulus.

Photo 7 Alisha and Clash demonstrate a side-pass. This complex maneuver could not be taught all in one day—it was achieved via successive approximations, or a series of small training steps that eventually added up to the advanced movement seen here.

gressively develop behaviors that you desire with the help of the reinforcements we just discussed. For example, in order to perform a beautiful side-pass, you need to control the horse's hips, shoulders, and nose position. You also want the horse to remain elevated, collected, calm, and willing. You cannot teach all this in one step. This advanced maneuver requires you to teach your horse many smaller responses that eventually build up to the side-pass (photo 7).

Understanding how your horse learns is the cornerstone to the Countdown to Broke, and enables you to train in a consistent, commonsense manner. There are no guessing games about whether the horse has found the correct answer or not.

The Five Control Points

There are five specific "points" on the horse's body that you need to control in order to one day have him prepared to execute any movement, and perform in any discipline (photo 8). All five points can move in six directions: forward, backward, right, left, up, and down. The five points are:

1 Nose
2 Right shoulder
3 Left shoulder
4 Right hip
5 Left hip

That's it. There are no other places on the horse's body that you need to be concerned about. As you take your horse through each lesson in the Countdown, you will begin to isolate these control points and condition each one to respond to your cues, as needed.

Spot, Direction, Motivator, and Release

In order to "condition a response," such as the movement of one control point at the appropriate cue, you will use a teaching process consisting of four equally important components: *spot*, *direction*, *motivator*, and *release*. This method requires you focus on the horse's small "tries" and successes,

Photo 8 By controlling all five of the "control points" marked here in white (nose, right and left shoulders, right and left hips), any maneuver is possible. My Countdown to Broke training program isolates each of these points and shows you how to condition a great response to your cue(s) for each.

and reward his efforts. By isolating a "spot" on the horse, you are able to see these small changes more easily and can accurately assess how the control point is responding. For example, in order to recognize a precise change in a shoulder, the lesson may suggest you focus on a front foot as the "spot," where it is easier to see the horse's progress.

In any lesson, your first step is to determine each of these four parts so that "the plan" is clear to both you and your horse from the beginning. So, begin by choosing a *spot* on the horse to "move." This can be the point of the chest, a particular foot, or really any other part you can easily focus on. Knowing *what* you want to make move keeps it simple. (Usually, but not always, the "spot" is part of the control point you are trying to influence—see p. 14.)

Second, you need to have a *direction* in your mind in which you want the *spot* to move. Your horse may take the spot in many directions, but the direction you have chosen is the important one.

In order to move the particular spot in the chosen direction, you must have a *motivator* to encourage the horse to respond to your request (see p. 17). A dressage whip is one example of a motivator.

And, the fourth component is the *release*. When the horse moves the *spot* in the *direction* of your choice, you have just "defined a response," and the *release* (or stopping the use) of the *motivator* tells him that his response is the correct one. By "getting it right," the horse sees that the motivator is no longer applied. The ideal moment to discontinue application of the motivator is called the *release point*.

This, in a nutshell, is the teaching method primarily used throughout the Countdown to Broke. Memorize these four components and apply them to every lesson plan. Let me provide a sample situation here—let's say your plan is to teach your horse "go forward" from the ground (photos 9 A & B). This is how to break it down:

1   **Spot** Choose a spot on the horse to watch for forward movement. A small, distinct area like the point of the chest helps you determine success more easily.

2   **Direction** You want your spot to move forward. Have a clear direction in mind.

3   **Motivator** You will use a dressage whip as the motivator. Tapping the horse on the hindquarters with it

Photos 9 A & B In this teaching situation, the spot is Clash's chest, the direction is forward, the motivator is the dressage whip tapping the hind end, and the release—stopping the whip tapping—will only happen once that spot has moved in the desired direction (A). Once Clash moves her chest forward, Alisha releases all pressure as a reward (B).

encourages the correct response. The tapping pressure begins softly and can be escalated as necessary.

4 **Release** At the moment the spot moves in the proper direction, offer a release with *negative reinforcement:* stop tapping the whip and stand quietly with the horse. Then offer *positive reinforcement*, such as a head rub and kind words. Together, the two types of reinforcement strengthen the chance of this desired response reoccurring in the future.

You have just begun to teach your horse a *conditioned response*: the horse moves the spot forward when the whip is applied to his hind end. If he does not move forward with initial tapping, escalate the firmness of the taps until he responds. Your horse will soon become uncomfortable with being tapped and quickly learn (through repetition—see below) he is better off responding promptly to the motivator in order to find the release.

Teaching Cues Separately

Many maneuvers require you to cue several body parts of the horse. But you must condition a response to *one* cue before you add a second. It is important to the horse's foundation that he can move each body part in response to an individual cue. If a horse does not fully respond—further, faster, and softer (see p. 20)—to an individual request, he will be difficult to correct and shape as maneuvers become more complex. For example, a reining turnaround (also known as a turn on the haunches, spin, or reverse arc circle) can be requested in three ways: inside rein, outside rein, and outside leg. By teaching a full response to each cue alone, the maneuver will be easily performed and correctly shaped when you ask for it.

To transfer the horse's short-term memory into long-term memory, you need to *repeat* this process many times. The response must also be practiced on a *regular basis* to keep the horse's long-term memory fresh.

A Word about Motivators

An essential piece of the teaching process is the *motivator*. As just explained, in order to move the *spot* in the *direction* that you want, you must motivate the horse to respond. Since you cannot verbally reason with your horse, you use a physical motivator. Understanding what your motivator is and how to use it effectively is crucial. Without proper use of escalating pressure, your horse will learn the wrong behaviors instead of the right ones.

Your aim is to evoke a correct response—one that you have previously taught or a new one—and in order to do that, you want to use the motivator with *just enough* pressure. If you do not use enough, your horse will be released while giving an incorrect response; something to avoid. However, if you use too much pressure the horse may show signs of avoidance behavior and lose trust in you. The right amount of pressure is just what it takes for your horse to respond correctly, and no more. Consistent use of reinforcements following the motivator's release will reassure your horse that you are fair and trustworthy.

Since you do not always know how much pressure it will take to get the desired response, always begin softly, increasing the application of the motivator until the horse finds the right answer. If your teaching step is small and you use your motivator effectively, your horse will continue to learn.

Bit pressure (a result of rein handling) is one of the most common motivators. You apply motivating pressure to the bit through your reins, and you release by slackening the reins and eliminating pressure in the horse's mouth. The reins *cue* the horse to respond (see discussion of cues, p. 18), but it is the withheld release or the escalating bit pressure that *motivates* him to change. Note: the use of bit pressure must always remain fair. Pick up your reins and apply pressure smoothly. This warns your horse what is coming so he can begin to think about how to respond.

Leg pressure is used in a variety of ways. Leg "bumping" can tell a horse to speed his feet up. Leg pressure also tells the horse to move a hip or shoulder to one side or the other. Legs are commonly used for cueing, but can also act as the motivator. The release is taking your legs off the horse and keeping them still. (Note: if you choose to wear spurs during later lessons, they can increase your ability to signal the horse with precision, as well as amplify leg pressure when needed as a motivator.)

A **lariat** (rope) is used to motivate movement in the round pen as well as from the horse's back. In early lessons in the round pen, body and vocal cueing is enforced with the toss of the lariat at your horse's hind end to entice him to move forward, and the horse learns to move when you are in the process of throwing to avoid being struck. In early (first 30) rides, you can reach back from the saddle and tap the horse's hind end with the tail of your lariat (or saddle strings) instead of using excessive leg bumping—if the leg bumping was not effective in achieving "forward."

Make use of a **dressage whip** to teach the horse some basic maneuvers in hand. It can act as an extension of your arm and be used to tap with increasing firmness until your horse responds correctly. Like many motivators, the dressage whip provides the cue for your horse to move, while the escalation of pressure in the tapping is the motivating influence. The release is to simply cease tapping and lower the whip.

You can use **hard work** as a motivator when training from the ground, as well as from the saddle. You cannot make a horse stand still, but you can make him move. When you want your horse to stand quietly next to you, make that the *only* place where he can relax. Rest is a *negative reinforcement* achieved by you taking away hard work (see p. 17).

Another common motivator is **halter pressure**. You can teach a horse to give to poll and face pressure through the use of a halter. When he yields to the halter pressure, he is able to release himself from the annoyance or discomfort created by the halter.

All the highlighted motivators I've mentioned are *applied motivators*, since they require *you* to create the

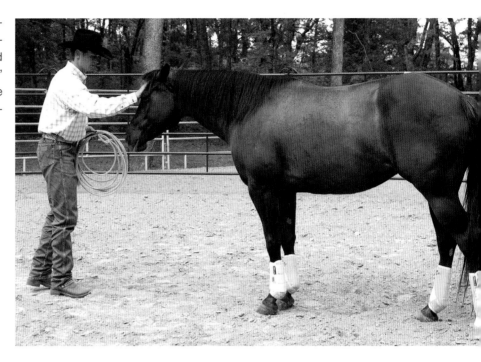

Photo 10 A young horse will quickly understand the significance of positive reinforcements, and kind words and head rubs will come to have a "calming effect" on him. This will not always be the case initially, but it will in time, as these actions will be associated with pleasure.

situation. There are also *natural motivators* such as: eating, resting, socializing, breeding, and surviving—although not created by us, these need to be recognized as influences on the horse's behavior.

The Difference between Cues and Motivators

A *cue* signals a horse to respond in a particular way. Through repetition of the teaching process—*spot, direction, motivator, and release*— a horse learns to recognize and respond to a cue. For this to happen, the horse must not only understand what is being asked of him by the cue, but must have a *reason* to change his behavior and make the effort to respond. This reason to change comes from the *motivator*.

A cue and motivator are closely related but not always the exact same thing. Figure out the cue you need by asking yourself, "How should I signal my horse to do what I want?" Then ask yourself, "What 'pressure' am I going to add (and escalate if necessary) until the horse gives me the proper response?" This *pressure* is your *motivator*. The motivator might be your cue used with greater energy, or it

might be something you add that is different. A cue alone, with no repercussions, such as a wagging finger, change in seat position, or vocal commands, will not work unless it is "backed up" with one or more motivators.

I'll give you an example under saddle: when you *cue* your horse to move forward, you use light leg pressure to make the request. The *motivators* can be tapping of the dressage whip, lariat, or saddle string on the horse's hind end, or escalating leg bumping until forward movement is achieved.

When you set out to teach your horse a specific lesson and you understand clearly in advance what your cues and motivators are to be and apply them fairly, the lesson will be far more efficient and effective. And, when you are consistent with your cueing and build up the escalation of your motivator as needed, your horse views you as reasonable and honest, and learns to behave within the parameters you give him.

Understanding the Release Point

The "release point" (as opposed to the "release," which is

Photo 11 To help build trust, tell your horse "That's all I wanted," by backing off and asking him to approach you. Predatory behavior does not back away, thereby proving your credibility. Here, I back away from Belle, giving her a full release.

the *act* of removing the pressure) is the moment in time when you as the trainer *should* remove the motivator. This moment is just as a correct response is achieved. When you accurately time your *release* with the *release point*, your horse will learn faster.

Horses do not enjoy pressure. This is why it is such a good teaching tool. In order for your horse to respond correctly, he must be motivated. Knowing that a release is pending motivates the horse to find the correct answer. Once the response is achieved, a release of the pressure teaches your horse how to find the same release in the future. This makes the response more likely to happen again.

As your horse finds many "releases" from you, he will become a better student. A horse that is new to human handling will take more time to find his release than one that is use to the teaching process. Highly trained horses will "hunt" the correct response. Your release is your "Yes" response to your horse.

So, as an example, let's say you ask your horse to move his feet faster by transitioning up from a walk to the jog, and you ask him with leg pressure as your cue and motivator.

The *release point* comes when the horse "thinks" about jogging and his body is beginning to respond—just as he starts to jog, *release* him from leg pressure. Should you continue to bump him with your legs, he will either continue to look for another—different—response, such as speeding up, or simply become desensitized to your leg.

Combining Reinforcements

Your release of the motivator is an integral part of the teaching process. If you fail to release the horse at the release point he will stop looking for the correct response and will become difficult to teach. *If the end is just as uncomfortable as the beginning, then what is the point?* As I've already mentioned, releasing your horse from a motivator is a *negative reinforcement*, a strong teaching tool. But to strengthen the effect even further, use *positive reinforcements*, as well, when appropriate (see p. 12).

This combination of positive and negative reinforcement will speed up both confidence building and skill development. There is no time or place where this is more evident than in the early sessions in a round pen. A young colt quickly figures out the significance of a soft head rub and kind words when he has given you the correct answer (photo 10). You are not only building trust through touch, but you are associating a physical action and tone of voice with a release from a motivator (photo 11).

Explaining a "Give"

Each time that you request a response from your horse, you are looking for a "give." A "give" comes in three stages, which are:

1. **Recognition of the Request** You want your horse to understand what is being asked of him. This is accomplished through previous teaching.

2. **Physical Response** You want your horse to respond correctly to the cue with a body movement of some kind.

3. **Control** Once your horse has recognized the request and responded accordingly, you have gained greater control.

The next question that you should ask yourself is, "What is a 'great give?'" This is when the horse recognizes a very subtle cue, and he responds quickly and accurately, giving you control willingly. If you feel that a cue you are using does not result in a "great give," you need to teach your horse how to respond better. Your horse's responsiveness will be in a constant state of flux. It is normal for him to make, as well as lose progress in his responses to your cues. If you effectively teach your horse how to respond on a regular basis, you can expect him to improve over time.

Further, Faster, Softer

When you teach a maneuver, focus on it being performed *further*, then *faster* and finally *softer*. For example, when you teach your horse to pivot on one hind foot and walk his shoulders around himself in a complete circle, you begin "small," teaching *one* step only. As your horse learns how to respond to the rein cue for this exercise, you can continue to ask for additional steps—that is, take it *further*.

Once your horse understands your cue, and how to find his release, you can progress by asking for the maneuver to be performed *faster* and with more energy.

Although it is true that you want to cue your horse with only the exact amount of pressure required, the third step here is to make the cue as light as possible—or *softer*. This occurs much more easily once your horse knows how to respond and can do so with some energy. As you give your horse the chance to "work off less," your goal is for the cue to become increasingly lighter and end up very subtle.

Muscle Memory

How much *mental* energy does it take to tie your shoelaces? Since you have been performing this simple task from a young age, you have developed what is called *muscle memory*. Your mind and body have memorized the movements you need to make the knot.

Your horse can also learn to perform maneuvers this easily by developing muscle memory, and when a movement is performed well consistently, you are encouraging good *habits*. Habits are created through repetition and are an extension of the horse's *actions*. An action is a result of your horse's *thoughts*. If your horse is thinking right, he will act right.

THOUGHTS ➲ ACTIONS ➲ HABITS ➲ PERFORMANCE

In order to perform in an exceptional manner your horse needs to begin with the right thought. And, if you see or "feel" a bad habit beginning to form, be sure to address the action involved. Remember, a good action is just as easy to practice as a poor one.

As your horse develops good habits, his body and mind will be used to performing a maneuver a certain way—and muscle memory is created. For example, when a reining horse is trained to do a good sliding stop at the lope, even when he is asked to halt while jogging, he will brace himself for a "bigger" stop, such as what he would need at the lope. This is muscle memory.

Learning Curve

With each passing day you can expect many positive behavioral changes in your horse. His respect for you will improve, his confidence level will grow, and he'll learn to respond to your cues. But, along with *improvement* comes *regression*. Sometimes instances will be insignificant, while others will seem major at the time.

Regression is a natural part of the horse's learning curve and is to be expected. If you know ahead of time that it will happen, then it should be no surprise when it does. You may be in the middle of a lesson, when all of a sudden your horse will not perform a simple request that you have asked for successfully many times before. At such moments, instead of remaining "stuck" on the current lesson, take a step back and focus on the incorrect response. Once you re-establish the correct reflex, you can move ahead.

This learning regression is not a "first-week phenomenon"—it happens at all stages. Even though frustration might set in, remain focused and know that working through moments of regression will make your horse even better in the end.

Building Your Horse's Confidence

Helping Your Horse Overcome His Fears

Horses usually take the path of least resistance and conserve their energy…a nice way of saying that they are inherently lazy. So why does a young horse surge in speed under saddle when a slower pace would take less effort? The answer can be explained by examining the horse's fear level. He needs to build confidence through *experience* and *habituation* (see p. 22). Building your horse's confidence is not just about desensitizing him to a saddle pad; it is an ongoing process every time you handle him or get in the saddle.

Expect your horse to be fearful of new experiences. Your job is to assist him in overcoming his fear. Here is a list of measures you can take:

▸ Use your hands and legs wisely. Your horse must completely trust your actions and intentions. Communicate through physical touch that is fair and pleasing.

▸ Apply motivators (see p. 17) consistently and fairly—smoothly and with warning. For example, when using a dressage whip, take your position and begin hind-end tapping slowly with increasing firmness. Never startle your horse with an unexpected firm tap. With fair application he'll learn to respond without ever showing signs of fear.

▸ Be reasonable and consistent with reprimands (see p. 25). Your horse needs to know where the line is, and that the line is *stationary*.

▸ Spend ample time in the saddle on a regular basis. This keeps your horse prepared and accustomed to his job as a riding horse. When your riding time is short and infrequent, he won't progress nearly as well. You want the saddle and rider to be a normal part of his routine, where fear and discomfort are not factors.

▸ Work your horse regularly in all three gaits. He feels the rider quite differently in each gait and is not always as confident, say, in the jog or lope. Make sure that you jog and lope daily, thereby allowing him to be comfortable responding to your cues at the faster speeds.

▸ When your horse becomes excited, take the time to work him through it. The more "scary situations" he "survives" in a relaxed manner, the more confident he will be.

▸ Purposely expose your horse to new environments and stimuli. I am always looking for ways to show my horse a new sight—whether on my own property, or even better, elsewhere.

▸ Be a kind and trustworthy leader. Your horse is looking to you for guidance. Prove that there is nothing to fear and that being with you is safe.

Habituation

Since your horse is a "prey" animal, his first reaction to a new, possibly scary item or situation—such as a saddle blanket or even you approaching him—is to run away. In the wild, this is what keeps him alive. He does not wait around to see if his fear was justified.

Your job is to prove to your horse that his fears are *un*justified. These fears may not always make sense to you, as the horse sees the world quite differently. However, with a thoughtful approach, you can build your horse's confidence so that you can interact more safely and move ahead with training. *Habituation* occurs when you expose your horse to items or situations that scare him, and help him grow comfortable with them. This is an integral part of a horse's education. If you don't deal with many fear issues early on, your horse may be, or become, unmanageable.

When a horse "runs" from an alarming situation and "escapes," he "burns" a memory—and so he is even more sensitive to a similar incident in the future. However, when he encounters something that scares him but cannot completely escape—as when in the confines of a round pen—the process of habituation can be started. There are three things to keep in mind during this process:

▸ First, give your horse a more powerful reason to "keep his feet still" and stay with you, rather than run away. In the early lessons of the Countdown, you will use hard work as a motivator (see p. 17) when teaching your horse to remain still and face you. As this response strengthens and your horse learns that it is much easier to stand with you than work around the pen, he will be more inclined to keep his fear in check. He will also come to recognize that standing with you is a "safe place."

▸ Second, conduct yourself as a leader without acting in predatory fashion. Predators stalk and do not back away. You need to establish a positive presence with your horse whereby you continue your role as leader, while proving to him that he need not feel threatened. By advancing toward your horse, *followed by retreating*, this realization occurs. When you only advance (and so act in a predatory way), your horse will want to flee.

▸ Third, as you'll learn in Lesson 29 (p. 50), introduce new items and situations slowly, and begin with short "exposures" that are easy for your horse to accept. Start with your bare hands, and then once you can touch your horse all over, move on to more frightening things, such as garbage bags, saddle pads, ropes, and other everyday items.

You can gauge your horse's level of fear by whether or not he moves. If his feet remain still, you can expose him to a "scary" item with increasing intensity, although always paired with *periodic retreats*. For example, perhaps a garbage bag begins as a small ball of plastic in your hand, which you rub on the horse's shoulder, and the bag is gradually opened a little more after each retreat. The end goal is to rub a fully opened bag all over the horse's body. If the horse's feet move at any time during the process, you will know that you have overdone it.

Once you start working to habituate your horse to an item or situation, it is imperative that you finish the lesson. If you expose your horse to a garbage bag, for example, and stop before your horse has accepted it, his fear may actually become heightened. This also commonly happens with normal daily practices, such as fly-spraying or bathing. So, never ignore a fear issue. Take the necessary time to work through the concern and maximize every training opportunity. Repeat the habituation process until your horse is not showing any signs of fear—flinching, head tossing, or tail swishing. You want your horse to be completely relaxed and accepting.

Knowing When to "Push"

As I have explained, when you request something of your horse, you need to *release* at the moment of a correct response. Similarly, when you expose your horse to a new item or situation, you need to end the exposure as soon as the horse is calm and *habituation* occurs. But, knowing when to "push" your horse further can be very helpful. By "push" I mean taking your horse to the next level, but in a way that continues to build confidence as well as skill. Here are some examples of how you might push:

▸ Increase a motivator's strength to evoke the requested response.
  Example: Tapping the hind end with your saddle strings to request forward movement.

▸ Increase a "fearful" exposure beyond the horse's comfort level.
  Example: Securing the saddle and asking for movement in the round pen for the first time.

▸ Make a request that you've never asked before.
  Example: Loping for the first time.

▸ Escalate a request to be performed further or faster.
  Example: Asking for lateral shoulder motion to be performed more quickly.

▸ Increase the duration of a workout.
  Example: Asking your horse to perform lope circles for longer than on previous days.

The lessons in this book will help guide you through the horse's education in a way that will help you know when it is okay to push. With experience, your ability to recognize when it is time to push will improve.

Replacement Theory

There will be times when you will sense your horse growing anxious and losing concentration. In such situations, you may feel you no longer have complete control and begin anticipating the worst. Instead of attempting to *contain* your horse's nervous energy, focus his efforts into a constructive "replacement" exercise that will give him a release.

When I take a young horse into a large riding arena for the first time, I don't expect him to have the same focus as he did in the round pen. I know that there is a lot more open space. This gives the horse an opportunity to think a little bit more on his own. So, once mounted, I *immediately* put him to work with a simple exercise that he has completed successfully many times in the smaller round pen. This returns the horse to his comfort zone. My time is productive as I can continue offering him releases, therefore strengthening his response, and in the meantime, my horse is becoming aware of his new surroundings without having time to dwell in on any one thing that may scare him. This proactive technique of substituting desirable behavior for potentially undesirable behavior keeps you and your horse progressing safely.

For example, with a horse that is new to being ridden in an open area or riding arena, I begin my teaching session with serpentines (Lessons 16, p. 131, and 10, p. 179). Working on serpentines is a good way to focus the horse's energy on forward movement, while also requesting changes in direction. The inexperienced horse begins to focus his attention and effort on his response to the bit pressure, and after a few sessions, I find his attention back on me and my requests (photo 12).

When you take your horse to a new trail head, show grounds, or riding area use this technique to warm him up. There will be a lot for your horse to take in that is different or strange. You do not need a full workout; just ask for some simple responses as if you were at home. Work your horse in-hand, asking him to move his hips and shoulders, and when you feel his energy level is high and he is nervous, just try safe exercises such as "go forward" (Lesson 21, p. 99) from the ground. Once mounted in your new surroundings, immediately put your horse to work. Avoid wandering aimlessly, allowing him to look around and find something to shy at. Be proactive!

Photo 12 If your horse is reactive to a "scary" object—in this case, a tractor—use "replacement theory" and work on an exercise that you and your horse are good at, such as trotting serpentines. This focuses your horse's attention on the exercise and gives you opportunities to offer releases and rewards while the scary object is still present.

Being Fair

Your horse is at your mercy. It may not feel that way when you are in the saddle at times, but in reality, you chose to care for him and are making decisions that affect him. You should have his best interests at heart and want to be fair.

You expect your horse to treat you with respect and respond to your leadership. This can be achieved effectively through *clear communication*. When he is not sure what the message is, he will not know how to behave or respond.

First of all, your "Yes" must be clear. You say "Yes" to your horse with the help of reinforcements (see p. 12). When it is a *negative* reinforcement, your application of pressure with a motivator must be *fully released*. For example, if you ask your horse to back up and he responds correctly, release *all* rein pressure. This tells your horse he did the right thing. If you only partially release the reins, your "Yes" is not as clear. To amplify the "Yes," you may be in a position to offer *positive* reinforcements as well. Through physical touch and kind words, you make your affirmation of his response even stronger.

Just as your "Yes" must be clear, so must your "No." When you have to respond to an act of aggression, your "No" must be immediate, decisive, and *in kind*. When it is not, your horse will not completely understand, setting him up for further reprimand, as he will be more likely to test you. I would rather say "No" with a sharp reprimand twice, and be done with it, than spend several years lightly flicking my horse's muzzle each time he nips at my shirt. I do not want to aggravate or annoy him with constant small reprimands; instead, I want him to know that I mean business and that actions I consider aggressive are not allowed. By being a "steady hand" with your "No" and making the line that should not be crossed clear, your horse will be less likely to test you (see further discussion of reprimanding below).

A good leader is consistent and predictable. When your horse knows that responding to your cue in a particular way will give him a release, he is far more apt to do so. But, if your release is early, before he actually responds correctly, he may only offer the incorrect response the next time you ask. Conversely, when your release is withheld even though a good response was given, he will not know what to do in order to get his release, and so offer a different response. The more consistent and predictable the outcome, the better the horse's responses will be.

In an effort to ensure fairness to all horses beginning my training program, here is a list to help remind you what is *unfair* to your horse:

▸ Inconsistent cues

▸ Infrequent handlings and workouts

▸ Constant small reprimands

▸ Lack of good training

▸ Unfair use of motivators

▸ Poor nutrition

▸ Lack of ample turnout and freedom to move

▸ Lack of cardiovascular exercise

▸ Ill-fitting saddle and other equipment

▸ Dirty saddle pad

▸ Setting unreasonable goals

▸ Poor hygiene and health conditions

▸ Unhealthy feet

▸ Starting a horse too late in his life

I know many a horse owner who is just unaware of what might not be good for his horse. At some place down the line, *all of us* are guilty of making innocent mistakes. Avoid causing your horse confusion, discomfort, or injury by avoiding as many of these as possible. I am sure that there are plenty more points that could be added to the list—it is a good place to start.

Thoughts on Reprimanding

A reprimand is form of punishment. An example of *positive punishment* is when a parent spanks a child—an unpleasant stimulus is added. *Negative punishment* is the removal of a pleasant stimulus, such as when a child's allowance is withheld. Since a horse cannot reason, using negative punishment, when a reprimand is necessary, is pointless. Your horse understands physical contact and "herd posturing."

In a natural herd horses establish a "pecking order"—a hierarchical social structure that governs the group. Signs of dominance range from a simple look to a violent fight. When a horse attempts to show dominance over another, the recipient has to choose whether to submit or retaliate. In the end, one or the other must back down.

Because of the above, when a reprimand is needed, I suggest physical positive punishment. Just as it is done in a natural herd, I use physical and verbal retaliation when a horse acts aggressively toward me. I know the horse will understand this form of communication.

Aggressive acts that warrant an immediate reprimand include: entering the trainer's personal space without an invitation; pinned ears; threats to bite or kick, and/or actual biting or kicking. Failure to deal with any one of these when they occur notifies your horse that he has moved up a rung on the leadership ladder, and he is likely to repeat the behavior in the future.

Your job is to respond toward aggression *in kind*. If your horse crowds you and steps on your feet, you need to make him move off—use your voice and give him an open-handed slap on the shoulder. If your horse nips or bites you, "attack" back with vocal condemnation, a sharp slap on the shoulder, or make him back up several steps. The more aggressive your horse is, the more you need to amplify your reprimand. Your retaliation should be bigger than your horse's act of aggression. (Note: generally, avoid hitting the horse on the face. A bite is the *only time* I might slap the bridge of the nose. I usually just use an open-handed slap to the shoulder or barrel, accompanied by a sharp, loud vocal, such as "No!")

Positive punishment must be dealt *immediately* after the aggressive act occurs. If two or more seconds have passed, you've missed your chance to make an impression. And, once you retaliate, leave it at that. Do not continue to be angry or aggressive. As the leader you need to be respected, but you also need to be fully trusted. If you continue to punish the horse even after the incident has passed, your horse will begin to be frightened by you.

It is important to understand that I respond this way to my horse out of love. I am not harming him in any way. I know he craves leadership, and when he is respectful to all his handlers, he will likely receive better care and more attention throughout his life. In truth, I rarely have to reprimand my horses. I am prepared to if needed, but I try to find other ways to gain respect and a "top spot" in the pecking order. For example, by making my horse move his feet, I avoid a physical altercation, while establishing dominance. Lead horses in a herd always make the others move out of the way, and so that is essentially what I do. As you repeatedly ask your horse to move for you, such as in Lesson 33, p. 28, your role as leader becomes increasingly secure.

Finally, a reprimand is *never* meant to be used when a horse makes a mistake or demonstrates a lack of understanding. If he appears afraid of something new, work on dealing with it in a calm, logical way. When he simply fails to respond to a cue, take a step back in your training and revisit the lesson where he first learned it before moving on.

Problem Horses

As you set out to gain respect from your horse, build his confidence, and develop his skill set, you are proactively addressing the three areas that will make him a safe and capable mount. A "problem horse" usually refers to a horse that is lacking in one, two, or all three of these areas. Aggressive horses don't respect you. Horses lacking confidence are more likely to buck, rear, run away, and shy. Horses that haven't had a proper education do not know how to respond to your cues, which makes them dangerous to ride and difficult to handle.

When faced with a "problem horse," start at the beginning of the Countdown and let the progressive lessons reveal to you where the heart of the problem lies. You might be amazed at how many of the horse's issues quietly go away as you work gradually through, from 33 to 1. If you have an overly aggressive horse or one that you are not comfortable handling, it's time to contact a reputable trainer to work with both you and your horse. I don't recommend just leaving your "problem horse" out in the pasture, letting him grow old without a job. The issue certainly won't be resolved by ignoring it, and should you ever have to find a new home for your horse, you haven't set him up to succeed. All problems have solutions, it's just a matter of time, patience, and persistence.

Part Two
The Countdown

Initial Movement in the Round Pen

The round pen should be between 45 to 65 feet in diameter, with 55 feet ideal. The larger the round pen, the less control you have. In contrast, a very small pen can be unsafe with an overly aggressive horse, and also dangerous to lope in, as a horse can lose his footing or injure himself in a tight circle. Small round pens and deep footing can also discourage movement.

Goals

Your aim is to move the horse around the pen on cue and to control the direction and gait in which he is moving. You will also introduce the lariat, as this motivator will be used in subsequent lessons.

Check-In

Since you are at the very beginning of the Countdown to Broke there aren't any prerequisites for this lesson, other than being able to get your horse into the round pen (see Modern Wisdom, p. 29). As long as your horse is healthy you can begin. (To answer specifically whether your horse is physically ready to begin a training program, consult your veterinarian.) You may be starting an untouched colt that does not even respond to halter pressure or building a new foundation on a "problem" horse. Regardless of the horse and his degree of education, this is your starting point.

Cues to Use

You will teach your horse to "move off" your body pressure with the *go forward* body stance. Throughout this training program, this position is your cue for the horse to move away from you. You will also use tongue "clucking" to tell the horse to "move his feet faster."

Spot, Direction, Motivator, and Release

Spot The horse's hip

Direction Forward, away from your go forward stance within the confines of the round pen

Motivator Lariat and body pressure

Release A complete withdrawal of body pressure, vocals, and lariat

Teaching Steps

STEP ONE

Begin with your horse in the round pen. Remove his halter if you are able. Establish yourself in a central position. Hold the lariat with half the coils in each hand (see more about handling the lariat on p. 31).

You will now move your horse around the pen by "driving" him with your body pressure and lariat motivator. To do this, square up your body by looking directly at the horse's hip and "push" him (photo 13). As you do, make a "clucking" noise with your tongue, take a step toward his hip, and if needed, toss the lariat underhand toward it. The horse has the choice to move or remain still, letting the lariat hit him. He will soon learn to move before it makes contact.

The amount of pressure required will vary depending on the horse. Your horse might move easily from your body stance alone, or he may need loud clucking and the lariat thrown at his hip. Either way, you need to continue applying pressure until movement is established.

Ideally, your horse moves forward at the jog. If he lopes right away, that is okay. Movement is the goal and speed control will come later with varying body pressures that he will learn to recognize. Once movement is achieved, use just enough pressure to encourage your horse to remain at a speed above a walk.

MODERN WISDOM

Getting Your Untrained Horse into the Round Pen

In order to begin Lesson 33, the first in the Countdown to Broke, your horse must be inside the round pen. If your horse has had some early training with a halter and being led, this will not be an issue. When your horse has only had limited handling and does not "give" to halter pressure, you will need to plan a safe way to guide him into the round pen in order to begin the first lesson.

Here are some options for getting your untrained horse into the round pen:

● Set up your round pen (permanent or portable) where you can easily open gates and make "lanes" to herd your horse into the pen from a larger area, such as his pasture.

● Set up your round pen (portable) inside a larger area and feed the horse his grain and hay ration inside the round pen, closing the gate behind him.

● Using a small catch corral, spend time handling your horse and accustoming him to the halter prior to beginning the Countdown. Begin leading exercises with him. Once he is safe to lead, you can move your lessons from the catch corral to the round pen.

I recommend consulting a reputable trainer or a quality book on the subject of halter-breaking and leading if you need further assistance in this initial step.

At this time, it doesn't matter whether your horse moves clockwise or counterclockwise.

STEP TWO

Now that you have movement—around the pen—maintain it by continuing to focus your body pressure toward your horse's hip. If you see him slow down, take a step toward the hip and cluck. If this is not enough pressure, "threaten" with your lariat by moving it as if you are about to throw it. If necessary, throw the lariat firmly underhand at his hip (photo 14).

In order to dictate the speed—walk, jog, or lope—gauge the strength of your body pressure, vocals, and lariat. You do not want your horse running scared. He should understand the request and be confident in carrying it out. Once you establish a cadenced jog, for example, hold back any increase in pressure. When he knows that the lariat is only thrown if he breaks gait, he will settle in and remain at a constant speed.

Increase your pressure to ask the horse to lope, if he is not already. Keep him loping for at least six complete revolutions of the round pen. Then, simply turn your back to him and walk to the edge of the pen. This alleviates all pressure and gives the horse a release. Rest for one minute.

It is okay if your horse approaches you during your one minute break. Give him a gentle touch to the face or shoulder, proving to him that you are trustworthy. After the break, simply walk back to the center of the pen and send him off with pressure as before, continuing the exercise.

STEP THREE

After you have "released" your horse with a short break, begin again by returning to the center of the pen and "driving" him in the opposite direction. Start with clear cues for

Photo 13 I am driving Belle around the pen by "pushing" her in the chosen direction. Note how I am focused on her hip with a square posture. My lariat is ready for use, as it is my motivator; it will be used to escalate pressure as needed. In order to stay behind Belle's midsection, I walk a very small circle in the middle of the pen—always remaining square to her hip.

Photo 14 Belle slows and attempts to transition downward on her own, so I toss my lariat at her hip to encourage forward movement. You must insist on continuous movement around the pen once you've asked, until you provide a release.

him to move, but without great pressure. Gradually build pressure until he is loping again. If your horse responds to just your body and voice, do not throw your lariat. Your escalation of pressure should be smooth. Avoid "jumping into pressure." Ask for movement and then gradually intensify your pressure until it happens. This teaches your horse to respond more quickly in time.

Ask for at least six lope revolutions around the pen and offer a full release of pressure as you did in Step Two. Repeat Steps Two and Three before moving to Step Four.

STEP FOUR

Now show your horse how your level of pressure—body, voice, and lariat—changes, depending on the gait you are requesting. Do not allow the walk, but use just enough pressure to encourage the jog. Once your horse is jogging, hold steady pressure. If he decides to lope, back off the level of pressure—this means quieter vocal cueing, less aggressive body posturing, and holding your lariat still in your hands. If your horse transitions down to a walk, increase pressure again.

Do not get into the habit of making "empty threats." It is okay to merely "threaten" with the motivator—your lariat—periodically if you feel that it alone will elicit the correct response, but do not shy away from using it and actually striking the horse with it when necessary.

Ask him to jog at least six full circles, then turn your back and walk to the edge of the round pen to offer a full release and short break. After one minute, request movement at the jog in the opposite direction. Then, repeat the exercise in both directions.

STEP FIVE

Now that your horse is beginning to understand that he needs to move when you ask him to, and that he should jog when your pressure requests it, you can begin requesting gait changes from the jog to the lope and back down again. Begin by asking him to lope in the pen. Back off your pressure until your horse transitions to the jog, allow him to jog for a full circle or more, then pick up the lope again. Once he completes a few transitions properly, walk to the edge of the pen and offer a break.

Continue transitioning between the jog and the lope. Pick different spots in the round pen to ask for each gait, and have him maintain it for varying lengths of time. Whenever you or your horse needs a break, walk away and provide a full release.

If you are new to round pen work, prepare to become tired! With time, you will become more efficient in your efforts, and it won't seem such a laborious task.

Rider's Block

● Handling the lariat can be tricky in the beginning. Since it is such a great training tool, it is well worth the effort to become handy with it. Practice such simple tasks as coiling the rope, throwing it underhand, and learning to swing a proper loop (photos 15 A–C).

● If you are unsure how much pressure is right for a situation, remember what Ray Hunt taught and "use as little pressure as possible and as much as necessary."

Roadblocks

● Sometimes, a horse stops every 20 feet or so and faces

Photos 15 A–C In A, my lariat is prepared for use: I hold one end ready to be tossed underhand, if necessary, and the extra rope is neatly coiled in the opposite hand. In B, you can see my underhanded toss of one end of the lariat toward the horse's hindquarters. My body reaches forward, helping to increase the pressure. Photo C shows me recoiling the lariat after use—you should do so quietly and quickly after each throw so that it is ready should you need it, and also to keep it from getting under your feet, or your horse's.

Photos 16 A & B If your horse decides to change direction on his own, as Belle does here, immediately cut off his path as I am in A, and redirect him in the desired direction, as in B. When he responds correctly, with forward movement in the proper direction, revert to subtle cues to keep him moving.

the outside wall or fence, or changes direction on his own. When he tries this, cut his path off with your body and drive him in the direction you asked for (photos 16 A & B). Use your lariat to motivate the proper response. The point of Lesson 33 is to establish control over the horse's movement, and you have not done so when he stops or changes direction without the appropriate cue from you. If your horse is not responsive, just stay focused on the exercise, continue to pick your spot and direction, use your motivator, and patiently wait for the release point to come. If you remain consistent, the horse will eventually understand what you are asking.

Be careful with an aggressive horse. You need to be physically able to move quickly if charged or kicked at, but while it is important to remain safe and out of harm's way, it is also necessary to remain dominant and show the horse that he cannot "move" you at will. Because of this, I

MODERN WISDOM

Warming Up and Cooling Down

You cannot train a lame horse. So, in order to avoid injury, spend sufficient time warming your horse up before pushing for speed or advanced maneuvers. Not only do you want to prepare your horse's body for work, but you also want to prepare his mind. Start every lesson with the "slow familiar" to create a positive beginning to the day.

A proper cooling down period is just as important. After a period of riding or groundwork, spend time walking the horse at a relaxed pace to allow his breathing, body temperature, and heart rate to come back down to the normal ranges.

never move for a horse, unless I am sure I will be injured. A horse that displays this sort of behavior needs to spend extra time on Lesson 33 in order for the trainer to establish control and respect.

● In contrast, when working with a fearful horse that attempts to escape pressure by "climbing the walls," back off. A horse that tends to be afraid does not need much pressure to keep him moving forward.

Lesson 33's Benefits

● By making the horse move, you gain a higher place in the "pecking order." This establishes respect and consequently, control.

● This lesson always utilizes a motivator and release. By consistently offering the release, the horse learns that a release always follows the correct response. As you move forward with training, the horse will start to look for this release in every lesson.

● The exercise establishes one of the main motivators used in training—the lariat—as something the horse needs to respect. This makes the next steps progress more quickly. Before long, the mere "threat" of the lariat will be enough to motivate a correct response.

● This initial interaction with a horse in the round pen tells you a lot about the horse's movement, attitude, and his overall "eye appeal"—important characteristics for those looking to purchase a performance prospect.

Green Light

Establishing forward movement on cue is the building block of all ground and saddle work. You can only move on to the next lesson once you can move your horse forward, at varying speeds, in both directions. The better your control over his speed and the more subtle your cues, the better off you will be in the long run.

The amount of time that I spend on this lesson varies greatly. If I am working with a "long" yearling and I want to establish forward movement because it might be too early to begin much else, I will work on this lesson in combination with Lessons 32 and 31 for a few weeks. If I am starting a two-year-old and this lesson goes well, I might only establish what I need as a foundation and move on after 10 minutes. The important consideration is whether both you and your horse are able to complete the lesson with ease and mutual understanding. If so, you can move forward.

Inside Turns

Just because the horse does not turn to the inside at first does not necessarily mean that you have assumed the wrong position or given the wrong cue. Your horse may not understand what you are looking for yet.

Goals

You are now going to change your horse's direction, while insisting that he turn to the inside of the round pen—toward the center—before resuming forward movement in the opposite direction.

Check-In

You must be able to move your horse around the pen consistently. If you have completed Lesson 33, you now have cues to request this movement, as well as motivators to back them up.

Cues to Use

In addition to the learned cues for forward movement—body pressure, clucking vocals, and the lariat—you will now teach your horse to recognize your body's position as a signal for a precise change of direction. Your cue will be an opening of your body's posture, while simultaneously cutting off the horse's path. I discuss this cue further in the Teaching Steps.

Spot, Direction, Motivator, and Release

Spot Horse's nose
Direction Toward you
Motivators Quick turns, body pressure, clucking vocals, and lariat
Release A softening of body pressure while allowing the horse to move freely around the pen

Teaching Steps
STEP ONE

If you simply want a change of direc-tion, you can easily cut off the horse's path. But, this wouldn't necessar-ily result in an *inside* turn—he might make an *outside* turn instead.

In order to condition the horse to respond to your request you must establish a cue—your body position. You want to cut off forward move-ment (jog or lope), so stepping toward the round pen panels and getting in front of the horse is important, but instead of taking a direct step toward them and trapping the horse's move-ment (driving his nose away from you), soften your request by angling your-self away from the horse. So, don't take a step directly toward the panel, or take a step backward, but instead "open" your shoulder and move back at a 45-degree angle. The body posi-tion should look as if you are opening a door. This gives a reasonable amount of pressure to encourage the turn, but allows your horse room to make it to the inside of the pen (photo 17).

STEP TWO

THE CORRECT RESPONSE

When your horse makes the inside turn correctly, there is a point where the horse is committed to the turn and facing you—do not drive or pressure him until he is past this point, or you will confuse him and cause him to turn to the outside instead or continue for-ward in the wrong direction (photo 18). Once he has completed the turn, gently ask for forward movement in the new direction with softer vocals and body

Photo 17 In order to encourage an inside turn, you must cut off your horse's path, while still allowing room for him to feel comfortable turning in toward you. Here, note how I am moving left toward the round pen panels, away from Belle, with my body positioned like "an open door." This "invites" her to turn to the inside. If I walk directly toward the Priefert® sign, I will likely cause Belle to turn to the outside. Horses feel subtle pressure—carefully gauge your pressure level so you do not "drive" your horse into the fence, resulting in an outside turn.

Photo 18 Wait for your horse to commit to the inside turn, looking to the inside toward you as Belle is doing here, before you drive him forward in the opposite direction. Once your horse is looking in to you, your pressure will result in an inside turn. If you apply the pressure too early—say, when he is stopped on the rail and looking away from you—it may result in an outside turn.

pressure, and allow him to move freely around the pen. This is your "Yes" response to the horse's correct turn inside.

THE INCORRECT RESPONSE

Should the horse change direction, but to the outside, you have likely applied too much direct body pressure "toward his nose." Immediately ask him to change his direction back again, but step back a little more and give him more room to make the turn toward you. *This must be done quickly.* I like to add my voice and increase my body pressure at this point in order to create an uncomfortable situation. This is your "No" response when a turn is incorrect. He will try to find a way to avoid the additional pressure, sharp vocals, hard work, and the toss of the lariat. Once your horse figures out that you are less aggressive when he turns to the inside, he will continue to do so on cue. It may take one—or many—tries for him to understand this, but as long as you

remain focused and execute your "Yes" and "No" consistently and clearly, he will begin to respond to your request correctly.

STEP THREE

Establish good forward movement and begin working on a series of inside turns from a lope or a jog, depending on how well the horse is maintaining the circle and staying forward. When he "quits" on you, keep him loping. He does not need to be "relaxed"—the exercise accomplishes this for you.

After a few consistent revolutions, ask for a turn (photos 19 A–D). If you get an inside turn right away, keep him moving comfortably at a lope or jog, asking for another turn every one, two, or three revolutions. The idea is to space the first turns out in order to avoid excessively pressuring and possibly confusing him: when you ask for turns too close together, your "Yes" and "No" responses may

Photos 19 A–D I establish forward movement to my left (A). I then request an inside turn by cutting off Belle's path—moving toward the round pen panels, while backing off some pressure by moving away from her (B). In other words, I move toward the panels, but at an angle away from Belle's nose. This allows room for her to turn inside. I wait for Belle to look inside, then add pressure with my left hand—holding the lariat—to push her right eye away from me and commit her to the turn (C). Once Belle has committed to the turn, I use body pressure, vocals, and the lariat to request forward movement in the opposite direction (D).

begin to look alike. Once you get inside turns consistently, change up the intervals and duration of movement between your turn requests.

If you are dealing with a horse that does not give you an inside turn at every request at first, be patient. Go ahead and ask for a turn every revolution, as long as you are in position to promptly offer your "No" response. Pressure your horse and make him uncomfortable, until he turns his face toward you—at which moment, especially with a tougher horse, immediately relax your pressure and offer a big "Yes." Let him face you for a few seconds before you gently drive him off in the opposite direction. Set your horse up for success by asking for an inside turn when it is likely he will respond correctly. When the horse is already looking toward you is an ideal time. But, when he is looking outside the round pen or loping at a fast pace, it is often best to wait.

If your horse stops, stands, and faces you at any point, withhold all pressure and stand still. Allow him to relax a moment and he will be far more inclined to turn inside toward you the next time you ask him. When he is facing you, you can always gently push him off and "complete the turn" from that point. If the horse stops and faces away from you, however, continue to drive him forward until he turns inside or stops to face you, then immediately release all pressure.

STEP FOUR

When able to consistently get an inside turn upon request, improve your accuracy. By asking for a turn at a precise point on the round pen, you improve your request as well your horse's sensitivity to it. Do not always turn at or near the same points, however, or your horse will start to turn without your asking.

Your cues requesting the inside turn will change with time. At first, they will need to be "big." As mentioned, you will have to not only "open" your shoulder, but may have to move a few steps or more on a 45-degree angle away from the horse to invite him to turn. In time, your horse will be very attentive to your body and a more subtle opening of the shoulder will be all it takes.

Since this lesson requires a lot of exercise, keep its duration to a reasonable level. With a young horse, you should only work 15 to 30 minutes. With an older horse, you may work 30 to 45 minutes. When you are able to give breaks, you can work longer. Be mindful of the weather and the horse's physical condition. In order to create a solid conditioned response from your cues, you must "rehearse," so I recommend setting out to complete 500 correct inside turns. You can do them in "sets" over a few days, at all three gaits, and always ending your session on a good note. Maybe you complete 25 inside turns your first session and then call it a day. In your next lesson, you can go ahead and complete another 100 to 200 inside turns.

Count your horse's correct inside turns. When you are new to this lesson, a few can feel like a lot. By keeping track yourself or with help from a partner, you will know for sure how many you have completed.

Rider's Block

● The inside turn cue can be difficult for you, the handler, to understand at first. Trust me, this is a normal and reasonable issue. Some of you will cut off the horse's path and encourage an outside turn without knowing it. The body position that encourages an inside turn gives the horse room to do so without feeling a lot of pressure.

Roadblock

● Some horses will not turn inside easily. I have trained many horses that offered consistent inside turns almost immediately, but I have also had some that would not look to the inside or turn toward me for an entire session or more. This may be because they are frightened; or your body position cue is "pressuring" them to turn to the outside; or,

One-Sided Horses

With nearly every horse you train, you'll find one side of him is easier to teach than the other. This may be caused by handling practices, an inherent trait, or both. If you know beforehand that this is a normal condition, you will not be surprised by it and can go about resolving the issue.

In the round pen, you may find your horse only lets you approach him from one side. He may also only let you "see" one eye, as he protects his "shy side" by angling his body away from you and refusing to turn inside toward you when the shy side will be exposed.

By following the Countdown's lessons and spending time proving to your horse that you are trustworthy, he will begin to let you approach and handle his shy side. Spend extra time standing on the shy side, until he is just as comfortable with you there as he is on his better side.

When in the saddle, you will find that the horse responds differently depending which direction you are traveling and which side you are cueing. You may find that one side of your horse is more sensitive and giving, while the other is dull and stiff. Never ignore a "bad side" or a less-than-ideal response. Work toward both sides responding perfectly.

---

sometimes, a previous handler lunged them for years without letting them turn in. It really doesn't matter why the horse is more difficult at this point as the reason will not change your approach: stay focused, and make your "Yes" and "No" responses clear and timely.

Lesson 32's Benefits

● You are beginning to establish specific control over your horse's movement. As you progress in the Countdown to Broke, you need to be able to move your horse where you want, when you want. The more control that you establish in the beginning not only speeds up the training process, but, if you keep the requests clear, allows the horse to build confidence and avoid excessive confusion. This exercise also trains you to use your "Yes" and "No" responses, and helps you understand how a release truly works when conditioning a response in your horse. You are also learning to become efficient in your groundwork and shouldn't become as tired during a session.

Green Light

If you can answer "Yes" to the following questions, then you are ready to move on to Lesson 31:

▶ Have you completed 500 inside turns?

▶ Can you complete at least 50 inside turns in a row without one mistake?

▶ Can you turn your horse precisely at a specific point along the round pen's panels?

▶ Does your horse turn well at a walk, jog, and lope?

▶ Does your horse look in toward you much of the time, as opposed to paying attention to what's outside of the pen?

Asking the Horse to "Come In"

Goals

You want your horse to face, approach, and stand with you on cue. This response is first trained in the round pen, but later transfers to all handling situations.

Check-In

After completing the previous two lessons you can now control your horse's movement. Not only can you successfully request different speeds in the round pen, but you can also ask for your horse to turn toward the inside before resuming forward movement in the opposite direction. You are ready for the next lesson in the Countdown.

Cues to Use

When you ask your horse to *turn*, *face*, and *approach* you in the round pen, your cue is similar to the *inside-turn cue* (see p. 34). Turn your horse toward the inside with a subtle opening of the shoulder, but instead of driving your horse around the pen, remain still with your hands and lariat held quietly in front of your body. This tells the horse that he can stop working and approach you.

Spot, Direction, Motivator, and Release

Spot The horse's nose

Direction Toward you

Motivator Hard work

Release No work, a neutral body position (stand still, with hands and lariat quiet), addition of pleasing stimulus

Teaching Steps

STEP ONE

You want to begin this lesson after completing enough revision (inside turns and forward movement) that your horse is at least slightly tired. You need to use this fatigue—the result of hard work—as your motivator. You cannot make a horse stand still; you can only give him the chance to do so. You can, however, make him move.

Begin by asking for movement around the pen. Prepare yourself for an inside-turn cue—open up your shoulder, wait for the horse to face you. When he is clearly turned and focused on you, relax your hands and lariat and remain still. This is your cue that *he* is now allowed to remain still, as long as he focuses on you. It is important to not even *think* about pushing or moving your horse at this point, as you do not want to give off any subtle incorrect signals.

STEP TWO

Two things might happen when you offer your horse this cue: he might see you open your shoulder, remember it means you want an inside turn, and turn quickly to the new direction, or he may notice that once he faces you, you do not drive him off and forward again—so he stands and looks at you, even if just for a moment.

Either way, when you offer him this cue, let him decide. If he stands and faces you, remain still as described in Step One. If he continues with the turn and/or is doing something else on his own, regain control of his movement

Work the horse very hard at a lope around the pen. You want him to feel short of breath. This is a stronger motivator than a gentle jog. You do not want the horse to become worn out, but you do want him to simply need a break. It is the difference between a 100-yard dash and a 6-mile run. You need the horse's energy in the lessons, so don't use it up with long slow workouts, just make him want a rest so badly that he actively looks for a release.

by pushing him around the pen, and simply prepare to offer another inside-turn cue along with the option to stand still and face you. He will soon notice that something is different, and with a few chances (and a little more work!) should stand still and look at you.

Ultimately, you are giving him two options: stand still and face you, or look away and so be pressured to move. The choice is his. Every time your horse faces you, remain quiet for as long as he looks at you. As soon as he looks away, add gentle pressure—such as a soft cluck or shake of the lariat—and prepare to move him off around the pen. If he then responds by looking at you again, assume your neutral pose, but should he decide to head off on his own path, regain control of his movement and begin again.

STEP THREE

Ask your horse to look at you for longer and longer periods of time. You will soon be able to keep his attention with a soft cluck, leg slap, or shake of the lariat. Lock eyes with his and only pressure him when he breaks contact, always rewarding him promptly when he "gives you his face back." Once you feel that he understands this part of the lesson and is complying, begin to look for that first step toward you.

Mentally compare how your body appears to the horse as you drive him around with your lariat poised and ready, versus the language you give off when you stand still and offer head rubs and kind words. There should be a big difference. When signaling to drive forward, your actions are deliberate and focused on the spot. When you allow the horse to relax, your body is more fluid and soft. With multiple lessons and more handling, your horse will easily recognize your "pressure-on" as opposed to your "pressure-off" signals.

STEP FOUR

Now that you have established your come to cue, you need to break down the lesson into smaller, more teachable steps. The goal is to have the horse come in from the rail and stand with you. The first steps, which we have established, are to have the horse face you momentarily from a position by the fence, and then face you for a longer period of time before he moves off or looks away. Now you want your horse to take one step toward you, followed by more steps until he is standing within reach—about 6 inches away (photos 20 A–G).

Build up the difficulty of the lesson by not only asking him to lock eyes with you, but also make a forward step toward you. Move your horse around the pen, ask him to stand and face you, but now when he stops and looks but does not take a step toward you, ask him to move off again. You are upping the ante and now only reward a forward step. Once he takes even a small step toward you, reward him with a longer rest—20 seconds or so. Then push him back off, and look for another stop, face, and step toward you. When he has done this several times, only

Photos 20 A–G Here, Belle is moving to the right around the pen and I ask for an inside turn, remaining still with my hands and lariat in front of my body (A). My body language is neutral. Belle knows to turn inside on this cue; she is actively looking for a break from work. I do not request a complete turn and continue to stay relaxed, showing no signs of pressure toward the horse (B). She is "wanting in" at this point. Belle's body completely turns toward me as she approaches—she is focused on me and "invited" by my neutral stance (C). I remain still until she is within reach—about 6 inches away—when I reward her with a head rub (D & E). She already knows this action means "Yes!" In order to strengthen her response, I back away a few steps, and wait (F). Belle comes to me, resulting in another "Yes!" (G). These small repetitions strengthen the horse's response and create lasting behaviors.

reward two steps. Continue building in this manner until he is standing with you in the middle.

STEP FIVE

If your horse will allow you, it is very helpful to reward him for coming in to you with a soft rub on the face and encouraging words, and then calmly walk away just a few steps, perhaps in a circle around him. The horse just might start to follow with his face—if he does, give him another rub and stand still, offering a comfortable rest period (photos 21 A–E). You should rub your horse on the face smoothly, without patting or smacking him. The face rub helps you tell the horse "Yes" in future exercises. It is also a calming and bonding act.

Not all horses will respond well to a rub on the face at this point. If this is the case, do not offer it as a reward; acceptance of this kind of touch will come with time.

The strongest motivator here is, of course, the release of pressure to work hard. Loping around the pen is quite tiring. Your horse will soon learn that the best place to be is standing quietly next to you, receiving a comfortable break. This is to become his "default position" in the round pen. Unless you request movement from this point on, it is

where your horse should always be—calmly standing next to you. He will soon love this spot, where he can relax and receive positive reinforcement.

STEP SIX

This exercise can be continually improved. With frequent and proper training, a horse should come in to you in a much larger area, such as a paddock or large riding arena (*further*). This will not necessarily happen right away, but certainly once the lesson is strengthened through repetition.

You may also build speed into the same lesson plan (*faster*). Once you have a horse that will come all the way in to you and fully understands your cue, start asking for a quicker walk or jog toward you in the middle. (As long as my horse does not dawdle or meander, I am usually satisfied with a steady walking speed.)

Finally, make your come in cue more subtle (*softer*). Soon, it will appear you and your horse are having a silent conversation.

Rider's Block

● It is important not to miss your horse's small incremental improvements. If he stops and looks at you for *just one*

Photos 21 A–E I ask Belle to come in to me, and she does willingly, so I reward her (A). I then move off to her side a couple of steps and wait for her to face me again; when she does not, I cluck and move my upper body, "threatening" her with movement (B). I move a few mores steps, with the intent of forming a small circle around her, and Belle follows with her face. I stop and reward her frequently (C–E).

you ask you will condition him to stay out, thus allowing him to misinterpret your cue, contributing to the length of time it takes for the horse to understand what earns him a release.

● You may find that your horse is easily approached at this point in training—or, he may not be. If he is, you can greatly speed up the steps in this lesson by rewarding him with head rubs after the slightest of correct responses, then retreating back to the center of the pen. He will be far more inclined to take more steps toward you on cue. If he is not ready for your approach at this point, continue with the lesson and know that you are working toward solving that very issue.

Roadblocks

● When the horse has taken two steps toward the middle but will not come in any further ("locking up"), "threaten"

second in the beginning, reward him immediately with a release. If you ignore this moment, or continue to miss release points, you will encourage him to just keep on moving. Give the horse a chance to respond properly. If you need to move the horse out, do so for a brief time—such as a quarter round of the pen—before you ask the horse to come back in. While it is not wrong to work the horse for a longer period, if that is all

Confining Your Horse

I want my horse to be just as comfortable in a stall as he is in an open field with his friends. The only way to accomplish this is to actually put him in one! If his stall is clean, dry, and has plenty of hay and water, he will learn to relax and enjoy his time there.

I am a big advocate of movement and feel that horses need ample opportunity and freedom to move. This will help keep your horse sound in both mind and body. That being said, I also want to have a quiet, safe, domesticated mount that is willing to be kept in a stall or trailer without being stressed. I believe that keeping your horse in the barn is good for him—there is a good chance that you will need to from time to time, anyway, say at a horse show or veterinary hospital. And, of course if you live in a region with severe weather or in less rural area where turnout is limited, stalling might be the normal routine.

As you begin working your horse through this training program, it is an ideal time to begin keeping your horse in a stall or small paddock for regular periods. If you take a two-year-old and work him for just one day, then turn him back out in a large field or range area, you may not be able to catch him readily the following day. You want to avoid any "games" starting where your horse thinks it is acceptable to walk away from you as you approach with a halter in hand. By keeping your horse close to the work area, and in a smaller confined space, he will not be able to start this bad habit.

to throw the lariat at his hip (act as if you will, but do not let go) once or twice and give the horse a chance to respond correctly. I find the horse often thinks, "If I come closer to the middle, I will not have to work and this trainer guy will stop bugging me." Since he has found releases before by coming closer, this may be just the prompt to encourage the response you are looking for. If your horse refuses, send him off with authority and work him hard before asking him to come in again.

Lesson 31's Benefits

● You now have the *come to cue* confirmed—your horse turns and faces you, and comes in to you upon request. You have established more control and working in the round pen will now be easier for both you and the horse. You have further conditioned hard work as a motivator. Your horse now "wants in." It's important to note that many conventional training methods never allow the horse to "want in" or make finding a moment of complete relaxation the horse's choice. Instead of always judging the amount and type of pressure that a horse receives, I worry much more about the timing and size of the release. It makes for a much more relaxed and confident horse, and with future lessons, these traits will only be strengthened. I want my horse to find confidence and pleasure *with me*, not away from me.

Green Light

Do you and your horse have a "default position" in the round pen? After working on this lesson you should be able control the horse in the pen, and he should stop, face, and approach you on cue. Beside you is your horse's new "happy place." If it takes your horse three round pen panels before he makes a requested turn in, and he then saunters to the middle with many small pauses in between steps, then he is not ready to move on.

Movement gains respect, allowing the horse to stand calmly with you gains trust. They are both very important to establish with your horse before teaching further skills, whether on the ground or from the saddle.

Facing and Following

Goals

You are now teaching your horse to always face you and remain close regardless of your location in the round pen. He must stay with you while you are in motion as well as standing still. Your horse should focus on and follow you, until you ask for a different response.

Check-In

You can move your horse, change his direction, and request he come to you in the round pen. He also stands quietly at your side. This lesson further improves this *come to* response. If you have a solid *come to cue* established, the following steps will be easily understood and executed by both you and your horse.

Cues to Use

Your cue for the horse to give you his attention, face you, approach you, and remain at your side will be a "kissing" sound or clucking vocal. Only use this kiss or cluck when your horse looks away, or does not step forward at your request.

Spot, Direction, Motivator, and Release

Spot The horse's nose
Direction Toward you (facing you) as well as coming close to you
Motivator Hard work
Release Allowing the horse to remain at rest by your side, as well as head rubs and encouraging words

Teaching Steps

STEP ONE

Ask your horse to approach you in the round pen. When your horse is calmly facing you within reach, take a step to your right (photo 22). Cue the horse to pay attention to your movement with a kissing or clucking noise. When he responds by looking at you, release him by standing quietly. The second you lose the horse's attention and the ability to see both of his eyes, ask again with the kiss or cluck. This looks a lot like Lesson 31 (p. 39), where you gave the horse two options: to remain focused on you and relaxed, or to look or move away, and as a result have to work hard around the pen. Given the choice and work you did in the previous lesson, your horse will soon give you his full attention.

If your horse will not face you, tell him to move off and work him, then begin again by asking him to approach you, move one big step to the right, and ask for his attention with your vocal cue. When he gives you his face—the ability to see both eyes—offer him a soft rub and kind words. Now take two steps to the right. Move in a small circle around the horse, working on one and two steps to begin with.

STEP TWO

At this point, your horse is beginning to realize that if he stays focused on you, you will offer praise and not ask him to work. As you move one, two, and three steps at a time, and he continues to focus on you with his eyes, his feet will eventually begin to

Some horses will already follow you at this point, and it may be tempting to move on to the next lesson. However, this step remains important and should not be skipped over. You do not want to leave any holes in your horse's training.

move in order to keep up with his neck. If you can "control his nose," the feet will follow. Build the response to the right, working on adding more and more steps. Stay on a small circle around the horse and only try to improve his "facing ability" at this point.

STEP THREE

Once you have your horse's face and attention consistently to the right, and his feet are beginning to stay with his body (meaning he is straight and not just stretching his neck around to follow you) you can start over again going to the left. Make sure that you treat both sides equally.

STEP FOUR

Make a full circle around the horse in both directions and moving at different speeds. Give frequent "Yes" responses when he responds correctly. Here is your chance to establish a "Yes" response that will last his lifetime. Softly rub his head and tell him he is doing well. Your horse will associate this head rub with relaxation and a release. In the future, you will be able to use this to encourage, relax, and bond with him.

STEP FIVE

Once you are confident in asking your horse to face you in a small circle around him in both directions, you are ready to move ahead. So far, you have asked your horse to move his feet enough to remain aligned with you. Now ask your horse to take forward steps while remaining focused on you. This is the beginning of him *following you.*

Continue to move in a slow circle around the horse, but start to move away from him at the same time. Visualize your body position and movement as a slow spiral away from the starting point—you are not only continuing to ask him to face you but also asking for *small forward steps* to stay close to you (photos 23 A–C).

Give your horse a lot of praise when he first steps "into" you. Instead of making the lesson more difficult right away, simply ask him to continue facing you and continue to offer rewards and head rubs. You want to give a big "Yes" response and ensure the horse he is on the right track. Start again in

Photo 22 As I take a step to the right, Belle maintains her focus, following me with her nose. Try to not "chase your horses head." If his attention wanders, cluck or kiss until he faces you again.

your slow spiral away from him. As he steps toward you, reach back and softly rub him on the face, continue to slowly walk around. If you are losing him, make your circle smaller again and start over. Keep your training steps small and build slowly.

Carefully watch your horse's feet to make sure that you reward his slightest effort to move forward.

STEP SIX

Continue building the number of steps between "Yes" responses. Start to walk straighter lines and change directions. If your horse "falls apart" at any point, go back to what he can do and begin again.

Try moving at different speeds and in various patterns around the pen. Work on the horse approaching you from

Photos 23 A–C Belle comes in to me willingly, offering me her face, and I reward her (A). I then step to the side and away from Belle, inviting her to not only face me, but take a small step toward me (B). When she follows me and offers me her face, I reward her again. We spiral outward from our starting point and soon Belle is not only stepping around the circle, but with forward motion (C). I now have a horse that wants to follow me.

Advance and Retreat

Scenario One: Imagine walking into a store to make a large purchase, say, a washer and dryer. You are already stressed out about spending quite a bit of money and buying something that you know little about. A salesperson with an aggressive posture approaches you. You feel trapped and would like to be left alone. The salesperson stands in your space and verbally badgers you with personal questions and a long sales pitch, all the while pretending to be your new friend. You cannot get a word in edgewise and find yourself backing out the front door to avoid the entire situation. This encounter just confirmed in your mind why you did not want to make such a large purchase in the first place.

Scenario Two: Imagine walking into the same store to make the same large purchase. You are already stressed out about spending the money and buying something that you know little about. A salesperson quietly approaches you with a kind greeting and then leaves you alone. You are now a bit more at ease with your surroundings. As you start to look around and find you have a question, the salesperson responds to you politely, and then again leaves you to wander on your own. You investigate some more products and when queried, he intelligently advises you whether or not they will meet your needs. His sincer-

ity is evident. You have a stress-free conversation with him and realize he is not trying to force you into anything. You conclude that this purchase is a good idea, even though your initial impulse was to put it off.

You want to build the same trusting relationship with your horse as the salesperson managed to do with the customer in Scenario Two. It is your choice as to how it starts out and how it will end. Even though comparing horse training to buying a washer and dryer set is not a perfect analogy, it does have some parallels—imagine what it is like for a scared young horse to be in the round pen for the very first time. Though maybe you are not as frightened, feeling "trapped" by an intrusive sales clerk can certainly be similarly bothersome and unpleasant.

Advancing toward a horse, just close enough to keep him from moving off, and then retreating back to a comfortable distance for him builds rapport. The horse begins to sort out in his mind that you are not going to come all the way toward him until he is ready. With each new advance you prove to your horse that you are not going to harm him. You can then use the horse's natural curiosity and ability to accept your role as leader, and not force yourself upon him. With each successful exposure, you gain a bit of trust, and the more you interact and establish control, the stronger the level of trust. It grows incrementally.

further out and following you from greater distances. This can be a fun exercise for both of you and will only strengthen the conditioned response you are after.

The horse has now "learned to be lead" without a rope, and this, when firmly established, will benefit you greatly in future training.

Rider's Block

● Your horse may refuse to take that first forward step toward you. There comes a point when you have to stop rewarding what he *already does* well and only praise him when he makes an *improvement*. When your horse is focused on you and will pivot around and remain locked on you, you are on the right path. But if you continue to give him your "Yes" response, he does not have any motivation to improve. Keep the request reasonable, but ask for some kind of *progression*. If your horse does not improve, move him around the pen and start over. Then, the moment a small forward step is taken, offer your "Yes."

Roadblocks

● You may have to deal with a horse that is overly fearful and does not want to be touched, especially on the face. This exercise can be successful without you rubbing your horse's face. It may take longer to complete using only a release of body pressure and vocal praise, but in some cases, this is exactly what you need to do. With time in your presence and the option to choose to remain relaxed, your horse's confidence level and trust will improve. Take your time. You may have to work on facing and following for a while before you move on, but once you are successful, the benefits will be great.

Lesson 30's Benefits

● Not only does your horse come toward you from the rail on cue, but he stays with you when you walk, change direction, stop, or speed up to a jog. This is a strong building block for future lessons in the Countdown to Broke. A quiet, confident horse that is relaxed when beside you will "assist" you with his "sacking-out," bridle work, saddling, mounting, and even transfer what he's learned to riding lessons.

● If your horse is already halter-broke, you have just significantly improved the way he interacts with you. If your horse is not, he can now be led without a halter, making him much easier to handle and work on the ground. He has also figured out by now that running hard around the pen is not a lot of fun, so most of the time, subtle pressure from your body or a "threat" from the lariat will be enough to evoke the proper response.

● This exercise gives you many opportunities to "love on" your horse, improving rapport and level of trust. Horses that are "loved on" with your hands and spend quality time relaxing in your presence grow confident. Do not confuse this with allowing your horse to become rude, pushy, undisciplined, or spoiled (in the negative sense). I still ask my horse to move when I ask and respond to my cues. I want a horse with a strong work ethic and a lot of "try," but when I "turn off" my pressure, I want him to cock a leg and remain quiet and content by my side.

Green Light

Since you are moving on to "sacking-out" exercises in the following lessons, the ability to have your horse remain quiet and focused on you is very important. If your horse is not comfortable around you, always wants to leave the pen, or remains inattentive, "sacking-out" will be very difficult. I recommend *not* moving forward until you are convinced that your horse is quiet, confident, and really wants to be with you.

28
27
26
25
24
23
22
21
20
19
18
17

"Sacking-Out"

The term "sacking-out" originates from the traditional use of an empty grain sack to desensitize the horse and prove that the strange, crinkly, noisy, and odd-shaped item is not going to harm him. The way in which this exercise has been (and is) done varies from trainer to trainer and region to region.

7
6
5
4
3
2
1

Goals

You want your horse to learn to "handle" his fear, *without* moving his feet. This means he does not shy away from an object, and shows no signs of distress or panic when touched or approached with something frightening to him. In modern-day training, this is known as "sacking-out." (There are a few different ways to achieve this, which I've outlined on the following pages; they are all helpful and work well together.) You will also introduce new items to be used in everyday training and teach your horse to stand still while willingly offering his foot for you to hold.

Additional Equipment Needed

▸ Small tarp
▸ Garbage bag
▸ Grooming brushes
▸ Hoof pick
▸ Baseball cap
▸ Other "scary" barn items

Check-In

In Lesson 29, you need your horse to "want in." This means he would rather stand quietly with you in the center of the round pen, than look away or wander off on his own. If you are uncertain that your horse "wants in," then you need to go back and work on the previous lessons again. I also recommend reviewing inside turns (p. 34) as well as facing and following (p. 45) right before you begin. This reestablishes some recently learned cues and improves your horse's desire to stand still next to you.

Teaching Steps

STEP ONE: "SACKING-OUT" WITH YOUR HANDS

Begin with your horse beside you in the middle of the round pen. Rub your hands on his neck, face, ears, mane, back, barrel, front legs…in other words, all over his body. At first it is reasonable to just ask him to accept his upper neck being rubbed. Use smooth but firm circular rubs to work on this "easy" spot first. You want the horse to remain comfortable while you prove to him that he can trust you. Proceed from there, gradually introducing new areas. To help the horse stay relaxed, keep a hand on a part of the body that he is familiar with you touching, such as the withers or neck, as your other hand reaches out and works on new territory (photo 24).

Some horses let you rub most of their body with very little trouble, while others have a hard time with the head and neck right from the start. When your horse dances around or moves away from your contact, give him a chance to calm down by going back to the areas where he accepts your touch before you venture on to new ones again. If your horse reacts with a small—but safe—flinch or shy, focus your rubbing on the trouble spot until the reaction goes away. When he reacts by moving his feet a lot or if he acts aggressive, send him off to work around the pen, and start over.

Photo 24 Continue to build your horse's acceptance level by rubbing new territory with your hands (and later, ropes—as I am here—brushes and other items that he might find scary). Keep one hand on the horse in a spot that is familiar to him—such as the neck or withers—as you work a new area with the second hand or item. This helps the horse relax.

Advancing toward your horse with a new exposure or contact, followed by retreating, is a highly effective way of building trust (see Advance and Retreat, p. 48). I like to approach my horse, rub him on an area that he is not crazy about, and walk away. I then ask him to approach me before I repeat the same step. If you continually retreat before he has the chance to move away, followed by your horse willingly re-approaching you, there's a much better chance he'll accept the new exposures and contact.

Depending on your horse, "sacking-out" with your hands may take a while. Never ignore a slight flinch or shy, as it will show up as a problem down the road. Deal with all fear issues that arise in this step. Do not move on until your horse is comfortable being rubbed all over his body: including the legs, ears, girth, flanks, dock, and croup.

Three tricks to help "sack out" a horse:
- *Retreat before he does.*
- *Don't quit until he is desensitized to the contact or object.*
- *Use hard work as the motivator to stand still with you.*

STEP TWO: DEALING WITH THE HEAD

If your horse is at all "head-shy," this is the time to fix it. I start by rubbing the horse's face, then smoothly pass my hand over his ears and onto his upper mane. The horse may flinch, but I move off the sensitive ear area before he has a chance to react further. I repeat this as long as it takes for him to accept me rubbing and touching him there. I may walk away and ask him to follow, or mix it up with rubbing another area, but I never ignore head or ear problems— these can be dangerous in the future and are certainly not a lot of fun to deal with if left unresolved.

STEP THREE: INTRODUCING THE LARIAT AND OTHER NEW ITEMS

Gradually build on the horse's confidence by now holding a lariat or lead rope in your rubbing hand, or using a soft grooming brush to make contact all over his body (photos 25 A–D). It really does not matter what you use, but include "everyday" items. Depending on your horse's progress with "sacking-out," increase the number of items used and the time spent on this step.

STEP FOUR: INTRODUCING PROTECTIVE BOOTS

As I mentioned in Part I, I believe horses should begin wearing protective boots early in training. I recommend putting boots on all four legs—they protect your horse from popping splints, acquiring lower-leg cuts and bruises, and they support his maturing tendons and ligaments. Young horses can be clumsy and once in training, there is the additional danger of hitting the round pen panels or arena fencing.

At this point in the "sacking-out" process, your hands, brushes, and ropes have been all over the horse, and you

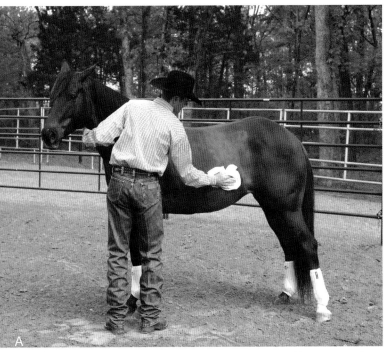

Photos 25 A–D   Your goal is to raise the horse's acceptance level of fearful objects, as you are preparing him to carry very precious cargo…you! Begin with a new object that inspires a low level of fear, such as the bunched up garbage bag I rub on Belle's barrel in A. First work on areas the horse is more comfortable with you touching, while continuing to venture out to body areas that the horse might be uneasy about. Increase the difficulty as I do in B, by opening up the bag and beginning again. If Belle moves, I will send her off and make her work hard for a few minutes, then allow her to return and stand quietly with me as I begin again. It is important to address the areas above the shoulders, including the face, neck, and ears. Belle reacts to the garbage bag on her face in C, raising her head and moving her feet, but I continue to work on the area until she stands quietly. Habituation can only occur when you work through the issue. Finally, in D I offer positive reinforcements as well as assurances that everything is copasetic… allowing for a calm ending to the lesson.

have a much better read on whether he is ready for you to put protective boots on him yet—or not. Begin with just one front boot, and send the horse around the pen. Invite him back into the middle, and add the second front boot—and so on, until all four are on and the horse pays no notice (photo 26). He might initially react with a kick or high step, so it is best to deal with each boot separately.

STEP FIVE: "SACKING-OUT" THE BODY

Use a soft rope or lariat, or both, and place it on and around the horse's body. Softly swing it, allowing it to strike the horse gently, until he no longer flinches or moves. Position the rope under each of the horse's forearms and rub it lightly back and forth. Run the rope down each leg to accustom the horse to rope friction and pressure on his legs as well as his body. Simulate front and rear cinch or girth pressures by wrapping it around the horse's barrel at the front and the back of the saddle area—apply sturdy pressure and slight friction for a few seconds, followed by a full release. Do this over and over again until the horse is downright bored with it!

STEP SIX: INTRODUCING THE SADDLE BLANKET OR PAD

The saddle blanket is important; it is large and scary, but it is an item the horse must accept comfortably. First, rub the horse all over his body with the blanket. Then, gently swing the blanket at your horse, allowing it to strike him softly from neck to tail. Increase the pressure by swinging it harder as you progress. Being rhythmic is very beneficial—in other words, bump or throw your saddle blanket to a consistent beat.

Continue until your horse does not flinch or react in any way. Finally, throw the blanket upward and let it land on his back—exaggerate what you normally do prior to saddling (photo 27). Make sure that there is absolutely no reaction from your horse.

STEP SEVEN: DEALING WITH SOUND AND MOVEMENT

Take a baseball cap or plastic garbage bag (folded up) and gently shake it while approaching your horse from the

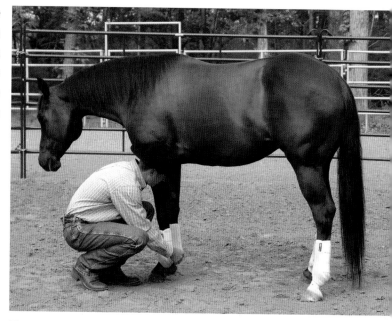

Photo 26 Belle stands quietly and trustingly as I add all four protective boots. Work your way up to all four, beginning with just one front boot, in order to give your horse the chance to familiarize himself with the new sensation on his lower legs.

Photo 27 I exaggerate the motion of adding the blanket prior to saddling, swinging the pad high up over Belle's back and allowing it to drop with sudden pressure. If she stands quietly with this kind of exposure, she will never have any problem with proper, quiet saddling technique.

front. Stop and retreat with the moving object *before* you think the horse might react. Remember: you are not trying to freak out your horse, but rather teach him to accept a reasonable amount of fear. If he does decide to move away from you, then immediately send the horse away with authority in order to make the action seem like your idea. Work him hard for a half circle or more and allow him to return to the middle and stand. In time, you can increase the size and noise of the item—unfolding the cap or bag and banging it against your hand or leg.

Photo 28 Accustoming the horse to sounds and movements overhead can be a time-consuming step—but it is worth working your way up from a simple object passing above the horse's ears (such as a brush or ball cap), to a "scarier" item like this swinging rope. Begin by swinging a short tail of rope far enough away that your horse doesn't react. Slowly come closer and move from side to side, and finally, overhead. The amount of rope and the speed of the swing (which affects the sound that it makes) can be increased in time. If in doubt, continue the action longer than you think is necessary. There must be zero reaction from your horse for a sustained time period to confirm habituation.

STEP EIGHT: GOING OVER THE HORSE'S HEAD

As you have progressed through the lessons so far, you may have noticed that your horse does not like sights and sounds directly over his head. If your horse had a tendency to be head-shy prior to "sacking-out," or seems especially skittish about movement and sound from above, build up to this step very gradually. Don't avoid this problem area—just realize it will require smaller steps for the horse to work through his fear issues.

Take "scary" items, such as garbage bags, ropes, or baseball caps, and approach your horse from one side and then the other so he sees them from different angles, until he shows absolutely no reaction. For example, hold a baseball cap out to one side of your horse's head, about 2 feet away, and move it up and down. Casually switch sides and work on the other side at the same distance. As your horse stops tossing his head and/or noticing the cap, move it around a bit more so it goes both overhead and under his chin. This may be where the problems begin, so be patient and revisit this exercise for many days until you are certain your horse is okay with it. Graduate to "scarier" exposures, such as open garbage bags, swinging ropes, and your saddle pad (photo 28).

STEP NINE: PICKING UP THE FEET

These early lessons are an ideal time to handle your horse's feet. Even if this has been done in the past it is an important skill for the horse to perfect. He needs to calmly hold his feet up and allow you to clean, trim, and possibly shoe them.

There are different ways to ask for a hoof to be lifted—some people simply grab the leg, while others press the chestnut. I like to use my thumbnail and press halfway up the cannon bone (photo 29). At the exact moment the horse lifts his leg, I stop pressing and just hold the leg. With a few repetitions, he will avoid your thumbnail pressure and lift the leg readily.

Once the foot is off the ground, hold it for just a moment—you want to start this step slowly. But, when the foot goes back down, it *must* be your idea. Never release the leg while your horse is moving or pulling away from you.

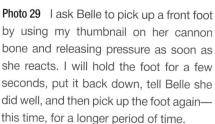

Photo 29 I ask Belle to pick up a front foot by using my thumbnail on her cannon bone and releasing pressure as soon as she reacts. I will hold the foot for a few seconds, put it back down, tell Belle she did well, and then pick up the foot again— this time, for a longer period of time.

Photo 30 I ask Belle to pick up her hind foot. My outside hand holds the lead line, in order to move her hip away from me if she acts up. Politely lift the hind leg above the fetlock in the direction of your horse's barrel. Hold it there for a second or two, and place the foot back down.

Most of the time you can hold on until he momentarily stops struggling, at which time you can immediately release. If the foot does get away from you, deny your horse time to relax and pick it right back up again. Release the leg soon after and start over. Gradually increase the duration (start with one second and build) as well as the number of times you pick up the same foot.

Work on both front feet, simulating what a farrier does—take a hoof and place it between your legs while rubbing and tapping it. Put the foot down, step away, ask the horse to turn and face you and begin again with the same foot or with the other front foot.

Once you can work on the front feet easily, move on to the hind feet, but *only* when the horse is already halter broke. If your horse is not halter broke yet, revisit this part of the lesson once he is (see Lesson 28, p. 60). *Do not* attempt to pick up the hind feet of a green or "problem" horse that is not wearing a halter. You will not necessarily get kicked, but the chance is there. Getting the horse comfortable with his front feet being handled is a great start, and you can be happy with that for the moment.

For those with halter-broke horses: halter your horse and with your outside hand holding the lead line, run your inside hand down your horse's hind leg and ask him to pick up his foot. Hold the hind leg up toward the horse's barrel, and keep your outside hand ready to pull the lead line and move the horse's hip away from you should he decide to react with a kick (photo 30).

If your horse shows signs that his hind feet are a problem, begin by picking one up with a soft rope. Loop the

Photo 31 If you feel unsafe or your horse is reactive to his hind feet being touched, work on this step with a soft lead line. Loop the rope under his fetlock and ask him to lift his foot in response to upward rope pressure. Hold the foot up momentarily, then release the foot back to the ground.

Many farriers do not have the time or patience to teach your horse to pick up his feet and hold them politely. In order to avoid a bad experience, you need to be proactive with this part of his training.

There is nothing more troubling for a handler and farrier than a horse that will not politely hold his own feet up, but instead pulls away and jumps around. To prepare your horse for farrier work, you can take the next step with your horse's hind feet (again, only if you feel comfortable doing so). Ask your horse to lift his hind foot, then fully extend the leg out behind him, pull it between your legs, and rest his foot on your lap as you crouch down over it (photos 32 A–C). This is how a farrier works on the hind hooves. The better a horse stands and holds his feet in place, the better a farrier can do his job.

Further Commentary

"Sacking-out" a horse is not something you do on one particular day or in one hour of your training time. It should be a continual process, from the moment you first handle your horse, until the day that you part ways (should that ever come). He will experience new stimuli—sounds, objects, people, movements, and animals—all his life. It is impossible for you to prepare him for all of them. Nevertheless, it's a good idea to expose him to as much as you can.

As I mentioned at the beginning of this lesson, there are many ways to "sack out" a horse. I have shown you a few, but intentionally avoided other methods that are, in my opinion, not only unnecessary but unwise. For example, tying a horse short and scaring him with a noisy garbage bag until he is pulling and rearing does not fit my training philosophy at all. This act only creates avoidance behavior—and a bad habit is encouraged by a high level of fear and stress. Another example of training I find unwise is actually attaching a tarp or set of tires, for example, to a horse that is already fearful. In such a situation, he will most likely come "unglued" because there is no escape and therefore no release. A good horseman would never purposefully blow a horse's mind that way.

rope around the fetlock and apply upward pressure until the horse gives in and lifts his foot (photo 31). Then release the leg. You are not tying or restraining the leg, just asking the horse to give to pressure and relax the leg while it's off the ground.

If you are not fully comfortable handling your horse's feet, this is as far as you need to go for the time being. Know that your horse will only get better with further practice. It is important to work on this step and pick up your horse's feet every day. Not only do you need to clean them to keep them healthy, but the act builds trust and improves your horse's overall behavior.

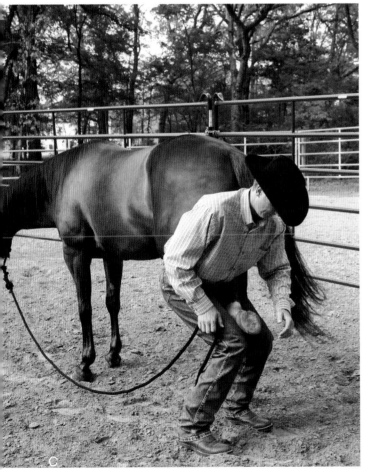

Photos 32 A–C   I prepare Belle for having her feet handled by the farrier. In A, I pick up the hind foot easily, rest the hoof in my hand, and wait for her to relax her weight into it. I only hold only the hoof capsule. Note: my outside hand holds the lead rope in case she reacts and I need to move her hips away from me. In B I bring Belle's leg between mine and extend the leg back behind her. Finally, in C I rest her hoof in my lap, as a farrier would, and allow her to relax. Practice this often, holding each leg in position for longer and longer periods of time.

"Sacking-Out" versus Bridle Control

"Sacking-Out"

It is important for your horse to become accustomed to being handled and exposed to everyday items, such as ropes, tarps, saddles, blankets and pads, jackets and hats, saddle bags, and clippers—to name just a few. However, the "sacking-out" (see Lesson 29, p. 50) portion of the horse training is ongoing and actually never ends. Your horse is always going to find new stimuli that frighten him. You cannot prepare him for every situation, even though you can take many proactive measures.

Bridle Control

In order to have control over your horse's movements under saddle, he must be taught to respond to bridle cues (see Lesson 24, p. 84). When he encounters something that scares him—while on a trail ride, for example—and he takes control of his own movement (perhaps all the way back to the barn!) it is safe to say that bridle control is nonexistent. Obviously, if your horse only responds to your bridle cues when he is not afraid, he is unsafe to ride in an open area.

As I mentioned with "sacking-out," your horse is always going to come across something new that scares him, but when the response to a bridle cue is taught well, he will learn to focus on the cue and respond accordingly. You will then know that your conditioned response is stronger than the horse's instinct to run away. This response keeps you safe and solidifies you as the leader of your "herd."

When your horse is conditioned to stand close to you as I suggest, and you introduce "scary" objects but allow him to move away and react, then you give him the opportunity to make his own decision and accept the exposure on his own terms. The end result—acceptance of the object and less fear—is therefore stronger and more meaningful. When a horse's fear is only increased in *small increments*, he will overcome it more readily with fewer traumas.

Rider's Block

● Two things can happen when you expose your horse to something new that causes him fear: he'll either become more frightened or desensitized to it. If you want the former, introduce the new exposure, let him run off, and then put it away. The next time he sees (or hears) the object, movement, or sound, he will know exactly what to do to avoid it—run! Whereas, if you want to desensitize him to it, continue to work with the item in a fair and safe man-ner until it's completely accepted. Follow up on subsequent days with the same exposure until you are sure he will not react to it in the future.

● When "sacking-out," you cannot rush the process. Sometimes you can only "win" by being simply more stubborn than your horse. For example, when you are working on rubbing his ears, he may shake and throw his head the first 200 times, but if you are persistent enough, he will eventually give up and accept that the motion and contact does not hurt him. *Make sure to finish what you start.*

Roadblocks

● When you are dealing with an overly sensitive horse that is frightened of just about everything you introduce, you have your work cut out for you! You may need to spend many days in a row beginning a session with movement, facing, following, and inside turns (see pp. 28, 34, and 45), followed by a short "sacking-out" period introducing easy items, such as your hands or a soft grooming brush. Give him time to accept you and your requests. This is the part in your horse's life and training that should not be rushed. A few extra days or weeks here is well worth it.

Lesson 29's Benefits

● The many advantages of having a horse that handles his fear well and without incident are almost too plentiful to put down on paper! This ability affects his overall demeanor and behavior, and contributes greatly to training success as he learns more quickly where fear and lack of confidence do not hold him back.

● In addition, you have now likely found the most sensitive parts of your horse's body and his nature. With this knowledge, you can use the round pen and later lessons to deal with these issues, and you'll be better prepared in the future for potential problems. For example, perhaps your young mare is highly sensitive around the flank area. Even if you successfully deal with the issue in Lesson 29, you may have to keep repeating this lesson to make sure that sensitivity in the flank area does not rear its ugly head when you first lay your leg on her during an early ride.

Green Light

If your horse does the following, you're ready to move on in the Countdown:

▸ Allows you to rub him with your hand all over his head, neck, torso, and legs.

▸ Accepts being rubbed with a lariat or rope all over his body.

▸ Does not move his head or feet when you approach him holding, shaking, or swinging noisy, "scary" objects, such as a plastic garbage bag, tarp, baseball cap, or rope.

▸ Wears protective boots on all four legs.

▸ Can be groomed with a curry comb and soft brush without flinching or stepping away.

▸ Allows you to pick up and hold both front and hind feet (note: as mentioned earlier, if you horse is not halter-broke yet, it is fine to move on to Lesson 28 before working with his hind feet).

▸ Has a quiet and willing overall demeanor and shows no signs of stress or fear.

Introducing Halter Pressure

The "release" is what you do to reinforce the behavior—in this case, "giving back" the lead rope and halter pressure—while the "release point" is the moment in time when this needs to happen.

Goals

You will introduce the halter to your horse for the purposes of leading, tying, and general control. You also want to teach him to "give" to the halter each time that he feels pressure on it. Set out with high expectations in this lesson—never settle for a horse that leans on or ignores halter pressure.

Check-In

At this point in the Countdown to Broke you have a horse that wants to stand beside you. You have rubbed him all over with your hands, ropes, and some "scary" items. He is not head-shy or flighty in any way. So, now you can introduce the halter and teach him to "give" to its pressure.

You may have a horse that is already "halter-broke"—that's fine. Regardless of whether your horse has worn one many times or never before, Lesson 28 is of benefit. Neither do I advocate waiting to halter-break horses until this point in their life—I like to do it with a newborn foal, if possible. But in the Countdown, you are starting with a "clean slate" and building a proper foundation for all ridden work, in any discipline, in the future. For this to work best, now is the ideal point to introduce and train specifically with the halter.

Cues to Use

The halter, in combination with a lead rope (or longer rope), tells your horse to move. The pressure he feels encourages him to reposition himself and "give" until there is no remaining pressure. You will use steady pressure (while you stand still or when you tie him—see p. 66), and moving pressure (while you are leading him).

Spot, Direction, Motivator, and Release

Spot The horse's nose

Direction In the direction of the lead rope's pressure

Motivator Halter pressure

Release "Giving back" or ending halter pressure

Teaching Steps
STEP ONE

By now, your horse should be calm, facing, and following you, and been "sacked out" all over his body. You have frequently told the horse "Yes" with a release and positive reinforcement. So, if you have any trouble putting on a well-fitted halter, there is a very large hole in your training somewhere! Go back to the beginning of the Countdown and make certain every step taken in the previous lessons was a solid one.

With your horse standing calmly in the middle of the round pen, simply approach him with the halter and put it on. The halter can be just about any kind, as long as it fits well—that is, it should not be overly tight or hanging loose. I choose a thin rope halter, as the pressure it applies to the horse's head is sharper and encourages a desirable response more quickly than one that is too soft and does not give a clear signal (one made of nylon web, for example).

Attach a lead rope to the halter, and while any length will work, I prefer a 12- to 15-foot line.

STEP TWO

Since the horse follows you in the pen already (see Lesson 30, p. 45), you can start "leading" him around. If previous groundwork has gone well, the horse will follow and face you without ever "hitting" the end of the rope. This is what you want.

Your goal with this exercise is to get the horse to start "giving" to halter pressure. To understand how to teach a horse how to give to pressure, I'll remind you about the *release*. You give the release when the horse responds to you by moving the *spot* you chose in the *direction* that you want. In this case, the *spot* is the horse's nose. The *direction* is toward you—the trainer holding the lead rope. In order to build this response quickly, you must try to *release* at the *release point* (see further discussion, p. 18).

Begin at the halt. Step toward the horse's hip without tugging on the lead rope or cueing vocally, and apply a small amount of pressure on the lead rope—that is, enough to bring the horse's head out of its resting position and hold it steady. This halter pressure is your motivator, and you are relying on it to generate a response. As soon as the horse decides to give in to the halter pressure, immediately release the hold on the lead rope. This release is your "Yes!" The "give" comes in two parts: first, your horse will offer you his head without leaning on the halter; and second, his feet will move and his body will realign to become straight again (photos 33 A–C).

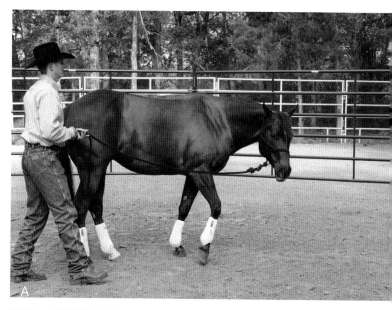

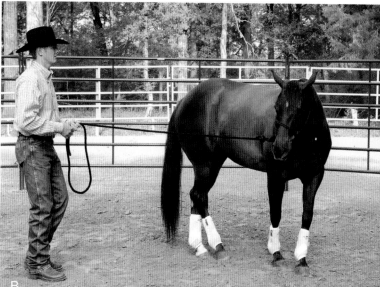

Photos 33 A–C I begin to teach Belle about halter and lead rope pressure by stepping away from her and around to her side. I pick up steady pressure on the lead rope (A). Belle looks for a way to eliminate the halter pressure—a release. She finds that "giving" in my direction is easiest (B). By holding my hand with the lead rope steady, as Belle moves toward me and realigns her body to become straight, the halter pressure goes away. She just found her own release: she "gave" with her nose, followed by her body and feet. This small "give" to halter pressure is a basic building block for everything to come.

Photos 34 A & B In A, the lead is looped around the bar of the round pen panel, and I apply steady pressure and wait for Belle's feet to move. She has to move toward the panel—rather than toward me—in order to find a release. Once she gives in to the pressure, as in B, the release is found.

It is your goal as a trainer to never give in to your horse. If you ever feel or see him "lean on pressure," or you encounter defiance, continue to ask him to "give" until he relents. Remember, a release of pressure is a "Yes," and if you say "Yes" to a horse when he does not give in, you just encourage undesirable behavior. That being said, a good horseman never asks a horse to do more than he is currently able to handle—so be sensitive to your horse's ability level before going a step too far.

If at first the horse decides to pull away from pressure on the halter, or simply remain still and lean on it, continue to hold the lead rope steady and don't give in to the horse. After a time, the horse will move toward the pressure and you can offer a release. Note: lead rope pressure from a position that requires your horse to bend his neck (from the side), usually allows you to offer a release sooner than a position directly in front of him. This is because when the horse's spine is straight, he has more power and stability, and it takes a lot more pressure to evoke the response.

Stand in many different positions around the horse and hold pressure on the halter until you get a "give," then release all pressure and reward him with a rub and kind words. Repeat this many times. Graduate to walking and jogging in different directions with the horse following you.

When you ask your horse to "give" straight ahead, such as when leading in a straight line, and he decides to slow down or stop on his own, hold steady pressure and step to the side, as far as needed until his feet become "unlocked." By taking your horse's body out of alignment, you will get your "give." With young and green horses, this is a common issue; just be patient and only release on a "give" to condition a proper response.

STEP THREE

Work on spirals, much as you did without the use of a halter (see p. 45). Circle around the horse with your body, applying pressure on the lead rope, and reward him when he "gives" and follows you. Make your circle larger, your horse taking more and more forward steps until you are "leading" him comfortably. Spiraling out is an excellent way to achieve your goal of "giving" to halter pressure, without ever having a "tugging war" or fight. You create a situation where your horse "gives" to you more quickly than when you try to pull him in a straight line right from the beginning.

STEP FOUR

Indirect pressure is an important learning experience, as well. Teach your horse to "give" to indirect pressure by looping your lead rope around a solid panel, post, or tree. Stand beside your horse and take the slack out of the rope. He will feel halter pressure from the direction of the panel, not from you. Apply small amounts of pressure and wait for a "give" (photos 34 A & B). This step prepares your horse for learning to tie by making him comfortable with indirect pressure from a solid object (see Lesson 27, p. 66).

STEP FIVE

If you have access to quiet, safe general surroundings—preferably an area that is still completely fenced in—lead your horse around outside the round pen. Bear in mind, this new experience is out of his comfort zone, and he only has you to rely on. This is another test of whether the groundwork you've practiced until now is solid.

As discussed previously, "sacking-out" is an ongoing process. During these early "outside" leading sessions, use your hands to rub your horse periodically and continue to build his trust. The halter and the pressure that it causes is the first real *trap* (constriction of his freedom) that you have shown your horse in this training program. It is helpful to do everything you can to keep the lessons moving along successfully.

A "trap" is anything that constricts, restrains, or causes claustrophobia. Since you are domesticating a fight-or-flight animal, a trap can be hard for your horse to accept. This is why small, easy-to-handle pressures and traps must be built on slowly.

STEP SIX

Progressively increase the number of steps that your horse must take before you stop and reward him. It is important to work on one, two, and three steps in the beginning, but once he understands the request, move on to more steps, straighter lines, and various patterns (*further*).

By adding vocals, you can now start to work on your horse jogging beside you while listening to the halter. And he should respond immediately to the pressure you apply via the lead (*faster*). In order to have your horse respond to *softer* halter pressure, you must continue to offer a full release once he does "give." If you don't, he will instead learn to lean.

Rider's Block

- Remember that teaching the horse to be near you *is not the same* as conditioning him to give to halter pressure. Even when you've done a good job teaching him to face, fol-low, and stay with you, you still need to make sure the horse learns Lesson 28.

- Never lead a horse with a tight lead rope—maintain pressure until the horse gives in, then *release*. When he's being led and staying with you properly, the rope should be slack. If you hold or continue to pull on the rope, you take away the release and simply condition your horse to *ignore* pressure and become increasingly less responsive—the horse learns he will not be rewarded even when he does what you ask him.

- Do not let your horse "walk all over you" or "invade your space." Just because he is young or untrained does not mean he can push you around; he would not be allowed to do that to the lead horse in a herd. When the horse is "leading you"—that is, his nose is ahead of your shoulder—take control of the direction and speed by turning him into a circle or arc. Be picky about where and how the horse moves when with you. This will establish much needed boundaries and teach him to conduct himself in a respectful, safe way while around you and other handlers.

Roadblocks

- If your horse is not absolutely calm and obedient in the round pen, do not attempt to take him for "outside" leading sessions until he is further along. He might be hard to catch if he manages to get away from you. For a change of scenery, practice leading in another riding arena, a corral or catch pen, or your barn aisle, if it is wide and clear of obstacles.

Lesson 28's Benefits

- It's very important the horse learns to give to pressure from the start. This is, in fact, what you are after with much of your training still to come: giving to various pressures from various angles. It transfers from one exercise or cue to the next, so forming a solid foundation with the halter and lead is imperative.

- Horses spend a lot of time being lead via a halter during

MODERN WISDOM

Ways to Increase Your Handling Time

I like to increase a horse's handling time in a variety of ways. I know that the more I interact with my horse, the more comfortable he will be with me and his surroundings. Here are a few suggestions:

- Take your horse "along for the ride" to a show, clinic, or training facility. Trainers do this on a regular basis just to introduce inexperienced horses to new places, sights, and sounds.

- Tie your horse while you are working around the barn or ranch, or finishing the chores (photo 35). I often ask my horses to stand tied in a shady comfortable place while I do busywork. I want them to be relaxed enough to do this regularly and have it be part of their daily routine.

- If you have more than one horse, tie one close to your riding arena or round pen, wherever you are training, while you work the other. This lets him absorb the commotion related to action in the ring that doesn't involve him, and encourages confidence.

- Plan a short workout and cooling-down period, tie your horse for a break as you work with another horse or finish chores, then return to your horse and work on something different—perhaps another riding session, some groundwork, or a bath. Always remember to warm up and cool down, but there is no reason why you cannot lengthen the duration of saddle time with a break in the middle.

- Lead or "pony" your horse down the trail. Your horse gets exercised while learning to respond to halter pressure, see new sights, and behave in the company of another horse.

their lifetime—even a horse that is never ridden (a broodmare, for example)—so it is essential that they respect and listen to its pressure.

Green Light

Since your goal is to teach the horse to give to halter pressure *every time* it is applied, you need to be sure that you have accomplished this before you move on. If your horse lifts his head before he gives in, he is not ready. If you can-

not move your horse forward at a steady walk around the yard, he is not ready. If you cannot trot your horse on a loose lead line, you should hold off moving ahead. If he shows any defiance or pulls back on occasion, you had better not tie him up yet—which is the next lesson. The more releases you can offer, the stronger and longer lasting his conditioned response to halter pressure will be—and only then should you move forward.

Tying

Have you ever had a horse that grazes quietly in the field while the tractor mows along the fence line beside him, but as soon as he is being led or ridden, this very same tractor—moving or stationary—scares him to pieces? As soon as a horse feels "trapped" in any way— thus giving up his ability to decide whether he stays or goes (see p. 64)—the combination of dealing with a frightening situation while responding to your control cues can be difficult for him to handle. It is your job to educate and "expose" your horse so that he can.

Goals

You will ask your horse to "give" well to halter pressure while he's tied, and you will expect him to remain relaxed and patient.

Check-In

You have already spent a lot of time teaching your horse to "give" to halter pressure and have introduced some indirect pressure, as well. Your horse's overall demeanor is more relaxed than before you began the Countdown. If you have not skipped or rushed any steps, you are more than ready to begin tying your horse.

Cues to Use

The cue is the same as in Lesson 28: the pressure from the halter and lead rope tells your horse where to position himself. The difference is that it is not you, but a fixed object, that is the source of the pressure. This solid object puts your horse in control over his own pressure-and-release exercise—and how much he is willing to endure before giving in.

Spot, Direction, Motivator, and Release

Spot The horse's nose
Direction Toward the post or tie
Motivator Halter pressure
Release Lack of halter pressure

Teaching Steps
STEP ONE

This exercise is an extension or "strengthening" of the work you did conditioning your horse to the halter. Now, you want him to respond to halter pressure created by a lead rope fixed to a secure object. Review Step Four in Lesson 28 (p. 63) where you looped the lead rope around a panel or post while you continued to hold one end, introducing him to the idea of pressure from a source other than you. Next, you will add a new element to this exercise.

STEP TWO

In the real world—away from the controlled environment of the round pen—your horse will no doubt be scared of something at some point while he is tied. This may be a bag blowing in the wind or a dog suddenly barking. So, it is time to add some stimuli to cause a reasonable amount of fear in your horse. Note: you have not yet "tied" the horse—you are holding the lead rope, present and participating in order to keep your horse safe and learning. This step should be practiced inside a fenced-in area.

As in Lesson 28, pass your lead rope around a strong panel or post. Continue to hold one end of the lead, stand off to the side of your horse's shoulder (not directly in front of him), and with your free hand create enough noise and motion with an empty garbage bag (or something similar) to cause your horse to react by moving backward. This should only be slight sounds and shaking—you are not trying to terrify him, just make him "look" and back away slowly (photos 36 A & B). Since you are holding the lead rope, it will become tight. At this point, just hold it steady; do not "give it back" or pull. Your horse will do one of three things:

▶ First, he may immediately give in to the halter pressure. If so, stop the noise and shaking. Praise him, calmly rub his neck with the garbage bag, and end on a quiet note.

▶ Second, he may "lock up"—that is, "freeze his feet." Your job is to hold steady pressure on the rope and wait for him to give in. Once he does, stop shaking the bag and rub his head. Calmly rub his neck with the garbage bag on the neck and end on a quiet note.

▶ Third, your horse might not be able to handle the "scary" item in combination with feeling "trapped" by the halter pressure and will bolt backward. When you get this response, you must rewind and work on a few things. Go back to the middle of the round pen and sack him out to the bag, because you have just *sensitized* (as opposed to *de*sensitized) him to it. Then, strengthen your halter work by repeating Lesson 28. Finally, try this step again using a smaller, less "scary" stimulus— obviously the bag was too much for him at this point.

Continue to practice with indirect pressure until your horse "bounces" off halter pressure in order to give himself a release, even when you are shaking a "scary" bag. Now, you can start tying your horse to a *secure* object.

STEP THREE

When first tying your horse, it is best to choose an enclosed area where he is comfortable, such as a tie-post close to where you have been training, or in a familiar paddock, or inside his stall. Always tie your horse "high and short" with a quick-release knot—you want the knot to be about 6 or 7 feet from the ground (about eye level), with enough slack in the lead line so your horse can relax his head comfortably. The reasons for the height of the knot are: 1) there is less

Photos 36 A & B   Here I repeat the exercise in indirect pressure from Lesson 28 (see p. 60), but this time, I increase the stress level by making sudden movements and introducing noise with a garbage bag (A). Belle looks, then responds appropriately by moving forward to relieve the halter pressure, and I allow for a full release when she steps into it (B).

The Do's and Don'ts of Tying

DO:

▸ Use an unbreakable halter, such as one made of strong rope.

▸ Keep your horse in his normal environment and "comfort zone" for the first few dozen tying sessions.

▸ Groom and spend time with your novice horse while he is tied.

▸ Tie your horse high and short, and always use a quick-release knot.

▸ Expect your horse to tie.

▸ Ask him to tie often.

DON'T:

▸ Use a clasp or buckle on your lead rope that could break.

▸ Tie to something weak, such as an "o"-ring on a barn wall or fence post.

▸ "Help" by untying your horse if you feel he is nervous or lonely.

▸ Expect him to tie without proper preparation.

▸ Tie where he could catch a leg or step in something unsafe.

▸ Ignore the weather and allow him to get chilled or overheated.

▸ Leave your green horse unattended.

▸ Snub (tie where there is no slack in the lead line).

of a "trapped" feeling (short and low is very restrictive for a horse); 2) if your horse does pull back or "sit down"—even for a moment—the angle at which he will pull is less likely to break the post or tree; and 3) the horse loses leverage by being tied higher, so is less likely to pull a neck muscle or, in an extreme case, flip over. The reason you tie a horse short is to keep him from catching a leg in the slack of the rope and getting tangled. A quick-release knot allows you to untie him quickly should an emergency arise.

Most likely, your horse will only lightly test the tie and then stand quiet. He may grow a bit anxious, paw the ground, call out to his friends, or dance around—this is completely normal. He needs to learn that such behavior gets him nowhere, and he might as well put his head down, cock a leg, and fall asleep (photo 37).

If your horse pulls back, but you have used a strong halter, lead line, and tie post, just stand back and wait for the "give." The worst thing possible is to reward his behavior by untying him. Plus, when he is pulling or rearing, your being in front of him to "help" him will only make him pull back harder. And you might get hurt in the process. Your horse needs to "hit" the end of the lead line, feel the uncomfortable halter pressure, and *find his own release* by moving toward the post.

I recommend tying your horse every day you handle him and even on days when you cannot ride or train.

Finish off the workday by tying him up; depending on the weather, one to three hours is great after a workout, cool-down, and/or bath. Remember, never leave a young or green horse unattended while tied.

Rider's Block

● Many times, a horse is blamed for not tying well, and an owner refuses to confront the issue. However, he may have been "taught" at some point in the past with a halter that broke, or tied to a weak post that fell apart. With proper preparation and the right tools, you *must* learn to tie your horse; one that cannot be tied is unsafe. It is a major hole in training and is inexcusable.

● It is not safe to jump the gun and tie a horse that has not been properly prepared with the previous lessons in the Countdown. Your otherwise calm and sedate horse might begin frantically pulling back as soon as you secure him, putting both you and him in danger. Don't skip steps to reach this one.

● Be sure to spend time working on indirect pressure exercises (see p. 63), so your horse becomes accustomed to your position hear his head—similar to that when you approach and tie or untie him. He should feel more confident with you beside him, but some horses (those not properly trained) will pull back when you approach in this manner.

Photo 37   Tie your horse in a safe and comfortable spot. Horses that are tied often learn to relax and remain still, as Belle is here. Horses that are not tied often may habitually fight the rope, paw, rear, pull back, and remain agitated and anxious.

Roadblocks

● You may have a horse that seems reasonable in just about every way until you tie him for the first time and walk away. He may rear, paw, whinny, and pull. This can last 30 minutes or 30 days. He will, in time, develop emotionally and learn to find his release. As you make tying part of your daily routine, your horse will settle.

Lesson 27's Benefits

● Whether you are training a recreational, show, or working horse, you will ask him to spend a lot of his life tied, whether while cleaning his stall, grooming, working on his feet, saddling up, or just securing him while you are busy with something else. This will become a large part of his domesticated life. It is your job to keep him comfortable and to establish the boundaries of tying early on.

Green Light

Your horse is going to tell you how you are doing at this point. He should respond well to halter pressure and his level of confidence and trust in you should be increasing. If you feel your horse is still lacking confidence or skill in *any area* that has been worked on so far, take the time now to go back and improve his responses.

Bathing

Teaching your horse to accept a bath is very beneficial for a number of reasons. Regular bathing allows you to:

- Lower the horse's body temperature after a workout or on a hot day.
- Keep the horse's skin and coat free of sweat, dirt, and other irritants.
- Limit the chances of fungal reproduction.
- Clean a scrape or cut that needs attention.
- Wash a foal's hind end during scouring (diarrhea).
- Keep reproductive organs clean and healthy.
- Maintain healthy and manageable manes and tails.
- Administer medicated shampoos for prescribed reasons.

If your horse has not been given a bath since he was a foal, or perhaps never, only attempt it once he is giving to halter pressure well (see Lesson 28, p. 60), and respecting your space. Then bathe him after a workout when the water will feel good and he is relaxed (photo 38).

In your wash area, which should be clear of ground clutter and objects that could pose a hazard to the horse, hold the lead rope in one hand and the nozzle of the water hose in the other. (Don't tie the horse for his first few baths, but give him a chance to accept the new experience.) Point the nozzle away from the horse toward the ground and slowly begin to spray it. If your horse moves, continue to spray the ground until he stands still again. You do not want to teach your horse that moving away from the spray will make it stop. You want to habituate him to the sight and sound of it.

Once the horse is used to the water spraying away from him, toward the ground, slowly bring the spray closer until you are lightly spraying his shoulder area. Use a comfortable spray setting and warm water, if available. Keep spraying if he moves his feet, and when he stands and relaxes, stop spraying and rub his head as a reward. Continue to spray the horse on the shoulder, barrel, and hind end on one side until he is completely relaxed and still, then switch sides and repeat.

Habituation occurs through prolonged soft spraying on his body and legs. Each day, make sure to spray every

inch of the horse's body, including under the tail, inside the legs, and under the belly. The more you bathe him, and the more areas you touch and wash, the quieter he will stand for you.

During the first bathing experience, avoid spraying the horse's head. You want this session to go well and your horse to become comfortable with the process. In later sessions, untie him to spray his face, and avoid getting water inside his ears. Only use a very soft mist and tear-free shampoo is a must for this part of the body.

For most days, a water rinse is enough. When you do wash your horse, there are some good shampoos that come with their own spray nozzle. These are designed for frequent (daily) use and are mild. When you use strong shampoo only do so once a week. You don't want to strip your horse's coat of natural oils and perhaps cause intense itching and irritation.

On a hot day, remember a cooling effect comes from evaporation, which involves air moving over the wet surface of your horse's body. So, after a rinse-down, shade and moving air (wind or fan) help the horse lower his temperature. If you soak a horse with water and then stand him in the direct sun, the effect is that of a wetsuit and the sun heats the water next to skin skin, resulting in an elevated temperature.

On cooler or cold days, use "cooler" blankets to keep your horse from experiencing energy loss and a possible chill. You want to get him dry as quickly as possible. Consult your veterinarian to find the best practices for bathing in your region.

First Saddling

Goals

Your aim is to introduce the saddle to the horse and have him accept you putting it on him and taking it off. You also want him to spend time moving under saddle to build his confidence.

Check-In

There are three considerations I feel are important before you begin your first saddling session. This is an exciting lesson and you want this time with your horse to go well, without incident! First, your horse should be confident and relaxed. If you have completed the previous lessons you have spent ample time with your horse and sacked him out to many items, including a saddle blanket or pad, protective boots, halter pressure, and rope pressure around his cinch or girth areas. Second, your horse needs to "want in." If he does not have a strong desire to be with you in the round pen, this exercise is bound to fail. You do not want to rely on halter pressure to hold your horse in position while you saddle him—you want him to accept the saddle without moving his feet. Third, your horse should understand how to move well around the round pen and make inside turns before you ever saddle him. This is because you need an exercise you know he can complete successfully while he is growing accustomed to his new saddle.

Teaching Steps

STEP ONE

You now have a horse that wants to be next to you, faces you, follows you, and "gives" to halter pressure. He is also able to handle his emotions and/or fear without moving his feet. Your next step is his first saddling.

Begin your training session with some movement around the pen, including a lot of inside turns (see Lessons 33 and 32, pp. 28 and 34). This improves your horse's desire to want to stand beside you and relax. (This is always important, but especially today!) Take some time to review and sack him out with your hands, ropes, and saddle blanket (see Lesson 29, p. 50). If he is not wearing them already, put on your horse's protective boots. Since you have already worked on all this, the time spent on these warm-up exercises should be minimal. However, you should never assume that your horse remembers anything during your early training lessons—always test him to see how he responds on a new day with a new lesson. This will keep you safe.

STEP TWO

Today, spend some extra time sacking your horse out with the saddle pad. Halter him, and work both sides evenly with plenty of head rubs and rest breaks. Repeatedly exaggerate the motion of throwing the saddle blanket on, let it land on your horse's back, and slide it off. Pull it up toward his mane; rub it over his hindquarters. If you find an area where the horse remains sensitive to the saddle pad, concentrate on that spot until he is calm.

Your horse might not display any signs of fear (i.e., flinching or moving) of the saddle pad while he stands still beside you. But once you ask his feet to move, he may behave quite differently and become anxious when the exact same saddle pad is thrown on and taken off his back. This is why sacking him out to the saddle blanket while moving around you is an integral step in the first saddling process.

Tips for "Sacking-Out" with an English Saddle

When using an English saddle for this lesson, some adjustments need to be made:

▸ Use a Western saddle blanket or something like it to "sack out" the horse (they tend to be bigger and heavier). At the point when the saddle is secured for the first time, a more suitable pad can then be used.

▸ Remove stirrup leathers and irons completely until it is time mount up (see Lesson 20, p. 110).

▸ If you can borrow one, consider using a Western saddle until Lesson 19 (p. 114) as the extra weight, wide fenders, and stirrups prepare the horse better prior to the first ride.

Now, continue "sacking-out" while your horse's feet are moving. Take a few steps toward his hindquarters, apply light pressure on the halter, and place the saddle pad on his back, then remove it, many times as he walks or jogs in a small circle around you (photos 39 A & B). Again ask the horse to stand still, and then repeat the movement exercise. Always finish "sacking-out" at a stand still—this will be the last thing your horse remembers before you introduce the saddle. When your horse has lost interest in the blanket and its movement, you are ready to go on to the next step.

Photos 39 A & B Belle and I review "sacking-out" to the saddle blanket (A). I exaggerate the motion of "throwing" the pad onto her back while gently moving her around me at a walk. I repeatedly put the pad on and take it off, from each side, until she is relaxed and accepting, and I reward her with a head rub (B).

STEP THREE

You now start "sacking-out" with the saddle. Prepare your Western saddle in advance by removing the breast collar and attaching both the front and rear cinches to the cinch keeper—the leather piece that holds your cinch buckles. If your saddle does not have one, lay both cinches

Photo 40 Introduce the saddle slowly. Allow your horse to examine it with his nose. Then, rub it against your horse's shoulder and barrel areas.

Photos 41 A & B When your horse is relaxed with the saddle, swing it smoothly onto his back, as I am in A. Allow the saddle strings and stirrups to rub and bump lightly. Belle looks back to see what I am doing, but she is not pulling on the lead rope or moving her feet. Settle the saddle in place, and always hold on to the horn or pommel in the beginning as I am in B, so that if the horse decides to move suddenly, you can keep it in place or pull it off quickly.

across the saddle seat. Leave your stirrups hanging naturally. (Note: I discuss aspects of "sacking-out" with an English saddle on p. 72.) Hold the lead rope loosely in one hand or lay it over your arm while you hold the saddle with both hands. Let your horse smell the saddle, then rub it against his shoulder area and lightly "bump" him with it (photo 40). Progress toward the back and barrel, continuing your rubbing and bumping.

Lift the saddle up and let it land softly against the horse's back. (Note: you are not using a saddle blanket at this time.) If he jumps around or acts afraid, take a step back and work with the saddle pad again. If he is not fazed, put the saddle directly on his back, keeping one hand on its horn or pommel, so if he moves suddenly you can either hold it in place or pull it off (photos 41 A & B). You don't want the saddle to fall off, and if it should fall to the ground on his offside, he will most likely shy into you—a safety hazard.

STEP FOUR

Put the saddle on and take it off from both sides of the horse. The more times you do this, the better the lesson will stick. Remember, the saddle is heavy and, unlike the soft saddle blanket, you need to be "polite" when you let it land on your horse's back. You want him to enjoy the interaction—not be given a reason to dislike the process.

It does not matter which side of the horse you work on to start, as both sides are treated equally in this training program. You no longer have to follow "rules" about only handling, leading, or tacking up on the "near" or left side. Your goal is a horse that is equally gifted on his left as he is on his right.

STEP FIVE

Create some cinch pressure without securing the saddle.

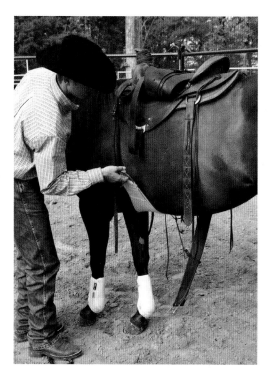

Photo 42 I apply cinch pressure by pulling the cinch around Belle and holding it tight for a moment, then releasing.

Photo 43 Before securing the cinch, I like to unclip the lead rope and loop it back through the halter under the horse's chin. This allows me to discourage movement when the horse decides to take a small step while I am in the process of an early saddling, but enables me to pull the lead quickly free once I'm ready to let my horse go with the saddle on for the first time.

One way is to release the front cinch from the cinch keeper, then simply reach under the horse and take the large "D"-ring on the loose end of the cinch in your hand. Pull the cinch tight around the horse's girth area, but only for a fraction of a second (photo 42). Release. Repeat pulling up on the cinch until he does not flinch or react. You want your horse to keep his feet motionless at this point. Start to hold the pressure for longer durations. Your goal is met when your horse doesn't react to the cinch being tightened or held in place.

Note: you should not loop the latigo through the "D"-ring (Western saddle) or fasten any buckles (English saddle) yet. This way, should the horse object, the saddle will either fall to the ground or you can take it quickly off. If your horse reacts with a quick sidestep or bucks with the saddle half on and you have attached the cinch or girth, the saddle can slip under his belly, which can result in a very traumatic situation for the horse, you, and your favorite saddle!

STEP SIX

At this point, unclip the lead rope and run it through the halter under your horse's chin, evening up the rope on either side (photo 43). This allows you to lightly guide the head, but pull the rope free in a quick manner—which you will do when you release your horse after saddling him and securing the cinch for the first time.

Hold the lead rope in your hand or drape it over your forearm. Place the saddle pad upon your horse's back, and the saddle on top of it. Adjust both to fit the horse's back properly. If you're properly prepared, the horse should not find this problematic, and should remain standing quietly.

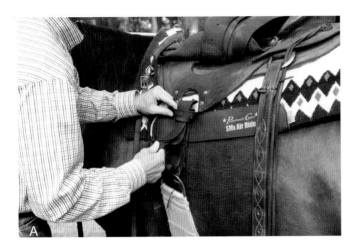

Photos 44 A & B With the lead line over my left arm, and the saddle pad and saddle in place, I secure the front cinch with a latigo knot (A). Then I secure the rear cinch (B). This should almost make contact with the horse's barrel on a full inhale, but remain a few inches away on a full exhale. If the rear cinch is too loose, your horse may catch a hind leg. If overly snug, it may create an anxious or explosive reaction to the new saddle.

Undo the rear cinch from the cinch keeper so both front and rear hang down. Ask your horse to keep all four feet completely still as you walk around him, adjusting the tack.

Begin doing up the front cinch first, but do not tighten it—you want to prepare your latigo knot first. After you have looped the latigo strap twice, complete the knot, and with a smooth but firm pull, tighten the latigo strap and secure it. Since you must avoid saddle slippage at this stage, you need the cinch to be quite snug—snugger than you would normally ride in. Reach back and carefully take hold of the rear cinch, tightening it so the leather is only a few inches from touching the horse's belly. You do not want to cause a "startle reflex" with a snug rear cinch; however, if it hangs too loosely a hind leg can get caught in it (photos 44 A & B).

STEP SEVEN

Now that the saddle is secured on the horse—for the first time!—carefully pull the lead rope free from where you've looped it through the halter. Back away from your horse and make your way to the center of the round pen. If your horse follows you, gently push him off and ask him to move him around the pen at a jog. If he remains standing where you left him, gently encourage him to move out once you've reached the middle (photos 45 A & B).

Move your horse around the pen, and do not let him approach you. This helps keep you safe, as you are still unsure how he may react to the saddle. Move him steadily at a jog for several minutes with periodic inside turns—keep the exercise mellow and allow the horse to "feel" the saddle and the two cinches attached.

The reaction you get from the first saddling is unpredictable. Even when you are well prepared your horse may still panic, run off quite hard, or begin to buck or rear. This is a natural reaction given this kind of new "trap" or restriction.

STEP EIGHT

Spend time moving your horse at a jog until he decides to speed up on his own, or you see that he has begun to settle. Signs that he is not settled are: running hard, a kinked tail, pinned ears, failing to watch and listen to your inside-turn cues, or kicking and biting at the saddle.

Once either you or he decides that it is time to lope, go ahead and work on inside turns at this speed (photo 46). It

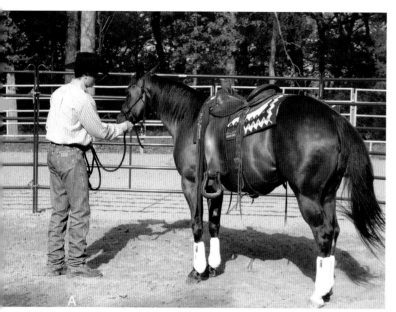

Photos 45 A & B I pull the lead rope free from the halter in A, and slowly back away from Belle in B. If she follows me to the center of the pen, I'll push her away and ask her to move around the round pen at a jog.

is important to work him at both the jog and lope, as the saddle and cinch pressures feel different at the two speeds.

When you are certain he is relaxed and accepting of the saddle, let him turn in and approach you so you can rub him on the face and stand quietly with him. (If at any time your horse starts to buck or act up when he is standing with you in the middle of the pen, immediately send him out and make him work.) Let him take a break for a minute or so to give him time to breathe and relax, then send him back out and work on some more inside turns and movement exercises at both the jog and lope. By giving him something that he can successfully do, such as speed control work and inside turns, you keep his attention and keep his mind off the saddle. This helps him become used to it.

Once your horse is doing well and has had a good workout, allow him to come stand with you, undo the rear cinch first, followed by the front cinch, then pull the saddle pad and saddle off the horse at the same time and walk away from him with them. Depending on the weather, it could be appropriate to either bathe the horse or tie him for a

while—just be sure to spend some quiet time handling him and reassuring him that life is still good.

Rider's Block

● Since you have a horse that "wants in," you can run into the problem of the newly saddled horse trying to move toward you in the middle of the pen. Because you're uncertain of his reaction to the addition of the tack, this is potentially dangerous at this point. Keep him in view and authoritatively move him away from you and around the pen until the end of Step Eight.

● Make sure that the front cinch is tight during these first saddlings. A loose cinch can cause the saddle to roll underneath the horse's belly. You then will have a scared horse that may injure himself.

● The rear cinch should not be too tight or too loose. When it is too tight, the horse has a difficult time accepting the constriction, which prolongs acceptance and creates avoidance issues. When the rear cinch is too loose, the horse can catch a leg if he bucks or kicks at his belly. During early saddling exposures, secure the rear cinch so the leather is a few inches away from the barrel on a full exhale, and almost makes contact on a full inhale.

● Don't worry if your horse bucks. Let him deal with his new "appendage" naturally. A lot of good, sane horses buck when saddled the first few times.

● Do not think that keeping your horse on a lead rope and only allowing him to walk the first few times under saddle is good for him. At some point, he is going to have to jog and lope and feel the new pressures associated with these gaits. So be proactive and deal all speeds right from the start.

● If you are unsure that letting your horse loose in the round pen after the first saddling is the best approach, I still recommend following this lesson as it is. It is true that many good horsemen keep their horses on a line at first—and I do as well, depending on the horse. However, if you are not used to handling a green horse during his first saddling, it is safer for both of you to do it this way.

Photo 46   I let Belle lope around the round pen and get used to the feel of the saddle, cinches, and stirrups. Most horses move off quickly when first saddled—prepare for a possible "big" reaction by keeping yourself safe and out of the way.

Roadblocks

● If you are lucky enough to have one of those horses that hates to be restricted around the barrel and will not stop bucking, you need to repeat this lesson many times, and do so with caution. Rewind and work on "sacking-out" and movement exercises, but be aware your horse will still need to spend many days just moving out with a saddle on. Be patient and allow your horse to gain confidence over time.

Lesson 26's Benefits

● This lesson prepares your horse for a rider. By completing this lesson now, you have the luxury of doing further groundwork with the saddle on your horse, giving him more time "under saddle" while you are still safely on the ground. The longer your horse wears a saddle, the safer your first

few rides will be. I am not sure what it is, but saddling a horse also seems to build a horse's confidence—I think it changes the way he holds himself.

Green Light

Before you can go on to more groundwork under saddle, you must be pretty certain your horse is no longer going to jump into you or kick unexpectedly at the cinches. Only move forward when you see confirmed signs of comfort, such as: standing quietly; walking, jogging, and loping quietly; licking, chewing, and lowering his head; and "wanting in."

Avoidance Behavior

Avoidance behavior is the defense mechanism your horse uses when a situation occurs that is unpleasant (water spraying in his ears) or scary (being approached with a noisy garbage bag). The horse looks for a way to avoid the stimulus or get rid of it—he runs away, shies, bucks, or rears. Here are some example scenarios:

Avoidance Behavior: The horse bolts away from you as you raise your dressage whip in the air.
Possible Causes: 1) Previous application of the whip has been unfair: release has not been given at the right moment, or the whip has been used too firmly. 2) The horse has not established this motivator is not something to fear, but to calmly respond to.

Avoidance Behavior: The horse moves his head away from your moving hand, anticipating contact.
Possible Causes: 1) The horse is justified in believing that he may be struck by that moving hand and is preparing to get out of the way. 2) The horse has not had enough physical contact to know that he can trust your moving hands.

Avoidance Behavior: The horse takes off running with you on his back, becoming inattentive to your cues.
Possible Causes: 1) The horse is growing frustrated with leg pressure, as a release does not seem to come no matter how he responds. 2) The horse is being ridden in an indoor arena on a windy day and his fear level has been raised until it is too much for him to handle.

Avoidance Behavior: The horse begins to buck violently while you are riding and is not responding to any form of cue.
Possible Causes: 1) The horse is not used to having a rider on his back and bucks out of discomfort and/or fear. 2) The horse is startled by the use of leg pressure and reacts in this manner.

There is a difference between the horse seeking a release point while looking for the correct answer, and overreacting and trying to avoid the situation altogether. Not all avoidance behavior is caused by improper handling. A horse that has not had time to build trust and experience will be more inclined to show it. Help your horse develop through thoughtful teaching and be aware of scenarios, such as these, that may not help him learn.

"Sacking-Out" under Saddle

Goals

Here, you aim to further build your horse's confidence under saddle.

Check-In

To spend time sacking your horse out with the saddle on, you need him to accept the saddle itself. If you have not spent enough time allowing him to move and turn under saddle (see Lesson 26, p. 71), you may "overload" your horse and cause undue stress. Make certain he can move around the pen at a jog and lope without bucking, approach you when asked, and stand quiet and still near you when necessary.

Teaching Steps

STEP ONE

Begin by standing quietly in the middle of the round pen with your horse fully saddled and both cinches secured properly. If you have a breast collar that fits, put it on now (if working with a young or small horse, and your breast collar does not fit him well, do not attach it).

Pass the end of your lariat through the honda (the small loop on one end) in order to make a small adjustable loop. Place the loop over the saddle horn and pull it tight, so that your lariat is firmly attached to the saddle (photo 47, and see sidebar, p. 82, for guidelines when using an English saddle). Holding the lariat in your hands, use your voice and body pressure to send the horse out to the perimeter of the pen and move him off at a jog. Drive the horse off in either direction.

STEP TWO

Tug on the lariat to put pressure on the saddle horn. This then puts pressure and friction on the front cinch, rear cinch, breast collar, saddle pad, and saddle tree, as well. Start with light tugs, and then increase the pressure, but make sure not to pull more than a couple of inches toward your body.

If at any point during this exercise you think that the front cinch might be loose, stop tugging, and ask the horse to come in. Tighten the cinch and begin again.

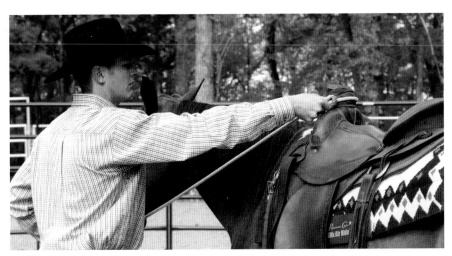

Photo 47 Belle stands quietly in the middle of the round pen as I create a small adjustable loop in my lariat and attach it to the horn of my saddle.

Photo 48 I've "pushed" Belle out to the edge of the pen and she's loping forward nicely. I now take the slack out of the lariat rope, putting pressure on the saddle horn. I tug and release, and repeat, allowing the horse to grow accustomed to the pressure that this causes.

Photo 49 With the lariat attached to the saddle horn, I swing it like a "jump rope" so it varies pressure, makes noise, and comes into contact with the ground.

You definitely do not want it to end up rotating the saddle around the horse's barrel!

When you begin tugging as the horse is in motion, he may not react at all, but he may run harder, buck, or show signs of annoyance. This is good—you are better off dealing with these things from a safe distance, because when you ride him you will be causing similar pressures and frictions. Apply these pressure tugs until you see the horse calmly accepts them in both directions. Move up to the lope and repeat the same work with the lariat (photo 48).

STEP THREE

Ask the horse to change direction with your inside turn cue while you swing the lariat over his head, gently drive him off and continue with movement in the opposite direction. So, if the horse is jogging clockwise, open your right shoulder—

If the lariat rope ever slips from your hand and is being dragged by your horse, just keep him moving until he appears calm. Then allow him to approach you and use the opportunity to pick the lariat back up. If he is running scared, keep him going, and work on some inside turns and speed control—familiar exercises—to take his mind off the dragging rope. Again, when you feel he is calm enough to come in, invite him to do so and begin again.

asking for the turn—and "flip" the lariat rope over his head as he turns. This keeps the lariat rope in a straight line between you and the horse—not wrapping around him. It could take a few attempts to get the lariat to do exactly what you want, but remember you can let it go if you are concerned the horse is

Photo 50   I get Belle accustomed to a rope dangling behind her hind legs. As she lopes around the pen, I allow it to make contact with her hindquarters and legs, but I'm sure to keep it from finding its way under her tail, where it could cause rope burn and possibly an undesired reaction on her part.

about to get tangled. With some practice you should be able to change the direction of your horse with ease.

STEP FOUR

With the lariat still attached to the saddle, move the horse around the pen at a jog. Begin swinging the lariat, giving it the action of a "jump rope." Your goal is to habituate him to the sight, sound, and feel of the rope action. It will create small varying amounts of pressure, "flashes" of movement in the horse's sightline, and whirring or whistling sounds. The rope can also be allowed to hit the ground, adding to the exposure. Repeat at all gaits and in both directions (photo 49).

Your horse will quickly realize that the rope does not hurt him. Only stop when your horse has completely accepted all the lariat rope actions you have created.

STEP FIVE

Ask your horse to jog, and swing the lariat over the horse's back so that it falls on the outside of the horse (closest to the panels of the pen) and behind his hind legs. To clarify what this looks like: the end of the lariat is secured to the horn; it then falls on the outside of the saddle and wraps behind and around the horse's hind end, and comes back to where you hold it in the center of the pen (see photo 50).

Let you horse become accustomed to moving with the rope dangling and rubbing lightly behind his legs, but do not let it get caught under his tail. This can cause a rope "burn" and give him—justifiably—something to really be upset about. As with all your training, you are trying to prove that each new step is just that—a new step—not something that will hurt him.

Repeat the exercise in both directions, at the jog and the lope (photo 50). Your horse will tell you when you have done enough. Once you feel habituation has occurred, remove the lariat from the saddle horn and reward your horse with a break in the middle and many head rubs. Perform some facing and following work (see Lesson 30, p. 40) to relax him before ending the day or moving on to the next step.

A horse that is scared tends to move or run (flight reflex). When he is moving at a faster pace, such as a lope, his stress level is already elevated due to the speed. Getting the horse to face fears and become accustomed to new experiences while he is already slightly stressed is an advantage. Where is he going to run to? He is already running and is still forced to deal with the "scary" object or sensation. This is why we perform all the steps at a lope, as well as a jog.

STEP SIX

Again form a small loop in your lariat. Run the end with the loop through your inside stirrup and up to the saddle horn. Attach the loop to your saddle horn firmly. With the remaining lariat rope in your hands, send the horse to the perimeter

Photo 51 I've run the lariat through the inside stirrup and attached it to the saddle horn. As Belle lopes, I lift the stirrup and then let it bang against her side and the saddle. This "sacks out" the horse to stirrup movement and related noise, which is very important in preparing for a rider.

of the round pen at a jog. Tug on the lariat so that the stirrup moves upward as you pull. Then allow the stirrup to fall back against the horse. This does not have to be pretty!

Continue to casually play with the stirrup as he jogs around, lifting and swinging the stirrup beside the horse as he moves. He may jump, buck, or run hard as this movement will be in his peripheral vision and there will be a new sensation against his side. Once he is accepting of the stirrup at the jog, move up to the lope (photo 51). As you progress and your horse grows more comfortable with the swinging stirrup, increase the pressure and even bang the stirrup off the saddle seat in order to create an unfamiliar noise. After some repetition, your horse will accept this, too.

When your horse is calm going in one direction, allow him to come in and offer him a break and a lot of praise. Undo the lariat and switch sides. Begin the exercise again and be certain to complete this new side with the same thoroughness as the first one.

Lesson 25 with an English Saddle

STEP ONE Make a large loop in the lariat, place it over the horse's head, and gently tighten around the lower neck of the horse.

SKIP STEP TWO.

STEP THREE Hold the rope low when you ask the horse to change direction. This will keep it out of the way of the horse's head as he turns to the inside, and it will still be in proper position once he has reversed direction.

STEP FOUR The lariat is closer to the horse's face than it is when attached to a saddle horn, so keep your "rope swinging" under control and limit it so it cannot strike the horse's face.

STEP FIVE Complete as described for the Western saddle, but with the lariat around the horse's neck, then run along the outside of the horse's body, around his hind end, and back to you in the middle of the pen. At no time should the rope be pulled tight around his neck.

STEP SIX Spend this time accustoming your horse to the lariat bouncing off the saddle flaps. You can also attach the stirrup leathers without the irons, then run the lariat through them and move them around as described for a Western stirrup.

This step is great for dealing with movement and noise issues that will occur on and around the horse's back when you begin riding him.

Rider's Block

● Lariat work can feel clumsy at first. Do not worry about it; instead, have fun with it! As long as you are not burning your horse's rear end or legs, you are probably sacking him out quite well. Remember you can always drop the lariat, bring your horse in, and begin again at any point.

● To decide how long to work on this exercise, pay closer attention to your horse. When he is in dire need of a break, give him one. If he is mentally done for the day, quit and plan to start over the following day. By keeping the steps small enough, you will find success more quickly. Small steps give you more "ending points" where both you and your horse can feel good about quitting for the time being.

Roadblocks

● If your horse has excessive issues with the lariat rope dangling behind him (see Step Five, p. 81), work with him at the jog and stay persistent. Be careful not to burn or catch the lariat under his tail. Wait for him to stop reacting: as soon as he stops kicking at the rope for a half circle of travel, let go of it (taking the pressure off his hind end) and let him relax. Some horses hate the rope behind them at first, but if you keep the exercise mellow and build slowly, they will get over it. It is worth taking care of the problem now: you do not want to ride a horse that will buck, kick, or scoot when a rope, jacket, saddle string, or other object unexpectedly touches him in his hindquarter area.

Lesson 25's Benefits

● In this lesson, you address some of the key fears that a horse tends to have when first mounted and ridden: cinch pressure and friction, flopping and noisy stirrups, moving ropes, and overhead commotion. You've dealt with these issues now while he is moving in the pen and you are safely on the ground.

Green Light

As I mentioned earlier, one of your aims is to show the horse that when it comes to the saddle, there is nothing to be afraid of. So make each step as small and safe, for him and you, as it can be. If your horse reacts to a moving stirrup on the saddle, he will no doubt react to a rider's moving leg! Minimize the horse's fear level as best you can prior to the first ride. If you have a lot of difficulty with this lesson, you'd be wise to end on the best note you can, and begin again the next day. Deal with issues as they arise and do not move on until they are worked through.

First Bridling

Goals

To teach your horse how to lower his head and hold steady while you show him how to accept and wear a snaffle-bit bridle.

Check-In

You should now have a horse that is much safer to be around than when you started. He should be far less reactive—in the negative sense—to being handled or approached with unfamiliar objects. He can handle a saddle blanket, saddle, and ropes, and is accustomed to being handled around the face—ears, muzzle, and nose—as well as the upper neck.

Cues to Use

To teach your horse to lower his head in preparation for bridling, the cue is pressure on the poll (the top of the horse's head, between his ears). The pressure comes from your hand—initially your fingernail and later your palm or forearm.

Spot, Direction, Motivator, and Release

Spot Poll
Direction Down
Motivator Fingernail pressure
Release Removal of fingernail pressure

Teaching Steps

STEP ONE

If you are just starting your training session for the day, warm your horse up by spending some time in the round pen checking your previous work. Move your horse, turn him inside, and ask him to approach you. This may take only a few minutes, but gains his attention and focuses his mind on you. Next, saddle your horse and send him back out on the rail to make certain he is accepting the saddle on this new day. Once you see him relax and "want in," allow him to approach you in the center of the round pen.

STEP TWO

Since you are going to be working around your horse's head, you want to double-check your earlier work and make sure he is not reactive to your hands on this day and in this new lesson. Offer him head rubs, while gently touching and rubbing his muzzle, ears, chin, and upper neck. If he seems unsure in any way, continue to rub and touch these areas until he is calm. Only when he is quiet with his head and accepting of your hands, can you move forward—a head-shy horse is not only difficult to work with, but handling and riding him can be dangerous.

STEP THREE

You will now teach your horse to give to pressure with the *head down cue*. The *spot* is his poll, the *direction* is downward, the *motivator* is a push, pinch, or "dig" with your fingers (whichever is enough pressure to evoke a response), and the *release* is the removal of the motivator together with a head rub.

Stand to the left of your horse, beside his head, and take your right hand and apply a small but sharp pressure on his poll with your thumb,

Just as rubbing your horse's head will become automatic as you are learning to constantly reward your horse, so will asking him to keep his head down. It is a wonderful and useful cue that makes simple chores—such as worming, shots, bathing, haltering, and bridling—easy and stress-free for both you and your horse.

index, and middle fingernails. Your left hand should be gently placed on the bridge of his nose. Your horse will lift, lower, or shake his head as you apply this pressure. Look for the slightest drop in head elevation. It may only be a fraction of an inch, but the second you see it, you must release the pressure immediately (photos 52 A–D). Give your horse some head rubs and a few seconds of break. Begin again and apply the same pressure at the poll while you wait for a response. If he lifts or shakes his head do not release the pressure, but once you see the slightest lowering, release him quickly. Repeat. Your horse will learn how to avoid this annoying pressure. It may take three tries, or it may take many.

STEP FOUR

As you see your horse come to understanding the head down cue, ask him to bring his head lower and lower. Continue to work on this exercise until you can get your horse's head near the ground (see photo 52 D). Walk away, ask your horse to follow or come back to you, and begin again.

Once you can consistently ask your horse to lower and hold his head in the position that you are looking for, you can begin to soften your cue. With repetition and correct releases, a light touch on the poll with your fingers will get the correct response. Graduate to using the palm of your hand to cue the horse to lower his head, then your forearm with your open hand spread above the horse's eyes. (This prepares him for the next step in putting on his first bridle.)

Once you arrive at this point, it is time to switch sides and start the exercise from scratch on the opposite side. Take the time needed to teach it over again properly from the new side. As long as your horse does not act aggressively, do not reprimand in any way if he does not lower his head. Just maintain the pressure until he responds correctly.

This cue is going to be a wonderful tool in your repertoire as it allows you to position his head where you want it while haltering, bridling, or in other handling situations. Slowly but surely, you are gaining control over more and more of his body parts.

Special Note on the "Snaffle-Bit Bridle"

In Western riding, a "bridle" traditionally includes a leverage bit, curb strap, headstall, and reins. When one says "snaffle-bit bridle," he is describing a training bridle that has a snaffle bit instead of one with leverage.

A snaffle is the bit that I use with all my young, untrained, or unfinished horses. The snaffle comes in "O"-ring, "D"-ring, and full-cheek varieties. The mouthpiece can be thick or thin and have smooth or twisted edges. All snaffle-bit mouthpieces have a break or hinge (one or two) in the middle. For this program, I recommend a mild, smooth, single-jointed mouthpiece.

In order to keep your snaffle bit in its correct position in the mouth, you can use a full-cheek snaffle bit, or as I do, an "O"-ring with a bit hobble. A bit hobble is a leather strap, nylon braid, or rawhide braid that is attached to both of the "O"-rings (it works with "D"-rings, too) and loops under the horse's chin. This bit hobble prevents the bit from shifting from side to side when rein pressure is applied.

Although split-leather reins are acceptable, I prefer to use a continuous rope rein in all of my groundwork and riding in the early stages of training. I then move on to split reins at a later point. I like slobber straps with a soft double-braided nylon rope that measures between ½-inch and ⅞-inch in diameter. (Note: you can find further discussion of bits and bridles on p. 3.)

STEP FIVE

It's time to put the snaffle-bit bridle on your horse. Begin with him calmly standing to your right in the middle of

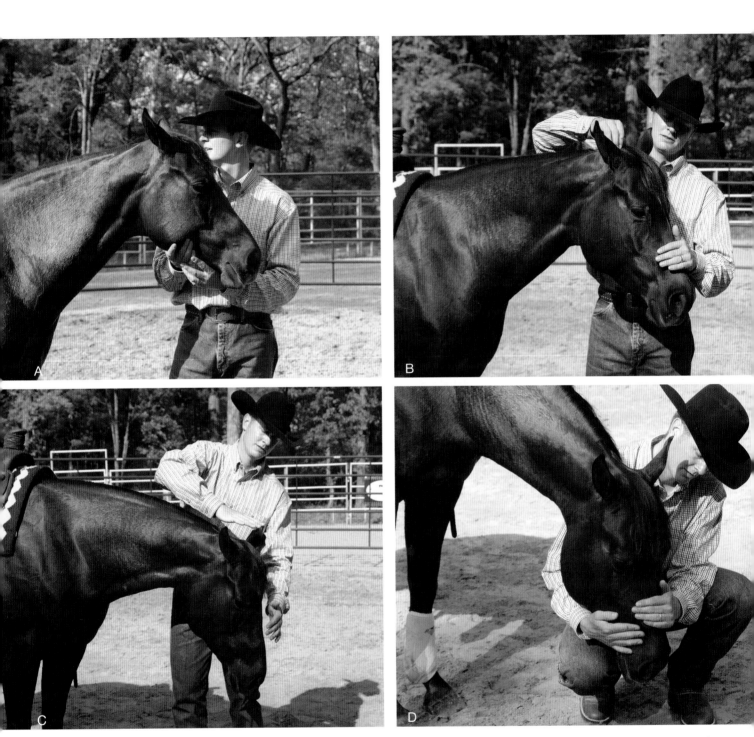

Photos 52 A–D I begin beside Belle's head, refamiliarizing her to the feel of my hands on her face (A). I ask her to lower her head by applying pressure to her poll with the fingers and thumb of my right hand (B). If your horse isn't particularly sensitive in this area, you may have to go so far as to "dig" your thumbnail into his poll to get his attention. When Belle seeks to escape the pressure from my fingers by dropping her head, I immediately release all pressure (C). It is important to continually prove to your horse that he can trust your hands. I reward Belle with soft strokes and words of praise (D).

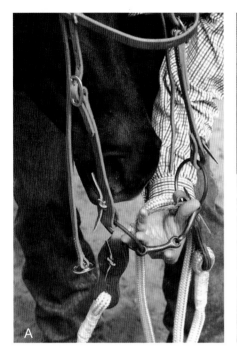

Photos 53 A & B Use this polite and effective method every time you bridle your horse: ask your horse to lower his head with your right forearm while your left thumb and middle finger touch the corners of the horse's mouth and your index finger remains in front of the bit (A). Gently insert your thumb and middle finger into the corners of the mouth and encourage the mouth to open. As the horse's teeth separate, guide the bit past the horse's front teeth with your index finger. Your right hand lifts the headstall and holds the bit in the horse's mouth (B).

the round pen. Ask him to lower his head to a comfortable height—so his neck is level. Spread your right hand out and lift your snaffle-bit bridle over your horse's face, so your right forearm is just above the horse's poll.

You are now in position to insert the bit: place the index finger of your left hand in front of the bit, while your thumb, middle, ring, and pinky fingers are behind it (but in front of the bit hobble). Next, gently use the thumb and middle finger of your left hand on opposite sides of the horse's mouth to encourage him to open it. You may have to insert them and touch him on the bars (the gum areas behind his front teeth, but in front of his molars). Once you see and feel his mouth opening in your hands, very gently and smoothly use your index finger to push the bit into his mouth. Avoid hitting his teeth with the bit. With your right hand, slowly lift the headstall upward until you know that the snaffle bit is in place (photos 53 A & B). Once the bit is in his mouth, you can put the headstall and browband over your horse's far ear first, followed by the near ear.

The snaffle bit should fit so that it is resting on the horse's bars, tight enough not to sag down from the cor-

ners of the mouth or touch the front teeth, but loose enough so there are no wrinkles or folds of skin at the corners of his mouth. Once you have adjusted the size, straighten the browband and secure the throatlatch strap. This strap should not be tight—leave 3 or 4 inches of slack under the horse's throatlatch.

Once your snaffle-bit bridle is on, take your reins and put them over your horse's head. Note: it is not a good idea to put the reins over your horse's head prior to bridling him, as it can be unsafe should he move suddenly or spook. I prefer to keep them looped over my left arm.

Rider's Block

Putting on the snaffle-bit bridle is a very big deal. Not only during the first bridling, but every time you do it. If you bump your horse's teeth, "jam" the gums, pull on his ears, allow him to lift his head, or bridle him in a swift impolite manner, your horse will learn to dislike the process. This can lead to him tossing his head, moving his feet, rearing up, or clenching his teeth shut in the future.

● If your horse moves his head when you are trying to bridle him, rewind and go back to work on sacking your horse out to your hands, and strengthening the head down cue.

● Be aware of where the snaffle bit is lying in your horse's mouth. Too loose, it moves around and bangs his front teeth; too tight, and there's constant pressure on the mouth's tender corners. As the trainer, you need to be in control of the pressure that your horse feels in his mouth—when you release your rein pressure, the bit should also be released. If the snaffle-bit bridle is adjusted too tightly, you cannot give your horse a full release of bit pressure, even with slack reins.

Roadblocks

● If your horse is suddenly reactive to the bridle when you are handling it around his head, take a step back in the training process. Work with your hands again, rub him all over, and tell him to drop his head. Slowly reintroduce the snaffle-bit bridle, beginning by rubbing him on the neck with it. Build up his trust by moving the new item around both sides of his neck, and then walk away. Ask your horse to approach you and repeat. Take it slowly and do not force

the bridle on your horse. It is your job as the trainer to prove to him that he has no reason to worry about the new piece of equipment.

● If your horse plays with the bit, or puts his tongue over the bit, realize that this is normal and okay. Some horses will not keep their tongue under the bit—where it should be—until they have learned to carry it for a while.

Lesson 24's Benefits

● Now that you can safely and easily put a snaffle-bit bridle on your horse, you are ready to begin groundwork that includes this equipment. You have also established a head down cue that aids you in all areas of handling.

Green Light

The aim of this lesson is to teach your horse to willingly accept the bridle. In the process you have taught him to drop his head, and reaffirmed that he can handle your hands and "commotion" around his face and neck area. When your horse is calm and confident in these three areas, you can move on.

Moving the Hips

Goals

You will teach your horse to move his hips over in response to a bridle cue. You are after a compliant response with a soft, lowered head and proper footwork. I teach hip motion in response to bridle pressure (rein cue) at this time for a few reasons. First, you will use hip motion to steer the horse when he is going forward. Second, you'll show your horse how to find a release from bit pressure: moving his feet correctly. Third, you begin bridle lessons with the "easiest" lesson—and hip motion is quickly taught.

Check-In

This lesson is your horse's first introduction to bridle pressure—pressure that is created by the bit-and-rein combination. If your horse is still head-shy, unsure about your hands, or uncomfortable with the saddle, this lesson will be more difficult because he'll always be preoccupied with something other than what you are trying to teach. (I like to maximize the horse's time spent wearing a saddle before the first ride, which is why I recommend you saddle up for this lesson.)

In addition to what your horse is ready for, I think it is just as important that you are also ready to move ahead. You have learned—and possibly struggled through—the earlier lessons in the Countdown. You now see the importance of making a clear request to your horse (spot and direction), as well as how to use a motivator with the right amount of pressure, followed by rein-forcements (full release or withdrawal of pressure and addition of pleasing stimuli). This understanding (theoretical) and practice (practical) is going to guide you through the remainder of the Countdown lessons and beyond. Stay focused when you train, with the intent to continually improve your ability to gauge pressure levels and the appropriate release point.

Cues to Use

You are going to teach your horse to move his hip laterally with bit and rein pressure. You draw the rein toward the horse's hip while standing beside him (see photo 54 B, p. 91). The pressure on the bit that comes from the tightening the rein like this is your horse's cue to move that hip over.

The amount of pressure you use depends on the response you get. As soon as your horse responds correctly, you must release. The horse's neck position (amount of bend) will be a product of this. Since your emphasis is on "teaching" and not "correctness," the amount of bend in your horse's neck will vary. In this exercise you will withhold your release until the horse moves his feet as much as you ask, keeps his neck level, and "gives" to the bit. If the amount of pressure it takes to gain these responses is great, the neck bends more; if it is light, it bends less.

Spot, Direction, Motivator, and Release

Spot Your horse's hip (whichever side you are standing on)

Direction Away from you

Motivator Bridle pressure (bit pressure caused by rein pressure)

Release Full release of rein pressure, followed by head rubs and a break

Teaching Steps

STEP ONE

In order to begin, your horse should be saddled and wearing protective boots. Warm him up with some movement and inside turns before you let him relax with you in the center of the round pen. Put on the snaffle-bit bridle, and loop the reins over your horse's head. You are now ready to begin teaching him to respond to a bridle cue.

Stand beside your horse and face his left shoulder. With your left hand, take hold of the rope rein about 12 inches (give or take) from the bit and draw the rein in the direction of the horse's left hip—that is, take the rein directly to the point of the horse's hip. Your hand does not have to reach the hip, it just has go in the direction of the hip. For your first few requests, use enough pressure on the rein to bring the horse's head around to where you can see both eyes (the neck will bend as you apply this pressure smoothly). Hold the pressure until you see your horse's left hind foot move away from you. At this moment, release the rein. Since you have continuous rope reins, it is safe to let go of the rein completely. This is a "full release" and your "Yes" response. Rub your horse's head, giving him further reassurance (photos 54 A–D).

You are looking for a very precise movement. You want the horse's left hind foot to move away from you and in front of his right hind foot. By looking for this exact movement you will know when you should release the rein pressure.

The way in which you apply the rein pressure is important. If you ask too softly, your horse does not have much of a reason to move. If you ask too sharply, he may react by lifting or throwing his head. You want to "enter" the rein pressure with a steady hand, allowing your horse a chance to feel the pressure coming.

I like to make this request on one side, have the hip

A Special Note on Hip Motion and Correct Footwork

When you ask your horse to move his hip over laterally, insist on correct footwork (see Forward Motion—Correct Footwork, p. 117), which in this context, is when the hind foot on the near side (the side you are on) passes in front of the opposite hind foot. In other words, a left-rein hip cue moves the left hind foot in front of the right hind foot. You may find that your horse does this on his own, but if he does not, ask him to take a step forward before you request lateral hip motion. This step forward will help your horse practice the proper foot placement.

move over one step, offer a full release, and casually walk to the front of the horse and rub his head. I then walk around to his right side and make the same request. After I get a good response there, I return to the left side with a head rub on the way, and repeat. At this stage, you are still only looking for one good step and a relaxed "give" to the bridle pressure—one without signs of avoidance behavior. You can work on this side to side for a while. The duration of the step will depend on how well your horse is doing. If you have difficulty moving your horse's hip over or have a horse that is not giving well to the bit, continue the exercise—only looking for this one step—until he is compliant.

This way of teaching the hips to move from the ground accomplishes many things. You teach your horse his first bridle pressure cue. You work both sides equally, changing the direction that your horse needs to bend his neck and respond with hip motion. I have found that it also relaxes the horse.

STEP TWO

Once you have been able to release on several "first steps," add another requirement to the exercise. As you pick up

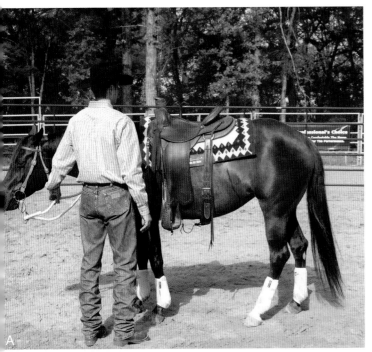

Photo 54 A–D   I begin with Belle in the middle of the round pen, standing quietly as I face her shoulder (A). I then draw the left rein toward her left hip. As you can see, the amount of pressure is enough to bend her neck, but I apply it in a smooth and fair manner (B). Belle finds the correct "answer" by moving her left hip away from the rein pressure. I am also pleased to see "forward motion" as her left hind leg passes in front of the right hind leg (C). I offer a full release of bridle pressure and give positive reinforcements (D). My release of the rein confirms that Belle gave the right response to "get out of" the bridle pressure.

The Semantics of Hip Motion

HIP ENGAGEMENT: think of putting your car *into* gear. You are adding the power of the motor directly to your tires, allowing the car to propel itself. When you engage the hip, you are asking the horse to move that hip in an effort to create impulsion as needed in: lope departures, side-passing, and turning on the forehand.

HIP DISENGAGEMENT: think about taking your car *out of* gear. You just removed the power behind the moving tires. When you disengage the hip, you are asking the horse to move his hip in such a way that you remove his impulsion—when the hind feet have to cross, the forward drive is removed. This is a useful tool to slow down or stop a young horse from incorrect or unwanted forward movement.

rein pressure, only release when the horse's head is level and soft to your hand—this is where you want him to place his head in order to find a release. From this point onward, never release your horse if his head elevation is high—above level height—or if there is pressure on your hand from his mouth, even when his feet are doing the right thing.

STEP THREE

When your horse consistently gives you one good hip step with a "soft nose"—he's not pulling or fighting the rein pressure—start to work on consecutive hip steps (further). Pick up the rein and only release the pressure when you see the hind foot take two steps away from you. Build slowly up to the point where your horse takes as many hip steps over as you want.

Once you get past the first one or two steps, your horse will start to pivot on his inside front foot (the one closest to you) as the hips move over. This pivoting action tells you that you have in fact isolated the hip with your cue and the

horse is responding correctly. If your horse walks forward, then you are not "isolating" his hind end enough. By releasing only when his front end is stationary and his hind end is in motion, you will teach him what you are looking for. If you remain still when you take up rein pressure, the horse is less likely to walk forward.

STEP FOUR

After completing many "gives"—where your horse responds well to the rein pressure by moving his hip—you can add some speed (*faster*). You are not looking to zip your horse around, you just want to add some increased pressure with your rein, as well as some clucking noises, and ask your horse to pick up the pace slightly. Three to six steps is more than enough.

You want your horse to know that when you ask for his feet to move faster (added pressure and vocals) that he had better do it. You do not want a horse that is lazy or slow with your requests. With speed comes emotion, so this is a good test to see how both you and your horse have done with the earlier steps. When your horse does not break the pivoting pattern, you are doing well. If you add rein pressure and cluck to him a few times, and he raises his head or moves laterally away from you with his front end, go back to the beginning and build the response again.

STEP FIVE

The beauty of this basic ground exercise is that your *softer* element will come quite quickly with repetition, if you allow for it. In time, you will notice your horse anticipating the motion and you will only have to pick up the rein lightly for him to move his hip over. This is a good sign. However, now you have another issue to deal with—anticipation—because you only want your horse to move when you tell him.

To combat anticipation—that is, you horse guessing what you want and reacting prior to the cue—you need to change the routine. If you have been walking from one side to the other and requesting a hip motion in the same rhythmic pattern each time, your horse will figure you out. Instead, occasionally wait at your horse's shoulder and don't pick up the rein. Take a few minutes and just stand with him. Rub him on the head and stand with him some more. Then, either ask him to move his hip over, by picking up the rein, or leave that side and walk to the other. Mix up the pattern by walking away and asking him to approach you, stand quietly in different spots in the pen, or revisit earlier lessons and ask for more than one movement at a time.

If you ever find that your horse does not respond as quickly (*faster*), or as far (*further*) as you are looking for, increase the rein pressure until he does. But when he performs the task well on a softer cue—one with less pressure—continue to decrease the pressure used for the request. In time, you will be able to ask to move his hip on a very soft rein cue.

Rider's Block

● If you are unsure what to look for in your horse's movement, you will not be able to release and reward him at the correct time. Look for a precise hip motion by watching where his hind feet go. When you see the hind foot closest to you move in front of the opposite hind foot, you have the proper response.

● Don't follow the rein pressure with your own feet or you will encourage the horse to follow you, as well. Stand still, and use rein pressure only to request the hip motion; he will then keep his front end—his shoulders—still and learn to "isolate" his hips, thus creating a pivoting "pattern" around the front foot closest to you.

● If you snatch the rein pressure quickly and are "annoying" in your request, you will create a jumpy horse that may complete the movement, but will not want to. Remember that "getting a horse to do something" and "teaching a horse to do something willingly" are two very different ways of training.

Roadblocks

● If your horse is not moving his hips with correct foot-

work, think about what you are doing that could cause this effect. I will use the left hip as an example: if I pick up the left rein too quickly or with a lot of unnecessary pressure, my horse might want to avoid bit pressure altogether and back away from it (since the bit is in front of him, his instinctual movement will be backward). When he travels backward, his legs cannot complete the correct foot pattern. Problems can also arise when you move your own feet, rather than just the rein, toward the horse's hind end. The horse actually thinks that if he backs up with you, you might let go of the rein.

Lesson 23's Benefits

● Bridle pressure has been introduced. Both you and your horse are starting to see where the hind feet need to be in order to get a release. This is a good start as you have a lot of pressure-and-release exercises to come! You are becoming a better teacher, while your horse is becoming a better student. As you complete more of these exercises, he will start to be confident in the fact that following pressure—whether from bridle, body, halter, or "other"—there is an inevitable release. Since he knows this to be true, as you have always been consistent and fair, he will willingly seek the answer. Horses that do not "believe" a release is coming are slower to respond—if they do at all.

● You have gained control over all five control points on your horse. You are able to move both hips over through rein pressure with the shoulder's stationary, and the horse's nose soft and low to your hand. You also insisted that the shoulders remain still as you isolate and move the hind feet over.

Green Light

When you can calmly ask your saddled horse to move his hips in either direction with a soft rein cue, while pivoting on his front end, you are ready to move on. If your horse is showing any undesirable behavior such as anticipation, anxiety, avoidance, or defiance, continue with this lesson until you have resolved the issue.

"Sacking-Out" with Hip Motion

Goals

Now you will continue building your horse's confidence level while also improving his response to a *hip motion cue*. By combining these two aims, you help in his emotional development. A constant goal throughout your training will be to test your horse's emotional response (heightened awareness, fear, or agitation), then to bring it down a notch. Another objective is to continually improve the horse's response to a cue when he is experiencing heightened emotions.

Check-In

At this point in the Countdown, your horse is comfortable wearing his protective boots, saddle, and snaffle-bit bridle. You have introduced a hip motion cue from bit pressure and successfully conditioned a solid response. If your horse happily accepts his saddle—so he does not buck or kick when you are close by—and is able to respond well to your hip cue through the bit and bridle, you are ready for this lesson.

Teaching Steps

STEP ONE

Warm up your horse (in his protective boots and saddle) around the pen, do some inside turns and following exercises. Once you see that he accepts the saddle and boots on this new day, ask him to approach you in the middle of the round pen. Put the snaffle-bit bridle on (see p. 84). Spend a few minutes reviewing the recently taught hip motion cue (see Lesson 23, p. 89). You should find your horse responds well to a light rein request. If he is unresponsive or requires too much pressure, work on this cue until it is as good as when you last visited it. Work on both sides equally. Once the horse is focused, you can start to add the next part of the lesson.

Standing on the left side of your horse, hold the rein as if preparing for a hip motion cue, but do not ask for it. With your right hand, softly slap the saddle's seat with a rhythmic beat, about three times. Then, ask your horse to move his hip over a couple of steps. Walk to his head, give him a rub, and repeat the exercise on the opposite side (photos 55 A–C).

You are not trying to move your horse away from you with this slapping—you are just proving that the sight, sound, and feel of it is nothing to fear. In order for the horse to fully accept this action, start small with a few soft slaps and build your way up until he accepts you smacking the saddle seat quite firmly and for an extended period of time. Work your way up to two sets of 30 slaps, with two steps of hip motion between each set, on both sides of the horse. By the end of the exercise, your horse will not think twice about your raised hand at his side, or the slapping of the saddle.

If you find that your horse cannot handle even three soft slaps in the beginning (he overreacts by running off or jumping around), try rub-

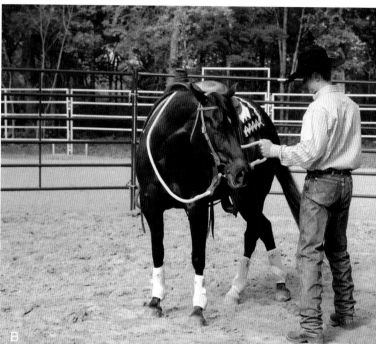

Photos 55 A–C   I stand beside Belle, sacking her out by slapping the saddle with my hand (A). If I detect a reaction from her, I'll continue slapping with rhythm until the reaction subsides. Intermittently, I ask her to move her hips to keep her from "locking up" (B). Since I am asking her to accept new pressures, noises, and movements, I continue to assure Belle that everything is fine with kind words and a familiar head rub (C).

bing the saddle and standing quietly with him before you move his hip over and switch sides. This exercise is meant to build his confidence, so if you have to start small, do so, and work your way up slowly. When your horse walks forward or away from you, immediately move his hip over. Then, rub him on the head, try fewer slaps, and start building again.

Do not hold your horse still with the reins. If you catch yourself doing so, just move his hip over, offer a full release, and begin again. Your horse needs to feel he is free to leave at any time, but if you see him thinking about it, ask for his hip to move before he does.

If your horse adjusts his balance or moves even half a step due to fear, keep slapping the saddle. The only time you

Photo 56 Here, I pick up the stirrup and snap it down loudly at Belle's side.

Photo 57 With my hand on the horn, I shake the saddle and move it back and forth on Belle's back. Tug on the hind cinch and continue moving the saddle around. You want to make noise and cause pressures that your horse is not accustomed to, proving to him that everything is alright and there is nothing to fear.

should stop early and move his hip over is when you think he is actually about to walk away from you.

Your horse should not be moving his hips all the time— you must request hip motion, reward him, sack him out, request motion, reward him, and so forth. What you are working on is "unlocking his feet." When a horse is unsure or scared, he tends to "lock up," similar to a deer in the headlights. Your horse may be thinking, "Okay, what's my next move?" By continually asking for movement throughout this exercise you keep his legs from staying still for long—whether due to tenseness or laziness—as well as proactively deal with fear issues.

STEP TWO
Continue building your exposures—scary actions. The exercise essentially remains the same, but instead of slapping the saddle seat, mess with the stirrups and fenders. Begin by picking up the left stirrup with your hand and snapping it downward (photo 56). At first, do it gently and don't make much of a noise. Move your horse's hips, reward him, and switch sides to repeat.

Increase the sound and feel of the stirrup snapping with more force. Build up the noise with many repetitions. When your horse reacts badly by moving off, move his hip, and go back to slapping the saddle or asking him to follow

you. Then, return to the stirrups and fenders, but use less pressure.

STEP THREE
Once you have slapped the saddle and snapped the stirrups a lot, add more stimuli. These include shaking the saddle with your hand on the horn, tugging the rear cinch with increasing firmness, lifting the cantle, and pulling on the breast collar (photo 57).

All of this messing around the saddle will continue to prove to your horse that you are not a threat. These exposures do not hurt your horse in any way—they are just noises and slight pressures on the horse's back. This is the time to have him grow comfortable with these sensations, as you are still on the ground and in control of his movement.

During Lesson 22 it is a good idea to step away from your horse often and ask him to face and come to you. Make this interaction "his" idea, so he is always approaching you. It is also a good test of your pressure level to see if he willingly comes back to you after you've worked through one of

Photo 58   Use a small item, such as a plastic bag or a baseball cap as I am here, to sack your horse out around his head and neck. Work on the areas above and below the face, as well as to each side. Continue moving the item around the head and neck until the horse no longer reacts to it.

the steps. If he doesn't want anything to do with you, revisit facing and following (see Lesson 30, p. 45).

STEP FOUR

Remember: you are trying to create a horse that is safe to ride. You are not climbing on yet, but work on this lesson with this in mind. For example, since you are going to be "over your horse's head" when you are on his back, you need to "sack out the air" around it.

I like to use a baseball cap to start. Show your horse the cap and shake it in front of him from a comfortable distance—maybe 3 feet from his nose. Move it from side to side. If your horse backs up, move the cap away from him—while still shaking it—and approach him with it again. Change from his left to right side, over his head and under his chin (photo 58). Spend quite a bit of time (anywhere from five to 20 minutes) shaking the cap on all sides of your horse's head until he is completely unresponsive to it in close proximity. Reward often with a head rub, assure him that he is okay, and go back to shaking the cap. I feel that if your horse cannot handle the "cap test," then you should not be in the saddle.

Rider's Block

● It is true that you have sacked your horse out before, but you can never "prepare him too much" for you as the rider. Now that he is wearing a saddle and bridle, it is a good time to continue this work. I sack my own horses out every day that I handle them.

● With "sacking-out" exercises, rhythm is your friend. Begin all your slaps and snaps with soft, steady beats. In time, you can change it up, but at first a steady influx of noise and contact is much easier for a horse to grow comfortable with.

● When you see your horse react to an exposure of any kind, do not "quit" the exposure. For example, if your horse tosses his head while you shake your baseball cap, though he is not moving his feet, continue with the shaking. You do not want to reward such behavior. Wait for him to quit—before you do. This is how your horse overcomes his fears.

● When you introduce a scary item or action, you must finish with it. This means that if you introduce a baseball cap and shake it around your horse's facial area, and he reacts by flinching or moving, you are now obligated to finish working with the baseball cap until he is 100-percent all right with it—that is, "desensitized." You must avoid "sensitizing" him instead, which happens when fear is created and habituation (see p. 22) has not occurred.

Roadblocks

● As with all "sacking-out" exercises, you may be surprised to find your horse reacts and is unable to handle certain things you took for granted—his stirrups being pulled or snapped, for example. When this is the case, start small—I mean really small!

Lesson 22's Benefits

● You have prepared your horse for his first ride by getting him accustomed to handling and "sacking-out" with his saddle on, and helped him grow comfortable and confident with all the noises, sights, and pressures that surround him. While doing this, you raised his emotional level by asking him to respond well to a bridle cue for hip motion, helping him learn how to still respond to a cue when under stress. On your first several rides, your horse will be under a high level of stress, but you still want him to respond to this basic cue.

Green Light

Conditions that must be met before moving on to the next lesson:

▶ You can walk up to your horse and slap the saddle loudly without him moving his feet.

▶ You can pull, flop, and snap the stirrups without any reaction.

▶ You can shake and lift the saddle without the horse caring or moving.

▶ You can move items around your horse's head, from side to side as well as over and under, without him moving his head or feet.

▶ He responds to your hip motion cue with a soft, low-headed "give," whereby his feet move properly with correct footwork (see p. 90).

▶ His overall confidence level means you have to use increasing levels of action, noise, and pressure to get a response.

Go Forward Cue

Goals

This lesson has four parts. Your initial goal is to teach your horse to move forward with the basic *go forward cue* from the ground. Second, you are going to teach your horse to reverse his direction while in-hand (attached to your lead rope). Third, you will teach him to change his direction with shoulder motion, while respecting your space. Fourth, you will test your go forward response by applying it to useful situations.

Other teaching goals include: giving to bit pressure; responding to a clucking noise to move his feet faster; respecting your personal space; accepting a dressage whip as a training tool; and recognizing when you are asking for movement and when you are not.

Check-In

This exercise combines many of your previously taught responses, while adding another training tool—the dressage whip. I have reserved this lesson for this stage in the Countdown in order for both you and your horse to find success more quickly. It is best taught when the following responses are already confirmed:

▸ Your horse moves forward in response to body pressure and clucking noises.

▸ He turns inside with a body cue.

▸ Your horse "wants in" and is comfortable standing still beside you.

▸ Your horse has been "sacked-out" well and is confident with the introduction of new items.

▸ Your horse has had time wearing a snaffle-bit bridle and responds well to a hip motion cue.

Cues to Use

You are now going to teach your horse to respond to a dressage whip. This whip will be both your cue and your motivator, as you tap the horse's hindquarter requesting forward movement.

Spot, Direction, Motivator, and Release

Spot Horse's chest
Direction Forward
Motivator Dressage whip
Release Cessation of whip-tapping

Teaching Steps

STEP ONE: TEACH THE BASIC GO FORWARD CUE

Begin alongside your horse—saddled and wearing protective boots—in the middle of the round pen. Have your dressage whip ready, placed on the ground nearby. Put the snaffle-bit bridle on, but before you put the rope reins over his head, twist them a couple of times so they are crossed under his chin, and fasten the throatlatch under them so they don't sag down and get in the way (photo 59). Then, attach your lead rope to the snaffle bit ring—either the left or right side.

Now, pick up your dressage whip

When working on Step One, you can attach the lead rope to either side of the snaffle bit. Pressure is pressure, and your horse will—and should—learn it comes from either side. I like to mix it up two or three times per training session by attaching the lead rope to one side for a while, and then switching it when my horse is taking a break in the middle with me.

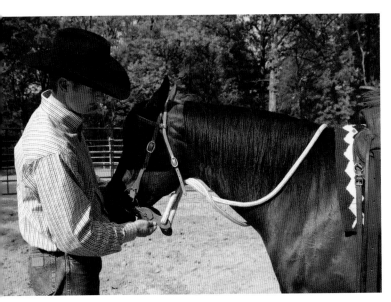

Photo 59 Once the horse is bridled, twist the rope reins a couple of times and put them over the horse's head. Loop them around your horn if they are long enough (mine aren't here) and use the throatlatch to secure the remaining slack. Another option is to detach the reins from the bit by undoing the slobber straps; however, many slobber straps do not have ties (like these from Schutz Brothers), so this is not an option. Either way, the goal is to keep them from getting in the way or creating an unsafe rope "loop" that your horse could step in.

ping firmness until your horse decides to take a step forward. Release your horse again and offer a head rub. After a few seconds break, repeat, this time asking for at least two steps, followed by three, and so forth (photos 60 A–E).

If you release your horse at the correct time, he will learn very quickly that he can avoid firm tapping by taking steps forward. Build the response slowly, as asking for too much movement, too quickly may cause your horse to become scared or perhaps angry. At this point, you can be satisfied with walking steps. Should he jog forward, that is fine as well. Allow him to come back down on his own and offer a break.

Work on building the go forward response *further*. As the number of steps your horse takes increases, he will begin to move in a circle around you (the distance the lead rope allows for—about 10 feet in diameter). Use your left hand to apply pressure to the bit when the horse leans on the lead rope and tries to travel in a larger circle. By keeping the circle small you have more control, are able to reach your horse with the whip, and can offer positive reinforcements. Again, you are satisfied with the walk, but a slow jog can also be rewarded. If your horse lopes—or attempts to—during this early stage, you are most likely adding too much whip pressure or have allowed too large a circle with a lengthy lead rope.

and stand quietly. Rub your horse on the head and let him relax. Right from the start, let your horse know that although you picked up the whip, he does not need to move until asked.

Let's say you are beginning on the left side of your horse. Stand at his shoulder, looking at the saddle horn or pommel, with about 3 feet of slack in the lead rope in your left hand. Next, raise your whip in your right hand and tap the horse softly on the hindquarters. In one-second intervals, gradually increase the firmness of the "tap." Continue tapping until you see the horse's chest move forward, even just slightly. At this moment, stop tapping, lower the whip, and offer a head rub.

Once you have your first release, repeat the process, asking for one good step forward. Raise the whip and ask for forward movement with a soft tap. Increase the tap-

Be mindful to never allow your horse to lean on the bit. As he travels in a circle around you, let your lead rope remain slack with a 3-foot allowance. Should he decide to make the circle bigger on his own, let him feel the end of the lead rope and corresponding bit pressure, and come back to the smaller circle. If he does not come back, increase the pressure by giving the lead rope a "bump" and bringing his nose toward you. The moment that he "gives" his nose and resumes traveling in the smaller circle, let the line go slack again. You have given your horse two parameters: go forward (or you will tap harder with the dressage whip); and stay in the circle size allowed (or he will feel unpleasant bit pressure).

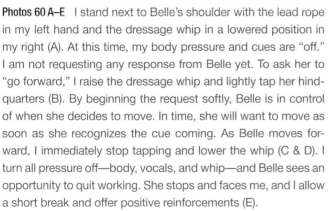

Photos 60 A–E   I stand next to Belle's shoulder with the lead rope in my left hand and the dressage whip in a lowered position in my right (A). At this time, my body pressure and cues are "off." I am not requesting any response from Belle yet. To ask her to "go forward," I raise the dressage whip and lightly tap her hind-quarters (B). By beginning the request softly, Belle is in control of when she decides to move. In time, she will want to move as soon as she recognizes the cue coming. As Belle moves forward, I immediately stop tapping and lower the whip (C & D). I turn all pressure off—body, vocals, and whip—and Belle sees an opportunity to quit working. She stops and faces me, and I allow a short break and offer positive reinforcements (E).

Once your horse completes a full circle around you, use your left hand to draw the lead rope in the direction of the horse's hip, requesting the hips to move over so your horse turns and faces you. Once he comes to a halt, release all the lead-line pressure and stand quietly with him, rubbing his head. Change direction and repeat the exercise. You want to establish a pattern in Step One to help with the steps that follow in the lesson. Moving your horse forward on a full circle or more, followed by a break in the middle for reward, makes him "want in" and discourages him from trying to face outward and leave you.

You need to teach your horse to recognize when you are asking for forward movement with pressure and when you are not. Even when you are standing beside him holding a dressage whip, you still want him to wait for the cue to move. You can teach him to recognize this pressure difference—"on" or "off"—a few ways. One, if he ever goes forward without your asking, move his hips over as you did in Lesson 23 (see p. 89). This stops his forward movement. Two, during breaks, spend time rubbing him all over his body with the dressage whip in a relaxed fashion. If he moves forward, stop him with the lead rope and continue rubbing him with the whip. This teaches him to recognize your "pressure off" mode—not asking for movement—before you once again take position and give him the go forward cue. By switching back and forth between pressure on and off modes, your horse will learn to recognize the difference.

When your horse travels calmly around you for as long as you ask, and he respects the circle size, you can insist he travel at a jog (*faster*). If he has already offered a jog, that's fine, but now you will insist on the jog. Give him another 2 feet of lead rope so that your circle is closer to 12 feet in diameter. If your horse only walks when you give the go forward cue, continue tapping with increasing firmness until the jog happens. Use your clucking noise (see p. 28) to associate this sound with your horse moving his feet faster. Repeat the jogging circles in both directions.

Note: at this point you do not want your horse to lope. This exercise has enough moving parts to work on without adding this element. If your horse is hard to manage, and he pulls on you or wants to break out of the jog, shorten your lead rope and try working him in a smaller circle. Many times I will increase my circle size only to decrease it when I see that the horse is not ready, or he needs to have something that was already introduced reestablished.

Once you have completed many go forward requests at both the walk and jog, you will notice that the number of taps it takes to cue him forward will diminish (*softer*). If you are requesting forward movement properly—by starting with soft taps and continually increasing the firmness—your horse will respond by moving on two taps, then one tap, then when you so much as raise the dressage whip. In time, you will be able to simply cluck for your horse to move forward.

STEP ONE QUICK-CHECK

▸ Does your horse stand quietly with you while you rub him all over with the whip?

▸ Can you maintain a symmetrical circle without your horse leaning on the bit?

▸ Can you move your horse into a jog with a soft tap of the dressage whip?

▸ Can you keep your horse jogging steadily for at least 10 circles without him breaking?

STEP TWO: REVERSE DIRECTION WHILE MOVING FORWARD

When you changed direction in Step One you asked your horse to move forward, stop, relax, and then move forward again in the other direction. You are now increasing the level of difficulty by asking for this change of direction with continuous movement—without letting the horse stop in the middle. Note: The horse will most likely make the turn by moving his hindquarters (hips) away from you and then resuming forward movement in the new direction. We will allow this type of turn in Step Two, but not in Step Three (see below).

Begin again standing on the left side of your horse in the middle of the pen. With your go forward cue, ask him to move counterclockwise, in a 12-foot circle at a jog. After he has jogged for at least half a circle, use your left hand to ask your horse to move his hips away from you as you did in Step One, by taking the slack out of the lead rope in the direction of his hip (your left hand will cross your body, creating pressure on the bit). You do not have to take more than one step toward his hip, as your previous work should allow you to make a subtle request. (Notice that I used the word "should" here. If you do not get the response that you want, increase the pressure—fairly—until you do.) This hip-motion request will stop your horse, and he will immediately turn on his forehand and face you—and likely expect a break! Instead of allowing him to stop and relax, switch the dressage whip to your left hand, move to your left to position yourself on the horse's right side, and ask him to move off in the opposite direction—that is, clockwise. This maneuver will not be fluid yet; your horse will pause slightly as you change sides and switch hands. However, do not let him take a break or reward the stop—until you really want him to stop!

In the beginning ask for one or two changes of direction, followed by a break. As you build the response and your horse learns what is expected of him, you can call for more changes, interspersed with forward movement from a half-circle to several complete circles in a row. Your horse will focus harder on you, as he'll be unsure whether you will let him stop or continue moving him. And, with repetition, your horse will stop and turn on his forehand with less pressure on the bit, and move off again with a more subtle go forward cue (*softer*).

This exercise is how I teach my horse's to lunge. I begin working on small circles, and when the horse responds correctly, I start to feed the lead rope out in 1- or 2-foot increments until he can respond to my requests at a 20-foot distance. If I ever feel that he is not attentive or is leaning on the bit, I immediately shorten the line and get it right. I am not fond of conventional lunging practices, as they seem to use fatigue as a "crutch" and allow the horse to lean on pressure and remain inattentive.

Your body language should remain quite relaxed. Do not yank your horse to a stop, jump over to his other side, or drive him off with great force. Calmly use only as much pressure as you need. By methodically building the exercise, you give him a chance to see what's coming next. This keeps your horse from becoming anxious or overwhelmed.

STEP TWO QUICK-CHECK

▸ Can you move your horse's hips over on the circle so he can come to a stop and face you with ease?

▸ Can you move your horse forward with a subtle motion of the dressage whip or a clucking noise?

▸ Is your horse relaxed and not trying to escape?

▸ Is your horse equally proficient in both directions?

▸ Are you comfortable handling the dressage whip and can you change sides gracefully?

▸ Does your horse anticipate the change enough to begin to move just before you cue him?

STEP THREE: CHANGING DIRECTION WITH SHOULDER MOTION

You will use your horse's "anticipation" to your advantage.

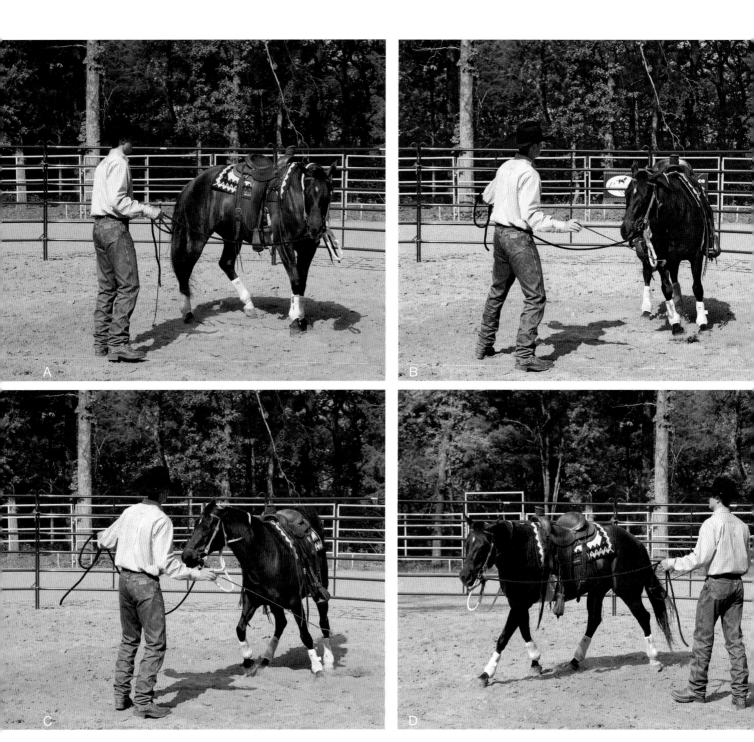

Photos 61 A–D In A, Belle moves forward on a small clockwise circle. In order to change direction, I quietly switch the dressage whip from my left to my right hand, and the lead rope from my right to my left. In B, I take a step to the right, as if I am asking for an inside turn (see p. 34). At the same moment, I extend my right hand and the dressage whip along Belle's right side. She responds in C, turning toward me. The lead rope pressure guides her nose in the right direction, and my body position and dressage whip cue her to move forward. Once she's changed direction in D, I let her jog along quietly as a release.

After Step Two, your horse will have figured out how and when you change his direction and move him back off again. So, continue with the same request, but ask for it in a different way, and expect a more advanced response.

Ask your horse to jog a 12-foot circle around you to your left—counterclockwise. Hold the lead rope in your left hand and the dressage whip in your right. Next, position your body for an *inside turn cue* (see p. 34) by dropping your left shoulder back and stepping to the left. At this time, switch the lead rope from your left to your right hand, and the whip from right to left. Once you see your horse stopping and his nose coming toward the middle of the circle, "push" him with a clucking noise and by extending your whip along his left side to ask him to complete the change of direction with energy and drive him off in the opposite direction. If your horse tries to "leave" the circle, back off the pressure and start again. "Too much, too soon" will make this lesson hard to teach. (In other words, keep the training step small until he doesn't show signs of avoidance behavior.)

Did your horse change direction? If he did not recognize the inside turn cue—the "opening" of your shoulder—and kept on going, immediately insist that a change of direction happens by reverting to Step Two (see p. 102). Then continue by asking for your next change as explained above. Repeat in the opposite direction (photos 61 A–D).

Once your horse knows what is coming—an energized change of direction—and he is respectful of both your space and the limits of the lead rope, he will begin to change direction by rocking his weight back and lifting his front end

Even though this lesson is in-hand, make sure not to let your horse invade your space. If he does, you must be bigger than he is with your voice, whip, and stature. In Step Two you used hip motion to turn him, which seldom results in a horse running forward and crowding you. Here, you are asking for an energized change of direction to the inside, in a small circle, and "space invasion" is more likely.

(shoulders) off the ground as he repositions himself for the new direction. This is exactly what you are looking for.

This type of direction change might not be very smooth for either you or your horse for a while. You are trying to switch the rope and whip, as you offer a body cue and learn a lesson all at the same time. If you ever struggle to the point of frustration, go back and work on Step Two again.

STEP FOUR: PRACTICAL APPLICATIONS
Teaching your horse the go forward cue is very useful in other daily applications, as well. You have a tool to use when asking him to pass through a gate, over a step, or into a trailer. Now is a good time to test how well this cue has been taught.

I work on this go forward exercise (Steps One through Four) with a thin rope halter as well. Sometimes I do so to warm up before a ride on the trail, or with a younger horse that is not ready for the snaffle bit yet. With young horses (five to 20 months), introduce the go forward response in short sessions (5 to 15 minutes) by following Step One and Step Two only. Younger minds and bodies need special consideration as they are not yet developed. Keep your goals small and easily attainable.

Pick something easy to begin with, even a test your horse has already passed without any problem, such as going through the round pen's gate. Stand at your horse's shoulder and ask with a soft cue, using the dressage whip, for him to move forward through the gate. Work on one step at a time and see just how calmly and confidently he'll move away from you through this gate on his own—you are holding the lead rope, but you are not leading him with your feet. Practice going back and forth through the gate a number of times.

Next, work over a low deck or teaching platform (photo 62). Again, ask the horse to calmly and willingly walk up onto the platform in response to the go forward cue. Ask him to take one step at a time, and wait for your guidance.

Photo 62 Your go forward cue will help you navigate stall doors, gates, decks, water crossings, and other challenges. You can build trust and responsiveness by practicing your new cue on a training deck (as Joe is doing with Shadoe here), over tarps, and through water.

Photo 63 Since the go forward cue was taught correctly, and small steps where taken to build Shadoe's confidence, the trailer loading seen here is a piece of cake. The dressage whip in this picture is only to demonstrate how it would be used in a training session, as by this point, Joe only clucks once and Shadoe willingly steps up into the trailer.

Once both of you are comfortable moving forward in open areas and have passed some easier tests, park your horse trailer in an inviting spot and work on loading and unloading a number of times (photo 63). Offer many rewards when your horse moves forward toward the trailer. If he stops or backs up without you asking him, keep his nose pointed forward and gradually increase the firmness of your dressage-whip tapping. The second that he moves forward again, release and reward him.

Spend lengthy breaks (from one to 20 minutes) on the trailer with your horse. This instills the idea that the trailer is a good place to be. Practice backing him out, stand, and load him back up again—just to take another long break. If you run into problems, go back a few steps and work on the go forward cue in another area, away from the trailer.

As you teach your horse to load into a horse trailer, remember a few things. One, your horse must know to move forward. Two, it is your job to make the trailer as safe and inviting as possible. Three, by working with him on a regular basis, you have become the leader and have earned your horse's trust—and this will help you when your horse is unsure or anxious.

Rider's Block

● Choose a tapping spot on the horse's hindquarters that is best for teaching purposes. I like to tap the meaty part of the hip muscle or above. Avoid the upper legs, stifles, hocks, and middle of the back (if working without the saddle). You do not want to create a struggle by picking a spot that is overly sensitive or one that could cause your horse to kick.

● If your horse is "blowing out" (all he wants to do is leave the entire situation, and you are being dragged around the round pen, tripping over your whip) you might be using too much pressure. This lesson can be very clear, relaxed, and extremely productive when the steps are addressed in small increments. If you are going to take extra time on a lesson, this is the one.

● Be cautious with the pressure you create with the lead rope as it is attached to the snaffle bit. Always avoid harsh pressure on the bit.

● This exercise will fail when you do not allow for many rest breaks. These breaks are built in to the lesson to help the horse understand the exercise pattern and what is expected of him.

● Once your horse is traveling on the lead rope, never let him lean on the bit—not even a little. You are going to spend the next 20 years training your horse to respond to the bit and give in to pressure, so it is best to begin that conditioning now.

Roadblocks

● Your horse may be very shy and nervous with the dressage whip. This can be caused by his personality, past experiences, or your application of this motivator and cue. Regardless of your horse's reason, it is your duty to spend extra time proving that in the right hands, a whip is nothing to be afraid of. You may have to spend a lot of time—many days—just rubbing him with the whip, for him to accept this training tool.

● If you have a dull horse that lacks energy and displays very little "try," you have to make the "right thing easy and the wrong thing hard," as Ray Hunt said. Some horses will require you to use more pressure than others.

Lesson 21's Benefits

● I have seen this lesson do wonders for the horse, building respect, responsiveness, and confidence. There are also many "mini lessons" within this lesson: your horse is giving to bit pressure; he must respect your space; he learns to move forward and use his front and hind ends; he learns to trust you; and all the while he most wants to stand qui-

What Makes Your Horse Buck or Rear?

Your horse will buck or rear for two reasons. One, he is afraid. Until a horse has grown accustomed to a saddle and rider, he may express his insecurity by bucking or rearing. By taking many precautionary measures (all of the lessons in the Countdown leading up to the first ride—Lesson 19, p. 114) you can decrease the chance of this happening.

Two, the horse is showing signs of avoidance behavior and has learned that bucking and rearing help him evade pressures that aggravate him. This is often the case with horses that haven't been taught a solid foundation. And, when a rider allows this behavior to happen repeatedly, he strengthens this bad response.

As you take your horse through the Countdown to Broke and prepare him for his first ride, it is helpful to know what might provoke him to buck or rear. This way, you can deal with it proactively.

- Overall tension and fear must be relieved before you place yourself in the saddle. A young horse should be able to stand still and remain relaxed with you on the ground before you get on. With each lesson completed and each day your horse is handled, the horse's overall tension and fear will be reduced.

- Pressure and friction created by the cinch or girth can cause bucking or rearing. From the ground, prepare the horse for the cinch with rope exercises (see p. 53). Once the saddle is in place, teach the horse to accept the cinch with lots of horn tugging, stirrup movement, and "up-downs." On a Western saddle, the rear cinch may also cause a horse to buck. I strongly suggest using this cinch right from the start so you have more time in the round pen (before you get on) for the horse to get used to it bumping his belly.

- Objects and noises overhead are a scary ordeal for the untrained horse. Teach your horse to accept these from the ground. Use various items such as ropes, bags, caps, and whips to create movement and noise, proving to him that there is nothing to be afraid of. The "up-downs" that you will perform in Lesson 20 (p. 110) habituate your horse to your body moving in this area of vision. This is important for when you eventually mount—you do not want him to overreact.

- Fast and sudden movements cause fear and tension. Prepare your horse for this by exaggerating fast movement when on the ground. Include fast hand movements, rope-swinging, shaking of a garbage bag, and any other "fast action" that might concern him. With prolonged exposure, your horse will learn to relax.

- Your leg pressure must remain quiet and still until the time is right. When you do get on for the first time, don't use your legs as a motivator yet. Even after a few rides, be aware of your leg pressure. If excessive, it can cause a horse to buck. If you find that he is not responding to leg pressure as a cueing motivator from light bumping, immediately begin to use "hind-end tapping" (with your hand, saddle strings, or lariat) or get help from another person on the ground in the round pen (see p. 128).

- Your horse might begin to buck or rear when he is moved forward under saddle for the first time—the first step on the first ride can be a big one. The early lessons under saddle in the Countdown keep your horse moving, helping him to accept and learn to handle a rider. "Up-downs" help him to prepare for his first step and your added weight, allowing him to position his legs for better balance.

- A poor riding seat can also set a horse off. This is not usually a factor at the walk, but when he's moved forward into a jog or lope and the rider is not sitting the gait well, he will find it uncomfortable—and early on in training, probably scary. Make it a personal priority to have a good seat and spend ample time on well-trained horses before attempting to school an untrained horse.

- A change in gait such as moving from a walk to a jog, and then a jog to a lope, is another hurdle. Asking your horse to transition up and down many times, he'll learn how to balance himself and carry the extra weight while staying relaxed and willing.

- A counter lead (see p. 211) in the lope causes the horse to be out of balance at first and keeps him from traveling smoothly. This can create anxiety. It is best in such cases to transition him down and attempt to have him pick up the true lead.

- Rushing your horse or asking too much (too fast a gait, too difficult a maneuver) can cause dangerous reactions, such as bucking or rearing. Some clear indications that your horse is not ready are pinned ears, a kinked tail, muscle-tension, high head carriage, and short-striding gaits. When your horse is walking with a smooth stride, low head, forward ears, busy mouth, and you feel his body relaxed under you, you know he is accepting the situation and ready for the next step.

Note: when you feel your horse's back arch up underneath you, this can be a warning he's about to buck. It's not always the case, but recognize this physical barometer, relax, and don't push him further.

By knowing what causes unwanted reactions like bucking and rearing, you can deal with them on your terms (from the safety of the ground). Your horse might never buck or rear—most do not after being properly prepared. However, some do, even when taken through all the right steps. Your awareness is key to safety—both yours and his.

etly with you—the leader—and take a break with his head down. By introducing the dressage whip you now have another tool to request forward movement, including into or onto something that your horse would prefer not to on his own, such as a horse trailer.

- As you move on in the Countdown and begin to ride your horse, having a go forward cue established in the round pen, as well as on the lead rope, will help transfer a go forward response to his back.

Green Light

Lesson 21 is an excellent test of how well you can put your previous work to use. Your horse is honest. His actions will tell you how the training has gone so far. If he is still showing undesirable behavior and struggling with the goals you are attempting to meet, take a step back and work on one or two of the previous lessons some more.

19
18
17
16
15
14
13
12
11
10
9
8
7
6

There is no "right" and "wrong" side of the horse to mount. You need to prepare him, as well as your own body, to get on with ease on either side. You should be able to mount on the high side of the trail or the off-side of your camp axe.

Preparing for Mounting with "Up-Downs"

Goals

This lesson will prepare your horse for the first time you get on his back. You want to advance his exposure level to sights, sounds, and pressures on and around the saddle area.

Check-In

You need to be certain that your horse is strong enough to handle being ridden—albeit lightly—at this time. If he is a long yearling or early two-year-old, check with your vet before going on with the Countdown. When he is physically able to proceed, and you have worked on all the previous lessons and the goals of each were accomplished, you can begin this phase of the program.

Teaching Steps

STEP ONE

With your horse saddled and wearing his protective boots, warm him up well. Revisit earlier teachings to see if they've stuck. When your horse is attentive and ready to stand quietly with you in the middle of the pen, you can begin.

This lesson specifically deals with saddle sounds, saddle pressures, a rider above the horse's head, stirrup pressure, cinch or girth pressure, and energized movement around your horse. By dealing with all this now, your first ride will have a much better chance of success—it is more likely your horse will be quiet enough for you to feel confident throwing that second leg over the saddle.

Put the snaffle-bit bridle on your horse. Stand on his left side, take the reins in your left hand, leaving a relaxed loop in them, and rest this hand on the horse's mane. You should not put any pressure on the horse's mouth. Lightly rub and slap the saddle rhythmically. Of course, your horse should not find this problematic at this point in the training, but you must still start small and build the exercise slowly. After a few seconds, switch sides and repeat your actions.

By starting small, your horse is going to quickly figure out that he is not being asked to move forward or away from you. If he does move slightly, ignore it and continue to rub and slap the saddle. If he moves forward more than one step, move his hips over with the rope rein (see Lesson 23, p. 89) and begin again.

STEP TWO

When he is relaxed and still despite the rubbing and slapping, add to your movements by energetically hopping, bouncing your body up and down (photo 64). Remember to start small with just a few bounces and switch sides. A head rub on the way by is a great idea.

As you build your energy level and the height of your bounce, increase the length of time that you stay energized. In the past, energy around the horse has usually included a request for him to move something. You now want him to know that noth-

Photo 64 I rhythmically jump up and down while touching and patting Belle all over her body, and slapping the saddle with my hand. If she decides to move sideways, I'll simply continue jumping and stay with her. If she moves forward more than one step, I'll move her hip away from me with the rein (see Lesson 23, p. 89) and begin again.

ing will be asked of him if he just stands there while you jump off the ground and slap the saddle seat.

Continue jumping in place as your free hand rubs and touches the horse's hindquarters, flank area, and upper legs. Stop. Walk around the horse's hind end with your hand touching him the entire time and repeat on the opposite side. I like to take a baseball cap or clothing item and add it to my moving hand—as it slaps the saddle—to increase what the horse sees and hears. Remember that you are preparing him for you being in the saddle. You cannot overdo this exercise; it will only make you safer. This early part of the lesson (Steps One and Two) can take anywhere from five to 20 minutes, and it is a good exercise to repeat over several days.

STEP THREE

Return to your horse's left side, continue to hold the reins

in your left hand (looped, without any bridle pressure), and place your left foot in the stirrup. Take it out again. Repeat. When your horse seems comfortable, start "up-downs" by hopping lightly up and down on your right foot, keeping your left leg bent, and beginning "small" then gradually increasing weight in the stirrup (photo 65). Be prepared to step down at any given moment. Once you have jumped up and down a few times, take your foot out of the stirrup, rub your horse on the head, and repeat on the other side.

STEP FOUR

You will now put more weight in the stirrup, so make sure the saddle will not shift or come loose. Straighten it and tighten the cinch or girth. Return to your "up-downs," hopping until you are off the ground enough to straighten your stirrup leg (photo 66). At this point you can start to stay in the stirrup for longer periods of time—beginning with one second. Keep your chest close to the saddle and use your own energy well, so you can partially mount the horse without offsetting his balance too much.

When you start to rely on the stirrup (you're not just hopping anymore, but actually putting pressure on it), hold some mane to steady yourself and avoid leaning back away from the horse or grabbing the horn or pommel. This offsetting pressure puts stress on a young horse's back and legs. And, it is also a safety issue as you could pull the saddle off your horse altogether and wind up in a wreck!

STEP FIVE

While remaining off the ground with your weight in the stirrup, slap the saddle and rub the horse's hindquarters with your free hand. Pet him on his neck and assure him that everything is all right (photo 67). Do whatever it takes to keep your horse relaxed. This might include walking away and having your horse come to you, and then beginning the process over again.

Photo 65 I introduce Belle to "up-downs": I put my left foot in the stirrup, then hop on my right leg, beginning with small hops and gradually stepping up higher and higher while putting more weight in the stirrup. Periodically, I'll step away and ask Belle to face me.

Photo 66 After many "up-down" repetitions, I can finally straighten my left leg and remain above Belle. I continue this, remaining above her for longer and longer periods of time.

Your goal is to make the horse comfortable with someone "over his head." Spend time waving your hands over his mane and head, "switching the eye" with which your horse sees this action. You want to know if he can handle moving objects in his "rearview vision" on both sides.

Be careful to only put part of your foot in the stirrup. I like to hold my weight on my toes and ball of my foot. When you have your boot in the stirrup too far, you can get "hung up" if the horse reacts badly.

Lean over and pull and flap the stirrup on the opposite side (photo 68). You are in a relatively safe position, but be careful not to put your stomach over the saddle horn or lean too far over your horse. Repeat this exercise on both sides

until you are tired and bored—if you are, the horse probably is as well. However, remember that although boredom in not your goal with most exercises, if the lesson falls into the category of "sacking-out," boredom is not all bad.

Rider's Block

● If you do not spend time building this exercise slowly, or if you grow tired and quit too soon, you are putting yourself at risk. You are preparing for that first ride and this is not the time to rush the next step.

● If you have a horse that is "built like an oil drum," lacking good withers, this exercise may well be difficult for you because your saddle will tend to slip with even a slight amount of pressure on the stirrup. I suggest spending triple the amount of time just bouncing up and down, and then get creative to sack him out over his head. You can sit on a fence rail and

Photo 67 As Belle grows accustomed to my actions, I reach over and rub her neck and hind end with my hands.

Photo 68 I spend more and more time half mounted and lean over, picking up the offside stirrup and sacking Belle out from her back. I'll repeat many times on both sides.

place your feet on and around the saddle. You can also pony him from another safe, experienced riding horse and reach over to add pressure and sounds to his back and saddle.

Lesson 20's Benefits

● The biggest advantage to this lesson is that you are taking one more proactive step toward remaining safe when you actually mount up.

Green Light

Can you:

▸ Act "energized," making quick movements around your horse without him moving a foot?

▸ Perform "up-downs" equally well on both sides of the horse?

▸ Place your foot in the stirrup and straighten that leg (on both sides)?

▸ Shake a baseball cap over your horse's ears without him raising his head or taking a step forward or sideways?

▸ Picture yourself swinging your leg over and sitting on him, or does he give you any indication that this would be a bad idea?

18
17
16
15
14
13
12
11
10
9
8
7
6
5
4

Remember that rhythm is your friend. During any "sacking-out" process, horses accept new stimuli much better when you offer it in a steady pattern. I like to perform "up-downs" with some kind of rhythm. Once you climb on if you are not sure what to do with yourself, you can provide continuity by reaching down and gently rubbing his neck, maintaining the same steady rhythm.

First Ride

Goals

Your aim now is to fully mount your horse. You want to do this in a way that builds your horse's confidence and keeps both of you as safe as possible.

Check-In

Go over a checklist of what your horse has learned to see how well he is accepting your new relationship. If he has struggled with any of the lessons and steps outlined so far, test these problem areas again and, if necessary, revisit them to make sure they are solidly understood. Truth be told, you'll never know for certain when he is ready for the first ride—or if he is going to bolt or buck once you are mounted. You will also never be completely certain you've done everything you need to prepare him for you as rider. No one can help you make the decision to mount up for the first time. It is your judgment call since you are the person who'll put a foot in the stirrup. If you do not feel completely safe or confident about this next step, then it is best to not do it yet. Hold off and practice other lessons in the Countdown—they won't go to waste.

Teaching Steps
STEP ONE

As I've mentioned, when you work your horse over many days (or weeks), you should spend time each new day testing that prior lessons have been properly learned before moving on to a new one. Do not pull your horse from the pasture or stall on Day Four and

decide within the first few minutes that you are going to mount today. First, take the time to review previous work to be sure he is still ready to move on—this can change on any given day.

So, begin with the steps you learned in Lesson 20 (see p. 110), and when you and your horse are ready, stand on his left side, place your foot in the stirrup, and swing your other leg over, properly mounting your horse with your legs on both sides of the saddle. Do not place your second foot in the stirrup on the offside. Sit a half-second, then take your leg back over the horse and dismount. Walk away.

There you have it. The first ride is over. Ask the horse to come to you and give him a lot of love for not killing you!

STEP TWO

Begin again by completing a couple of "up-downs" and mount the horse. This time stay up on him for a few seconds. Dismount. Repeat this process, staying on your horse for longer periods of time. Rub your horse on the neck and talk to him with a casual voice. By speaking to him, you can avoid a "startle" reflex because he'll be aware of your position the entire time.

STEP THREE

After several mountings from the left side of the horse, switch sides and repeat on the right (photo 69). Do not teach a horse to be mounted from the conventional left side only. This is not good horsemanship.

Photo 70   Once I have completely mounted Belle, I do not stay motionless. I keep moving by rubbing her mane, neck, and hind end. Fluid, rhythmic motion prevents the "startle reflex" common when a horse is surprised. Here, I have placed my opposite foot in the stirrup in preparation for dismounting from that side.

Photo 69   Practice good horsemanship and teach your horse to be mounted from both sides.

As you repeat the mounting exercise many times from both sides, stay casual and active. When your body language is relaxed and moving—as opposed to tentatively holding your breath—your horse will feed off you and feel the same way. Wait and watch his large "exhales" and a "busy mouth." This is one of the ways he will tell you everything is okay on his end. In between climbing on, walk away and ask him to come to you. This will keep the process fluid, and he will be more willing to accept you on his back.

If at any point when you are sitting on him, the horse decides to walk off, do not panic. This is okay. Some horses move on their own, while others do not. Remain calm and confident.

Read through Lesson 18 (p. 118) in the Countdown to learn more.

Once he is very comfortable with you mounting from both sides, sitting and rubbing your hands on him, put your other foot in the open stirrup and dismount from the opposite side you mounted from (photo 70).

Rider's Block

● Do not climb into the saddle nervously. Your previous work and recent "up-downs" should allow the next step of "throwing your leg over" to be a natural progression. So, step into the stirrup and climb on with confidence.

● If you think that the possibility of "hitting the dirt" could be the end of your riding career, then do not get on your young or green horse for the first ride. Find someone who is more at ease to take this step for you.

● Remember to stay fluid and active with your body. If you have been energetically climbing all over your horse during the previous lesson, and then put your second leg over and sit in "still-and-eerie silence," your horse might wonder, "What the hay?" Instead, continue to move your legs around, adjust your seat, talk to your horse, rub his neck, reach back and softly rub his hind end.

● At this point, leave your reins slack and do not pick them up in order to deter your horse from moving forward. You don't want to interfere with the "go forward" impulse—not yet.

Lesson 19's Benefits

● You are slowly but surely dealing with many of the issues that will keep your horse from bucking, rearing, and bolting (see What Makes Your Horse Buck or Rear? p. 108). Sacking your horse out to a rider in this manner is a great way to proactively keep yourself safe—all the while building your horse's confidence instead of diminishing it.

● Mounting your horse for the first time is also a psychological victory and a significant milestone in your horse's training. You can be very proud of yourself that you have gotten your horse this far in the Countdown.

Green Light

Before you move on to asking your horse to move forward with you in the saddle, you need to be sure you've done everything necessary to prepare him. If your presence on his back is no longer a scary issue, the next phase will go a lot more smoothly. When you have climbed all over him, rubbed and touched everywhere on his body, sacked him out above his head on both sides, and spent time in the saddle, you are setting the next lesson up for success. If you do not feel that your horse is completely comfortable and "bored" with you working on mounting exercises, do not move on until he is.

Forward Movement vs. Forward Motion

Generating Forward Movement

There are three steps to generating movement:

1 Get the horse's feet to move.
2 Keep the horse's feet moving consistently.
3 Choose the direction in which to move the feet.

You can successfully generate movement by doing the following:

● From the very beginning, teach your horse to move at the requested speed around the round pen (see Lesson 33, p. 28).

● Never allow your horse to slow down on his own.

● Teach your horse to "go forward" from the ground (see Lesson 21, p. 91).

● Never discourage forward movement during the first rides on your horse. Let him know it is okay to go forward.

● Spend plenty of time asking your horse to walk, jog, and lope. When you ask for all three gaits on a regular basis, he will "think" forward and not show signs of reluctance to transition up in speed.

● When you cue your horse to move forward, never "quit your cue" until forward movement is achieved. Your horse will be more inclined to move forward the next time if you are consistent with the timing of your release.

● In each day's lesson, include an exercise that encourages forward movement, such as lope circles.

Getting your horse to move forward is one of the basic building blocks of his education. Without movement, you cannot train him. True, not all horses are willing to move each time you ask, but once asked for, consistent releases from you at the right moment when he does move will teach him that moving is easier than standing still (or remaining at a slower gait).

MODERN WISDOM

Ranch and outfitter horses have the luxury of purpose in their work. They follow the horse in front, track a calf, head to the range, arrive at camp, or go home. All these jobs affect the horse's willingness to move, and are wonderful ways to begin a horse's career. However, even with this type of experience, your horse must be taught to move forward from your cue 100 percent of the time!

Forward Motion—Correct Footwork

"Forward motion" refers to the way in which the horse's feet are placed during lateral shoulder and hip motions, and does not refer to him "moving" forward. In order for maneuvers to be balanced, fluid, and continuous, the horse must place his feet with "forward motion." This means:

- When you move the horse's shoulders to the right, the left front foot must pass in front of the right front foot (photo 71 A).

- When you move the horse's shoulders to the left, the right front foot must pass in front of the left front foot.

- When you move the horse's hips to the right, the left hind foot must pass in front of the right hind foot (photo 71 B).

- When you move the horse's hips to the left, the right hind foot must pass in front of the left hind foot.

Whether you are on the ground or on the horse's back, you must insist on correct footwork at all times. If you do not you will be practicing "mistakes" that will create problems for you later (see Muscle Memory, p. 20).

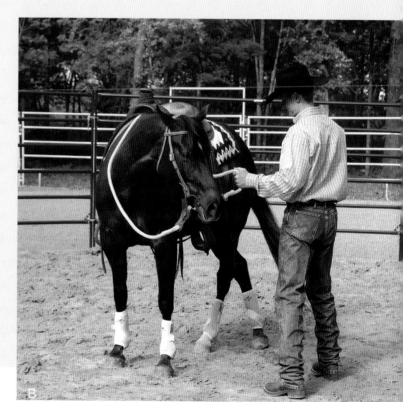

"Moving Out" while Mounted

Each of the horse's eyes sees the world differently, so in order to teach our horses to accept new experiences calmly, we must deal with both eyes equally and as if they were attached to "separate brains."

Goals

Your goal now is to get your horse's feet moving, first via the hips moving over, then walking forward. You want to keep your horse confident, relaxed, and accepting while making this new request.

Check-In

By now your horse has already been mounted many times. You are confident climbing up onto his back and remaining in the saddle. The natural progression is, of course, to have the horse now move out with you in the saddle.

As you begin this lesson, here is a list of situations that may send your horse into panic mode:

▸ The difference in pressure and weight combination as the horse takes his first step or steps.

▸ The sight of the rider in one eye's view, and then the other.

▸ The horse "locks-up" (see p. 8).

▸ The horse's hind feet come into contact with his front feet—especially in deep footing, a young or green horse's balance and legs are not yet skilled in carrying your weight.

▸ Movement in the saddle in response to his own.

▸ Your legs bumping or putting pressure on the horse. (If you worked on touching him and moving your legs a lot during Lessons 20 and 19, this should not be a problem.)

▸ Sudden pressure on the reins: an unexpected yank or pull can frighten and hurt your horse. It can also make your horse lift his front end and begin to rear. Not using the reins to hold and guide a young or untrained horse is counterintuitive for many conventional trainers, but it is the goal!

▸ The restriction the horse feels from the rear cinch or breast collar (increased if he takes off at a lope): any form of constriction or restraining force is categorized as a "trap" in my mind, and each horse deals with being "trapped" differently (see p. 64).

▸ The moment of a gait transition (i.e., still to walk, walk to jog).

You have prepared for these scenarios already, but from the comfort and safety of the ground. I list them not to frighten you but to warn you, so that you do not unintentionally encourage bolting or bucking once on board. And of course, there are other factors and variables that can cause a horse to become afraid. What might have not scared him while on the ground may frighten him now. The bottom line is to be careful and aware of what can set the horse off as you go forward with this lesson.

Cues to Use

You introduce three new cues in this lesson while in the saddle:

▸ First, you will ask the horse to move his hips over with the reins. This is very similar to the hip motion cue you used from the ground (see Lesson 23, p. 89). Hold the rope reins in the middle with one hand, and use the other hand to draw rein pressure in the direction of the horse's hip on that side.

▸ Second, you will establish "leg bumping" as a cue for your horse to move his feet. In this lesson, you ask for forward movement, so a lack of rein pressure and leg bumping at the cinch (directly below your seat) tells your horse to move out.

▸ Third, you will use a "clucking" noise—this should be the same vocal cue you used previously in training round pen movement, as well as with the *go forward cue*. Consistency helps make this new lesson easier for your horse to understand.

Spot, Direction, Motivator, and Release

HIP CUE

Spot Hip

Direction Away from rein pressure

Motivator Bit pressure

Release Cessation of bit pressure

LEG CUE (FOR FORWARD MOVEMENT)

Spot Chest

Direction Forward

Motivator Leg bumping on sides of horse

Release Cessation of leg bumping, rest, and neck rub

Teaching Steps

STEP ONE

After a good warm-up session that includes movement, "up-downs," "sacking-out," and quiet time, you can fully mount and remain on your horse. Your horse will do one of two things: he will either stand there or move off on his own. Both are normal and acceptable at this stage.

If you have worked on mounting a lot, as you should have, he will most likely remain still. Pick up your rein on either the left or right side and slowly apply rein pressure in the direction of the horse's hip on that side. Do not surprise him; this should be the same pressure you applied when moving the hips from the ground (see Lesson 23, p. 89). Hold the pressure until his hip moves over, then give a full release with the rein and let him move off if he chooses to. When the horse again stops going forward, pick up the opposite rein and slowly bring the horse's head to the hip on that side and ask it to move over (photos 72 A–C). Give a full release with the rein. The horse might or might not move his front feet forward. Both are okay. Continue to move your horse's hips from one side to the other, followed by full rein releases, to keep him moving.

If he does move out on his own after you get on, and it is a safe walk or jog, allow the movement to happen. If it is a dangerous "come apart," pick up one rein and hold the pressure to discourage him from moving out. At any time you need to stop, simply hold one rein, moving the hips over a lot, to discourage all forward movement and stop the horse.

Hip motion gives you two options at this time. It can stop forward movement, by asking for a lot of hip motion, or, it can steer forward movement, by asking for only some hip motion. When looking to encourage forward movement, be sure to not apply too much rein pressure.

Once the horse is moving, you have two choices: you can let him continue moving forward without concern for

Photos 72 A–C If your horse does not walk out on his own after mounting, ask for hip motion with one rein as I am doing with Belle in photo A. Remember, you have already taught this in-hand, and you want something to move at this point! Once you achieve forward movement, do not discourage your horse from moving out by picking up your reins—keep them slack as mine are in B. Stay calm and confident. Rub the horse's neck and mane in order to help alleviate any anxiety. When the horse comes to a stop again, ask for the other hip to move, as shown in C.

the direction, or you can pick up one of your reins and slowly move his hip over. It is best to let him move out on his own for a bit, and then steer him in a slightly different direction.

You want two things to happen at this point in training. You want forward movement and control over his hip motion in order to steer the horse's direction of travel. Do not discourage either. If he is moving forward nicely, but you continue to turn him by asking for his hip to move, you only discouraging forward movement. That being said, don't remain on the horse for too long without using rein pressure to ask for some hip motion. You want to improve both by asking your horse to move forward—and become relaxed—as well as responding to your hip motion request.

In the early stages of your horse walking forward under saddle for the first time, let him walk. When he is walking steadily, only pick up your rein once in a while. If and when he "surges," change directions more often.

In these early stages, do not use any leg pressure or vocal cueing yet—allow your horse to become relaxed with moving his feet. Carrying a rider is all new to him. After some time he will begin to relax. Note: you can move on with the lesson when your horse is walking well, or even if he is not—as long as he is comfortable with you in the saddle and moving his hips for you.

STEP ONE QUICK-CHECK

▸ Is your horse willing to calmly stand still when you sit in the saddle?

▸ Can you move around in the saddle without your horse reacting?

▸ Can you move your horse's hip over with the rein cue?

▸ Is your horse relaxed and not showing signs of tension such as: a kinked tail, pinned ears, an arched back, touchy sides, a high head, or quick movements?

STEP TWO

You are now going to teach your horse to move his feet in response to "leg bumping." While in the saddle, at the halt, very lightly rock your legs so they bump his sides at the same time you ask him to move his hip in one direction or the other with a rein cue. This helps "give him the answer" in the beginning. If you just keep bumping him, he may get annoyed, but if you give him a cue he understands, you can release him sooner. When you bump him and ask for hip motion, and he responds by moving his hip—followed by moving his feet forward—you can offer him a release from both leg and rein cues.

Avoid "squeezing" your horse with your legs—the cue calls for "bumping" your horse's sides. There are three reasons for this that I can think of: One, it is hard to increase the strength of a squeeze when you need to apply more pressure. Two, many horses do not like being squeezed, and since you are on an early ride, it is best not to "look for a problem." Three, you will not use a squeezing action to ask for forward movement in the Countdown in the future.

When your horse stops moving his feet, move his hip over and bump with your legs at the same time. Every time you pick up a rein and ask for the hip to move, you are improving the horse's response to that pressure through the release and repetition. And every time he does not respond, keep applying pressure until he does. The release is the teaching tool. When you bump with your legs and the horse moves forward, stop bumping.

Also add a "clucking" noise when you use your legs—you are trying to convey your leg cue means to "move his feet." In time, he will recognize this and respond accordingly. It could take two minutes or a couple of rides—it depends on the horse and your timing.

When the horse moves off on his own at any point, allow him to, and lightly apply some leg bumping to coincide with the walk, or as he moves into a jog. Again, you want the horse to associate his movement with your leg pressure. If you feel that he moved or accelerated pace due to fear, pick up the rein and ask for his hips to move. This will give him something else to think about.

You are working toward asking your horse to move forward from a stand still without having to move his hip over first with the reins. If you bump your horse on the sides, add some vocal encouragement, and your horse walks off, you are making progress. Repeat this step until your horse has completed many correct responses. The more times you can say "Yes!" by releasing him and letting him walk out, the better the cue will be taught.

STEP TWO QUICK-CHECK

▸ Does your horse accept your leg bumping without overreacting?

▸ Does he recognize leg bumping and vocal clucking as go forward cues and respond accordingly?

▸ Can you steer your horse—with hip motion—without discouraging forward movement?

▸ Can you bring your horse to a stop—with hip motion—if you choose to do so?

▸ Does the horse walk forward with his head down, showing he is calm and relaxed?

Rider's Block

● A horse will usually shy or move away from a scary object. For example, when you walk up to him with an unfamiliar item he'll likely back away. When you make a strange

noise behind him, he'll tend to go forward. And, if you decide wearing spurs on a first ride is a good idea and use them—purposefully or accidentally—then expect the horse to be scared upward in a bucking motion. It's your call!

● When riding during these early sessions, you will most likely be nervous. That's okay. Stay active with your voice and body, stay fluid with your motions, and keep focusing on what the goal is at hand. It will help take your mind off your nerves.

● Once you add a cue—which sets up a teaching process—you cannot "quit" on that cue until you have accomplished what it was meant to do. So if you add a rein cue and your horse stands still and ignores it, you must persevere. It is your job to finish the request by waiting for the correct response before offering the release.

● Remember, on these early rides, only use cues that have been taught from the ground in previous lessons. You can ask for hip motion and forward movement. Avoid asking your horse to stop, back up, neck rein, and move laterally in sophisticated ways. It will only confuse and frustrate him.

Roadblocks

● Your horse may react by surging, side-stepping, bucking, crow-hopping, or rearing during the first few riding sessions. This may be due to something that is unforeseen—the neighbor's cows are loose—or simply your horse getting used to the new circumstances. With the preparation the earlier lessons in the Countdown has provided, the likelihood of a bad reaction has been significantly minimized, but it could still happen. If it does, stay centered in your saddle and do not panic; smoothly, but firmly, take your rein and ask for your horse's hip to move to deter him running off with you. If he starts to buck, commit to "staying on" and hope that his fear is short-lived!

Lesson 18's Benefits

● Establishing a go forward cue from your legs is an

important step in the Countdown to Broke, as all future training requires movement. When your horse does not respond well to this cue, you will struggle in all riding work. Understand, though, you have to have reasonable expectations of your horse, and there will be a need to work on this go forward cue for many months to come.

● Asking for hip motion (the easiest, and so far, the only control cue you've taught) gives you influence over the horse's movement. This cue allows you to teach your horse to give to the bit with a soft neck and light response, while creating a better student as your horse "learns to learn" and looks for the release. When you teach your horse well—with clear lessons and "Yes" responses—you will show your horse that it is always worth trying.

Green Light

When your horse accepts you on his back, gives to the bit in response to your hip motion cue, walks forward from your leg bumping and clucking, and shows signs of relaxation and comfort overall, you have done a great job! Now, he can be moved out at a jog and lope (see Lesson 17, p. 124). Sometimes you can move ahead after a short time (10 minutes) while in other cases it may take a few days for both of you to feel confident progressing to the next step.

Jogging and Loping for the First Time

"Clucking" is actually going to be a "pre-cue" later, as it will be followed by a motivator. The way that it will be used in this lesson is to teach your horse to "associate" a specific noise with increasing the pace—movement can be forward, backward, or lateral.

Goals

You now want to walk, jog, and lope on cue. You want to work on these exercises in such a way that continues to build your horse's confidence as well as your own. Remaining safe continues to be your primary aim during these next steps.

Check-In

At this point your horse moves forward at a walk in response to your leg bumping. You can also control your horse's direction of travel with your reins by moving his hips over. The more control you have the better before moving into the faster gaits.

Cues to Use

You will use "leg bumping" just as you did in the previous lesson (see p. 118). Leg bumping is your "unrefined" *go forward cue* during early rides. It tells your horse to "move his feet faster" at this stage in the training. You will also use your "clucking" noise to encourage your horse to move out more, which strengthens this vocal cue, as your horse learns by association.

Spot, Direction, Motivator, and Release

Spot Chest
Direction Forward
Motivator Leg bumping
Release Cessation of leg bumping

Teaching Steps

STEP ONE: INTRODUCING THE JOG

At this point you have developed a response to your leg bumping—you have worked on it at a walk, while backing it up with the hip motion cue if forward movement did not occur. You'll now take it one step further and ask for movement with leg bumping with increasing pressure.

Begin on your horse riding the perimeter of the round pen at a walk. When you and your horse are ready, lightly bump your legs against the horse's sides—being careful not to startle him—and add your voice with a "cluck." Think "Jog," and energize your entire body. Since your horse should be comfortable with your legs to some degree, now use them as your motivator. Remember, once you add a motivator, you must not offer a release until you have what you are looking for. This is important. If you "quit" on your motivator and give a premature release, you just taught your horse to ignore the leg cue!

Continue to build the pressure by increasing the firmness of your leg bumping and elevating your vocal encouragement—go crazy and throw in a "whistling" noise if you must! With an energized body, firmer leg bumping, and elevated vocals, your horse will most likely break into a jog at some point. It may take a few steps, and it may take longer, but that is not as important as your perfectly timed release (photo 73).

Once you feel your horse speed up to a jog you must immediately do three things: First, stop using your motivators and "become quiet." Ceas-

Photo 73 When Belle responds to my leg bumping and vocal cues by moving into the jog, I immediately "go quiet": I cease adding pressure with my legs and discontinue clucking, rewarding her with a well-timed release. I keep my hands and arms close to my body so as not to alarm her with flapping movements in her peripheral vision.

ing these actions is the reward, and this release is the learning moment for your horse. The horse was shown that leg pressure means speed up, and he was rewarded when he increased the pace. Second, sit the jog smoothly. If you bounce in the saddle, your horse may become frightened and bolt or buck. "Feel" your horse jog and move with him. Third, keep your arms and hands close to your body so they are not moving and flapping in your horse's peripheral vision.

After this very desirable result (your horse is jogging), and once you have rewarded him by remaining quiet and flowing with him, allow him to break down into the walk on his own. If the horse jogs for 10 minutes, let him, and if he only jogs for three steps before slowing back to a walk, let him. You are satisfied with the initial transition from the walk to the jog.

Every time that you add "speed" to a horse, you also instill a heightened emotional level or state of awareness. By allowing him to break out of this new gait when he wants

to, you tell him that everything is fine, and he's okay. So, next time you ask him for the jog, it will be less of an issue than it was the time before.

STEP TWO: MAINTAINING THE JOG

Ask for several transitions up to a jog. Once your horse consistently responds to your legs by increasing his pace, try to keep him jogging. This means that every time you pick up the jog and the horse decides to break down to a walk on his own, you must quickly ask him to jog again. The earlier step focused on getting your horse to initially move into the jog by building his confidence as well as improving his response to your legs. Now he must remain in the jog until you let him walk again. Work on this faithfully, as it will be very important throughout the rest of the Countdown. If you cannot keep the horse's feet moving, you cannot teach effectively.

So far in this lesson you have not used bridle pressure. You have been more interested in the horse moving out and maintaining the jog. At first, I would not suggest "getting in his way" with too much directional work. If you need to move off the rail or change the direction of your circle, that is fine, but avoid turning him very much—if at all—while you are working on getting him to understand the go forward cue. At the point your horse is moving forward well— he is quickly and correctly responding to your leg cue and remaining in the jog on his own for many circles at a time— you can start to work on gentle turns. Continue to focus on encouraging forward movement, but you can start to dissect the circle with a light rein cue, moving your horse's hip over slightly (photo 74). If your horse starts to slow down or "quit" on your leg cue, retrace your steps and avoid rein cues while you work on forward movement again. This can be a bit of a balancing act. Err on the side of more forward movement than directional work at this point—you are still in a round pen and your horse cannot go anywhere!

Throughout all of this, you are "sacking your horse out" to a rider as he walks and jogs. The commotion on his back, coupled with added leg bumping, is building his confidence. You will need this newly bolstered confidence when you move him out to the lope.

Photo 74 Once Belle understands the go forward cue and willingly maintains the jog on her own in a calm, relaxed manner, I add gentle rein cues and "dissect" the round pen circle. Here we leave the rail as I use my right hand to move her right hip over.

STEP THREE: ASKING FOR THE LOPE

Your horse should now understand that leg bumping and "clucking" are his cues to move his feet faster. You have also gained valuable "sacking-out" and confidence-building time in the saddle. At this point, your horse needs to "feel the lope" for the first time. This may happen to be—accidentally or intentionally—on your first ride, or it may be many rides later, but it needs to be when your horse is both relaxed and willing to move forward off your leg pressure.

Begin on the perimeter of the round pen at a jog, and when you and your horse are comfortable, add leg bumping and loud clucking. Begin with "soft" leg pressure and vocals, and increase their firmness with each passing second. "Use" your riding seat (change the rhythm with which you move with the horse) to encourage the cadence of the lope. Continue using leg pressure, a "driving" seat, and vocals until your horse breaks into a lope.

Your horse can feel you move with him. When you are in rhythm with him, you are encouraging whichever gait he is traveling. If your body motion is not the same as his, you make it harder for him to travel. When you want to jog, think "Jog," and allow your body to simulate what a jog feels like. And when you want to lope, think "Lope," and use your seat to drive the horse's movement forward.

Just as you did with the jog, immediately cease leg pressure and vocal cues the moment your horse takes his first lope stride. He may want to only take one stride, or he may continue for quite some time. Stay centered, relaxed, keep your hands close to your body, leave his mouth alone, and ride him until he breaks back down to a jog on his own (photo 75). You can then allow him to break down into a walk—letting him do this reassures him that this new request was nothing to be afraid of, and you are more likely to be met with a willing response the next time you ask for an upward transition.

Start over at the walk, followed by one or two jog circles, and then again request the lope. If he does not respond, increase your motivators until he does. Follow the lope departure with an immediate release of leg pressure and vocals, and then allow your horse, once again, to break down all the way back to a walk. As you repeat these steps—taking him up to the lope and back down to a walk—you build his confidence. Try your best to work equally in both directions, even though it will likely be harder to achieve the lope one way or the other (see p. 38).

Your horse may not want to move out for you in the lope. This may be caused by a number of reasons. He may simply be tired: if you work extensively on the ground prior to riding him, you could deplete his energy. You want to warm up your horse, yes, but be aware that long durations of movement prior to mounting can interfere with his willingness under saddle.

If your horse does not respond to your leg bumping and vocal cues, try slapping your own thigh. The action and resulting noise helps to encourage movement.

Another reason that your horse may not move out enthusiastically is that you have done a great job getting him relaxed. Sometimes, this gets in the way of a horse wanting to move. If you were to jump on a flighty, sensitive animal without all our previous work, your chances of forward movement—and fast forward movement—would definitely improve, but at what cost and risk?

There are also horses that are just less sensitive and lack the desire to move. With this type you might have to use greater pressure to encourage forward movement. As long as you approach the lesson with a reasonable goal in mind and do not "quit" on him, your horse will learn to increase his pace on command.

STEP FOUR: KEEPING THE LOPE GOING
Now, you can request that your horse remain in the lope. This means that when you are already loping, and you feel him "thinking" of transitioning down (or he actually does), use your motivators to encourage him to stay at the desired speed.

When I tell you to keep your horse jogging or loping even when he wants to transition down, I am not including lameness or another medical condition as a possible reason for his desire (or need) to stop. If you see any sign of pain, discomfort, or a physical ailment, call your vet. Your horse's health supersedes any training or timeline—you can pick up where you left off when he is 100-percent sound.

Photo 75   When Belle first picks up the lope, I sit quiet and still, and leave her mouth alone. She might be a bit unbalanced and speedy at first, but since the goal is to encourage forward movement, not discourage it, I go ahead and let her lope until she breaks back down to walk on her own.

I like to plan on completing a number of circles and work on keeping my horse moving at a lope until I have finished them. On an early ride, such as the third day in the saddle, I might set out to complete 10 circles to the left and 10 to the right. On a young horse that is just getting the idea of moving out under a rider, this amount sounds reasonable to me. It is enough to get the point across without pushing him too hard for too long, thus making him less willing the next time.

You will begin to see a big change in your horse's demeanor after you have worked on jogging and loping under saddle. He will be much more calm, and happy to stand still when allowed. He will be much more accepting of you as well. Since there is a lot going on in the horse's mind, make sure you constantly tell him everything is okay with head rubs and vocal praise. It's a good idea to occasionally offer complete "mental timeouts" by dismounting, rubbing

Additional Motivators

If you are struggling to get your horse to lope and you feel that your "excessive" leg bumping—as it has now come to that—is just annoying him and frustrating you, there are additional motivators you can turn to.

HIND END TAPPING

Tap the horse on the hind end with another motivator to help achieve the response you are after. Options include your saddle strings, lariat, or riding crop, or an open-handed slap. I really like to use my saddle strings as they can be easily managed and dropped again at any time (photo 76).

Use one of these new motivators and your leg bumping and vocals simultaneously, as you want to rely on your leg and voice cues in the future, not these additional motivators.

ROUND PEN HELPER

Another way to establish forward movement into the lope—as well as the jog, if necessary—is to have a helper in the round pen with you during this lesson (photo 77). If your horse learned his earlier lessons and knows to move out with someone pushing him from the center of the round pen, you can usually get an immediate response.

I only allow someone that I trust in the round pen with me, and I ask him or her not to move the horse forward with the lariat unless I request it. I do not like a lariat being thrown or a lunge whip being snapped as this startles the horse into movement. If the horse will not move off at a light body cue from the trainer in the center, then previous groundwork lessons were not taught thoroughly enough.

I ask the horse to move out a walk and then a jog. If the horse does not respond, I ask for a "push" from the helper in the center. This means he offers the go forward cue from the ground at the same time I use my legs and voice. I do the same thing for the lope. I ask my helper to wait while I request the lope myself. If it does not happen, I ask for a "push" from the center. Once the horse lopes, I quit leg bumping and just ride.

With a horse that doesn't want to go forward, I also ask my helper to keep the horse jogging or loping for me—we combine efforts until the lesson has sunk in.

Photo 76

Photo 77

Photo 78 After some time spent jogging and loping, it is always a great idea to dismount and give your horse a mental time out. Here I give Belle a short break and positive reinforcement, again proving that I am trustworthy before I mount back up and repeat the process. Every time you start and stop, approach and retreat, ask and reward, you effectively teach the horse.

him, and walking away, then asking your horse to come to you before you remount and work some more (photo 78).

Rider's Block

● You still have not taught your horse to stop. This poses a dilemma for many new trainers. It shouldn't. Since you are in a controlled environment—a round pen—you should feel safe. Where is your horse going to go? Believe it or not, you have control. You are teaching him to go faster with your legs and to respond to the reins and move in the direction you want. You should also know by now that if you truly want or need to stop, you can just ask for a lot of hip motion and the horse will break down to a standstill.

● Just because your horse decides to buck a bit, it is not mandatory that you apply rein pressure. If you are an expe-

The Thing about Leads

When you are first establishing the cue for your horse's feet to speed up in response to leg bumping and "clucking," you want to avoid giving him a "No," when he does it. We first need the feet to move, before we choose how they move, so I allow my horse to pick up either the "true" lead or the "counter" lead.

This lesson allows your horse to transition down on his own many times before you insist that he stay moving at the lope. During these early "breakdowns" and resumptions in gait, your horse will most likely choose the most comfortable lead for him. Considering that you are riding in a round pen, the direction of travel will help encourage the true lead. If, despite this, your horse consistently chooses the counter lead, disregard it and continue with the lesson. You will soon have more tools to help you teach your horse to shape his lope departure and encourage the "requested" lead. (Since I purposely "counter lope" my horses, as well as lope them on the true lead, I do not use "right" or "wrong" lead to describe what I see or what I am doing. I like to use the term "requested" lead.)

With experience you will learn ways to encourage the true lead even during an early lesson on loping. These include: asking at the opportune time; asking the nose to look in with slight upward rein pressure; bumping the inside shoulder with your foot; and even speeding the lope up until the true lead is the only comfortable way of travel.

rienced, able rider, just ride it out, and continue to ask for forward movement. With the groundwork, "sacking-out" exercises, and other lessons in the Countdown under his belt, your horse may have a short-lived desire to buck, but he will not likely have a panic-stricken "coming apart" bucking fit. This type of hard-to-ride incident usually only comes with an under-prepared horse.

● Once you begin asking for jogging and loping, don't feel like you're home-free. It is best to continue work with your horse on a regular basis. Infrequent lessons are not good for building his confidence.

Roadblocks

● Some horses are annoyed with leg bumping at first. If you feel your horse "sullen up"—he tends to go slower, rather than faster, with increased pressure—move right along and begin to use hind end tapping or a round pen helper (see p. 128). The goal is to have your horse move off of your leg from the start, but some horses need another approach.

Lesson 17's Benefits

● In the Countdown to Broke there are two constants: One, you continually build your horse's confidence level, and two, you are always teaching new skills. In this lesson, you have accomplished two of the most exciting, important, and difficult steps in any training program. Your horse has accepted a rider and learned to move his feet on cue. You are entering a new phase and can begin to focus on riding exercises as you build your horse's experience level.

● You have also improved your ability to troubleshoot problems that will (likely) arise down the road—such as insisting on forward movement when your horse may feel otherwise—as you now understand what it takes to teach the skill initially.

Green Light

This is not one of those lessons where once you arrive at "A" you can just move on to point "B." Your need to encourage and insist on forward movement will be an ongoing lesson as you advance through the Countdown. I like to spend 10 or so sessions asking for good forward movement before I move on to Lesson 16 (see p. 131). This gives me a stronger, confirmed response to my leg cues, as well as ensuring my horse is truly comfortable carrying a rider.

Once I do move on, I revisit this lesson in part as I see the need. When you start to ask for lots of directional movement, you may need to restore forward movement at any given time.

Hip Serpentines

Goals

The purpose of asking your horse to perform "hip serpentines" is to combine and improve previously introduced cues. The responses you will improve are: moving the feet faster; staying in a requested gait; "giving" the nose and neck to bit pressure; and moving the hips.

You will also encourage desirable behavior from your horse, such as: a willingness to stand still; speed control; acceptance of a rider; a lowered, relaxed head carriage; and an improved work ethic. Plus, you'll establish a routine that both you and your horse can perfect and use when you need to. You will be able to begin many future riding sessions with this relaxed, beneficial exercise—a great starting point for the day.

Check-In

In order for this exercise to go well, your horse must understand two cues. First, your hip motion cue should have been worked on both from the ground and the saddle. Second, "leg bumping" should result in your horse moving his feet faster and transitioning up to a jog or lope. In an effort to keep the teaching steps small and manageable, confirm your horse's responses to these two before you combine them in this exercise.

Cues to Use

This lesson focuses on two cues: one, the *go forward cue* (via leg bumping and vocal clucking), and two, the *hip motion cue*, which you ask for by drawing the rein on one side toward the horse's hip on the same side.

Spot, Direction, Motivator, and Release

GO FORWARD (FROM THE SADDLE)
Spot Chest
Direction Forward
Motivator Leg bumping
Release Cessation of leg bumping

HIP MOTION (FROM THE SADDLE)
Spot Hip
Direction Away from the engaged rein
Motivator Bit pressure
Release Cessation of bit pressure

Teaching Steps
STEP ONE

In all of these early rides, make sure to warm up your horse's body and mind. Once he is saddled and wearing his protective boots, move him in the round pen, ask for some inside turns, and finish with him coming to you in the middle. Spend a few minutes sacking him out with your hands and snap the stirrups a number of times. If you see or feel that on this new day he is not ready for a rider, take the time to prepare him for a successful lesson.

Perform some "up-downs" and mount. Ask for forward movement with your legs and walk your horse around the pen for a few minutes. You can periodically control his direction with your reins, asking for the hip to move over as you move forward. Once he is listening to you, ask for the jog.

You may have to reach for more or less rein in order to apply the right amount of bit pressure. You know that the bit pressure is right when your horse's neck is bent enough—giving him a reason to move. As you see what it takes to get the desired response, adjust your request. The amount of rein needed will depend on the length of your rope reins as well as the horse's neck.

Jog in both directions until your horse lowers his head and relaxes within this gait. Ask for the lope and count off your pre-determined number of circles (see p. 127). Make sure to work both directions equally. This step's movement in the round pen will help your horse think forward.

STEP TWO

It is important to understand what to do with your hands before going on with this lesson. This is a "one-rein exercise," meaning only one side of the snaffle bit will feel pressure at any given moment. To ensure this happens, place your right hand in the absolute middle of the rope reins and hold them 2 inches above the horse's mane. The reins on both sides are completely slack and there is no pressure on the bit. Next, reach down and grasp the rein with your left hand about 12 inches from where your right hand is positioned (once you begin the exercise, adjust the distance based on your horse's response), and draw your left hand back about 12 inches toward the horse's left hip (photo 79). Hold for a moment, and then release the rein with an open hand, allowing it to drop. Next, replace your right hand holding the middle of the rope reins with your left, thus freeing up your right hand to complete the same steps on the right side.

By forcing yourself to hold the middle of the rein with one hand at all times, you cannot inadvertently apply pressure to the other side of the bit while you learn to focus on the bit pressure that you do want to apply. The manner in which you release is also very important. I like to see a complete open-handed drop of the rope rein in early lessons, for both the rider's and horse's benefit. This way the rider can see what a "full release" looks and feels like and the horse profits from precise bit pressure, which can be easily understood during early learning.

The hand-to-rein action needs to be consistent. Your ability to perform this motion will improve as you repeat it many times.

STEP THREE

During this exercise there is going to be one continuous

Photo 79 In a one-rein exercise, only one side of the snaffle bit feels pressure. In this exercise, you hold the middle of the rope reins with one hand, while creating bit pressure with the other. In this photo I demonstrate holding the reins in my right hand and cueing with my left: I reach about 12 inches down the rein and draw it back toward the horse's left hip. This creates a soft bend in his neck and allows you to influence his direction.

request: your horse must remain at a jog. If at any time this is not the case, immediately use leg bumping and clucking to insist that he picks his speed back up.

Begin jogging around the pen to the right. Hold the rope reins in the middle with your left hand 2 inches above the horse's mane. Reach down the rein about 12 inches with your right hand, grasp the rein, and draw it toward the horse's right hip. Pull the rein back about 12 inches, holding the pressure steady with a firm grip, but a steady hand. Your horse's neck will bend as his nose is pointed in a new direction (photos 80 A & B). Do not hold the horse in an extreme bend—it should be a gentle turn only. Note that you have just set up the learning process: you are not pulling on your horse, as your hand is steady, but you will not give the rein back until he gives you the response you are looking for.

The first requirement is that your horse must "give" his face to your hand. This means that he cannot pull or lean on your rein pressure. The second requirement is that your horse must respond with hip motion away from your rein cue. So, when you cue with your right hand, the horse should move his hips to the left and follow his nose roughly in the direction that you have pointed it.

Never release your horse while his head is elevated or when he is leaning on your hand. If you teach your horse now he will find a release only when his head is low and soft to your hand, you will find success down the road more quickly.

Once you feel your horse "give" his face to the bit, perform the requested hip motion, and continue following his nose at the jog, open your right hand and release the rein (photos 80 C & D). This shows him he can eliminate bit pressure in the future by repeating these actions. Allow him to jog a few steps as you switch your middle hand on the reins and repeat the process on the opposite side. Allowing him to travel unimpeded for a few steps is further reward for his correct response. When you rush picking up the rein on the other side, his reward is cut short and learning progress is slowed. If it helps, count to three slowly ("One-steamboat, two-steamboats, three-steamboats") before picking up the next rein cue.

After several rein requests and releases, your pattern of travel will look like a series of "S" shapes, hence the name "Serpentines."

STEP FOUR

The next step is a big one! Not only are you going to continue this exercise, but you are going to do so outside the round pen—in a riding arena! You can work in any appropriate area, as long as it is enclosed, flat, and has safe footing.

Each horse is different, and the amount of time it takes to get one horse ready for the arena is not the same for another. The arena's space will build confidence and encourage forward movement better than the round pen. Of course, the question is, "Is he safe enough to ride in the arena yet?" If you move there too early, your horse may be more likely to bolt or buck. I suggest waiting until you feel that your horse is very relaxed and confidently performing walk, jog, and lope sessions. This may be after your twelfth or twentieth ride; it all depends.

Mount your horse and sit still. Rub his neck and talk to him. He is going to be a little bit nervous and unsure of the new practice space, as you may be, too. Ask your horse to walk and let him look around a bit. If he is calm, and looking and feeling relaxed, keep walking. This is good for him. However, if he seems at all anxious or nervous, immediately move on to Step Five and start serpentines to keep his attention on you and the task at hand, rather than on the surroundings.

STEP FIVE

Ask your horse to jog and remain jogging for 10 minutes or so. Ready your hands and begin cueing your horse to perform the hip-serpentine exercise. After several repetitions, you will feel a big difference. Your horse will start to "give" his face to your hand with less and less pressure on the snaffle bit. He is learning that there is no need to bump his own mouth on the bit and to stay off that pressure. He will also

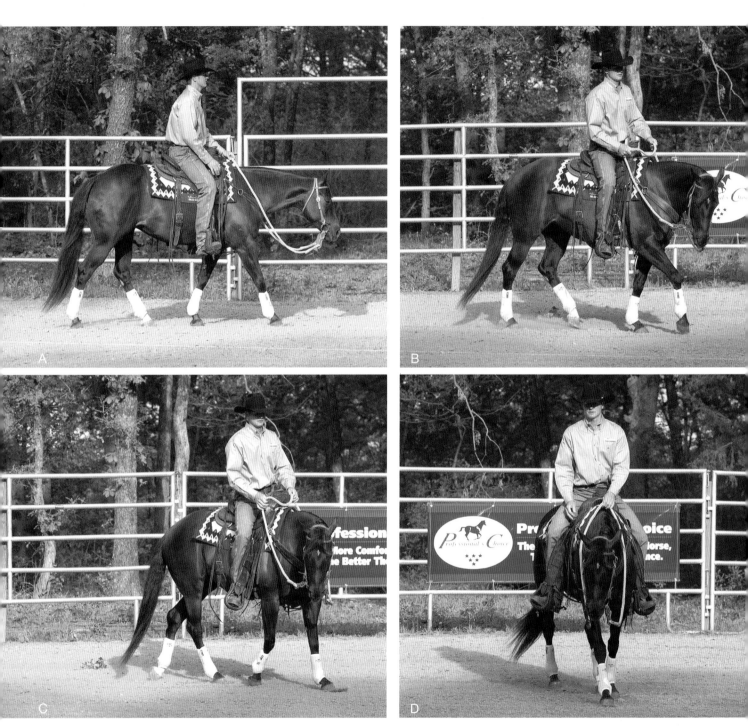

Photos 80 A–D I ask Belle for a steady, relaxed jog to the right, and my left hand holds the middle of the rope reins about 2 inches above her mane (A). I reach down with my right hand, grasp the right rein and draw it back, holding steady pressure in the direction of Belle's right hip (B). My left hand remains in the same position and the left side of the rope reins is slack. This is how I request Belle moves her right hip and follows her nose while remaining at the jog. My release point comes when she responds correctly: moving her hips to the left, softening her nose to my right hand, keeping her head level, and following her nose roughly in the direction I pointed it (C). Because Belle responded correctly, I let go of the right side of the rope reins—her release (D).

Photo 81   As we work in the larger area, Belle begins to follow her nose and move her hips over much more quickly when I cue her with the rein. You can see here that she has softened her nose nicely and kept her head low. My release will follow.

begin to "follow his nose" by moving his hip during forward movement with a much better response time (photo 81). After another steady 10 minutes of work, take a break and let him stand still for a while with you in the saddle. Three 10-minute sessions are usually about right on a young or inexperienced horse. End on a quiet, relaxed note.

Rider's Block

⬤   In order for the response to your rein cue to improve, you have to give your horse a chance to *work off less pressure*. In the beginning, I instructed you to take 12 inches of slack out of the rein and hold steady. After a number of releases, apply the cue with your hand only 11 inches down the rein, and as he continues to show improvement, take up less and less. If at anytime you need to go back to 12 inches, do so. In time, you will only lightly pick up the rein, and he will "offer" you his face and turn in the direction that you are looking for. You want your horse to work off as subtle a cue as possible, and it's by continuing to give him a chance to respond to an increasingly softer cue that you will get this result. If you always apply your cues with the same pressure, he will never learn to respond to less.

● Avoid picking up the reins and applying pressure to both sides of his mouth. You may have a "wandering" middle hand that inadvertently puts pressure on both sides of the bit. Work on keeping your hands smooth, steady, and consistent. If your horse speeds up or spooks, hold steady pressure on one rein only, as the necessary hip movement will slow him down.

● When you allow your horse to "break down" the speed, you are not doing him any favors. You will find in all of your riding work that a horse that willingly stays in the requested gait and has a good work ethic is worth a lot. In these early sessions, insist that he think and go forward. If you are struggling to keep him forward as you turn, ride some straighter lines or go back to the round pen for a lope session. Get him "thinking forward" again.

● This exercise is all at a jog—you can work on it for longer than you think. You want to do it long enough so that your horse becomes soft, stays forward, and accepts the new situation. Ask him to work in 10-minute sessions, and complete three or four of these. Your horse will improve his speed control—he will be less inclined to accelerate—as well as be more willing to stand still when asked.

● The "hip serpentine" exercise is not meant to be performed in a perfect "S"-shaped pattern all the time. It is a good idea to start with that in mind, but then begin to change the size of the arcs, and even stop using the "left, right, left, right" pattern. Change it up. As you will find out,

when you wait for your horse to respond to the bit pressure, you'll be creating your own pattern anyway. The important thing is that you release when the requirements of the lesson are met.

Roadblocks
● You may have a horse that was very relaxed and willing in the round pen but does not make the transition to the arena very well. This is quite normal. Spend time with him in the new area just standing quietly, performing groundwork from previous lessons, and completing some "up-downs." He will recognize the exercises and grow comfortable with the familiar even in a strange place. When you feel that he is calm, begin the new exercise. This is how you expand his comfort zone.

Lesson 16's Benefits
● **Work Ethic:** Your horse now works at a steady pace for longer, and "gives" to bit pressure. By insisting that he remain at the jog—with no walking—he learns that in order to avoid leg bumping, he must continue working. He is finding that he cannot quit just because he wants to.

● **Speed Control:** Each time your horse even "thinks" of speeding up, turn him. This is a great way to regulate his speed. As he learns there is no point in going faster, he will abandon all thoughts of acceleration and settle into a steady jog. At first, there may be some surges, but after a few sessions of hip serpentines, his desire to speed up will vanish.

● **Standing Still:** By insisting on constant forward movement, you'll find your horse will begin to take advantage of being allowed to stand still. This lesson is not the result of holding him back or forcing him to remain in one position—in fact, you are doing the opposite by asking him to work. And in the end, he'll figure out that standing at a halt when he can is a great option.

● **Rider Acceptance:** Sure, you had already ridden your horse prior to this lesson, but with these more

MODERN WISDOM

Speed Control

Asking for more speed—and getting it—is rarely a problem with a young horse, but "downshifting" to a slower level while staying in the requested gait is something that takes time and training.

When you drive down a busy street and encounter several sets of red lights, you usually figure out that another stop is coming up, so you do not accelerate quickly toward the next set of lights. Your horse thinks in the same manner when you work on starting and stopping exercises. He learns to anticipate a stop and so stay at a slower speed. By teaching exercises where he must repeatedly start and stop, you can make use of this anticipation to help with speed control.

Changing direction, as performed with hip and shoulder serpentines (see Lesson 16, p. 131, and Lesson 10, p. 179), is another method of controlling speed. When you ask for movement to be directed from one side to the next, you take the horse's focus away from surging forward and replace it with seeking a release. It is also easier for him to change his direction at a slower speed. Continue with an exercise such as hip serpentines until your horse travels more slowly in the desired gait. Don't quit early while your horse is still thinking forward rather than thinking forward-but-slower.

Another way to control speed, when necessary, is to ask for prolonged movement, thus requiring substantial effort. Loping for 10 minutes in each direction could be all it takes to get your horse to slow down. By asking for faster movement, your horse will show his "lazy" side. However, be sure to not let him slow down on his own—keep him loping for the full 10 minutes each side. If after all this he still surges forward, full of energy, repeat the circles again for the same amount of time.

Trained in these ways, a horse that has speed control issues preserves his confidence and yet conserves his energy. Now, you'll be able to ask for speed when you want it.

---

advanced requests, he is getting quieter, carrying himself with a level head, and showing little or no signs of fear.

Green Light

Before you teach your horse to stop and back up—which comes next—you want to introduce bit pressure one side at a time. This lesson does just that. By working only one side you are introducing a "trap" that is easily understood and a release easily found. If you take hold of your horse's face with both sides of the bit on your first ride, you will likely find yourself dealing with a negative reaction.

Horses that move their feet well, back up well. By insisting on him going steadily forward, your horse is learning to agree to requests for movement—and this transfers into a better backing response. Once you have worked on this lesson for a few days (or more) and feel your horse moves forward consistently, and "gives" his face and hips on a light cue, you can begin the next lesson.

Backing-Up—Part I

14
13
12
11
10
9
8
7
6
5
4
3

The rein cue that indicates to your horse he should move his hips is the easiest rein cue for him to understand. The rein cue to move the shoulders can be more difficult, initially. This is why this lesson comes later in the Countdown.

Goals

In this lesson you are setting out to teach your horse to move a shoulder backward from a one-rein cue. This new *shoulder rein cue* allows you to begin backward movement from a standstill, walk, or jog. Your aim, as always, is for your horse to respond to bit pressure with a soft "give" and willing feet.

Check-In

First and foremost, your horse must confidently accept a saddle and rider before you begin this lesson. Your time in the saddle up to now has helped your horse grow comfortable moving his feet while carrying the weight of a rider.

Second, your introduction of the snaffle-bit bridle and *hip motion cue* has shown your horse that a release follows an action. This helps your horse predict the outcome when you apply bit pressure. When you don't teach the (easier) hip motion cue first, he could react quite negatively to any new, uncomfortable pressure of the bit.

Finally, be certain that consistent forward movement has been achieved. Without good movement, this exercise is not possible, as you are going to teach him to respond to your cue from a walk and jog.

Cues to Use

You will introduce two rein cues. One: pick up the right rein and take out the slack, holding it just to the right of your saddle horn or pommel while leaving the left rein slack without any pressure on the bit. This is your cue for the horse to move his right shoulder back. The amount of pressure used with the cueing rein will vary depending on your horse's response. The second new cue is the same configuration but on the left side, using the left rein.

Spot, Direction, Motivator, and Release

Spot Front left or right foot (depending on rein)

Direction Directly back toward six o'clock (see p. 167)

Motivator Bit pressure

Release Cessation of bit pressure

Teaching Steps
STEP ONE

Warm up your horse under saddle with forward movement and hip serpentines in the round pen, or if your horse is comfortable, in the riding arena. You'll continue this lesson in the arena.

Begin on your horse at the halt. With your left hand, hold the middle of the rope reins 2 inches above his mane, slide your right hand down the rein and draw it back to a few inches to the right of your saddle horn or pommel where you hold it steady. This should be enough pressure to bend your horse's neck around until you can see the full side of his face (photo 82). This rein pressure is both your cue and your motivator.

The response you want is for your horse to move his front right foot back. At this point, "back" can be anywhere

Photo 82   To give the one-rein back-up cue, hold the rope reins in the middle with one hand (here, my left) about 2 inches above the horse's mane. Slide the other hand (my right) down the rein and draw it back so it is a few inches to the side of the saddle horn or pommel. This should bend the horse's neck so that you can see the side of his face. Maintain the pressure until he takes one step back with the rein-cue-side front foot.

Photo 83   Alisha picks up a good amount of pressure with her right rein, and holds it steady. Clash lifts her front right foot and takes a step back, which is the response Alisha is looking for, so she'll give her a full release. It is important to use enough rein pressure for this cue at first. When you only pick up a small amount of pressure, your horse may confuse this new cue with the hip motion cue, and offer you endless circles as he moves his hip away.

behind the foot's initial position. Of course, where your horse actually moves (if he moves at all) is up to him. He may step anywhere but backward, or he may confuse the new rein cue with the hip motion cue that you taught previously. What-ever his reaction, focus on holding steady pressure a few inches to the right of the saddle horn or pommel until you see that front right foot take a step backward (photo 83).

At the precise moment he takes that step back, release all rein pressure by opening your right hand and dropping the rein. This "Yes" response helps show him that the action he took earned him a release. He might not understand with the first release what he did to warrant a reward, but with repetition it will become clear.

Continue to hold the middle of the rope reins with your left hand and pick up the right side of the reins—cueing your horse to take one step back. Practice this one-step response followed by a full release of pressure until the response is immediate and correct, then, continue asking for it as you work on something else—such as hip serpentines—until you have completed 30 repetitions.

STEP TWO

Now that you have shown your horse what this new cue means, and practiced it, you can ask for *two* steps back.

In order to improve your horse's response, insist on some additional conditions. First, only release while he is moving his foot. This means: let go of your rein at the very moment he is actually moving so you reward him for moving back as well as his "intention" to do so. Do not release while your horse is standing still, before or after the step is taken.

While you are asking for the shoulder to move back from this one-rein cue, it helps to think "Back up," as if you are riding a horse that already knows what you are looking for. This helps you stay centered in the saddle and gives a clearer, more consistent signal.

Second, you want your horse to "give" to the bit. Your right hand should not feel your horse leaning or pulling on the bit in any way. Only release him when he stays off the bit pressure. Any form of contact with the bit is "leaning" on it and should never be rewarded with a release.

Third, your horse's head should be level with or lower than his withers. When you release your horse when his head is higher than this, you tell him that this position is okay. Throughout your training, always insist that his head elevation is correct in order to get a release.

Continue asking for two steps back, with a soft face and a level neck line. If your horse stops, changes direction, lifts his head, or leans on the bit, maintain the pressure until two "good" (meeting all your conditions) steps are taken. Complete at least 30 repetitions at this level.

Remember, you are not rewarding the completion of two steps back. You are rewarding the actual move-ment backward, with a release coming as the second step is taken.

STEP THREE

You can now build on the number of steps your horse takes with his right foot. Stay at each step level for at least 30 repetitions, until you can get 12 steps perfectly. As the number of steps increases, your horse will either move straight back or on a slight angle away from your cueing hand. Either is fine at this point.

If you imagine your starting point is the middle of a clock face, your horse's right front foot should step straight back toward six or on an angle toward seven o'clock.

As you increase the number of steps you ask for and you see that he is giving the right answer most of the time, give your horse the chance to work off less bit pressure (photo 84). If at any time he stops responding correctly, immediately go back to asking with more rein pressure.

STEP FOUR

You will now increase the difficulty of the exercise. Walk your horse forward with your left hand still holding the center of the reins 2 inches above his mane. Reach down with your right hand and pick up the rein as you did before. The requirements are the same—you want your horse to move his shoulder back from this rein cue. But now you are looking for the horse to move forward (walking), cease forward movement (stopping), and perform backward movement (backing up). Just so you know, this is a "roundabout" way of teaching a "stop." (We further examine the "stop" in Lesson 12, p. 158.)

At first, your horse may turn or simply continue walking on an angle, but if you hold the rein steady, he will soon give you the backing response he has been from the halt. During this new phase of the lesson, change up the number of steps you ask for in order to keep him guessing.

Continue asking your horse to walk forward a number of steps (again, change it up) and pick up the rein to request the shoulder to back up. He should start to stop in his tracks and begin backing with only the one-rein cue. Practice until you feel he fully understands what you are asking, and he no longer wanders or turns.

STEP FIVE

Once your horse stops and begins backing his shoulder up on cue from a walk, ask him to jog. Pick up the rein cue as before and ask him to back his shoulder up (photos 85 A–D). Again, at first you might not get the perfect response, and with additional speed, you can count on your horse to be confused. So if he struggles to understand the cue, take a step back and work at the walk before trying the jog again. With a number of well-timed releases, your horse will come to understand.

STEP SIX

Work at all speeds on the right side until you can back his shoulder with the one-rein cue, and keep his neck almost perfectly straight—meaning, you can ask with a very soft rein cue and get the correct response. With repetition, and some anticipation working to your benefit, you will find your horse stops forward movement immediately when you ask and begins backing up with cadenced, deliberate steps. Continue with the right side until he can do this.

STEP SEVEN

Repeat Steps One through Six on the left side. Approach this new side with the full knowledge that your horse does not understand this cue on his left side yet. It is important not to assume that anything he learned on the right will be transferred to the left. Do not skip any steps or rush—treat it almost like a whole new lesson.

Rider's Block

● During your first several applications of this rein cue, you may be tempted to change your hand position in order to "help" your horse find the answer. But, your goal is not to

Photo 84 In a short period of time, you can expect your horse to move his shoulder in response to only a small amount of rein pressure on either side, and step back with a soft nose, "giving" to the bit. The position of Alisha's hand has not changed (compare to photo 83, p. 139), but the amount of pressure she is using has decreased with each correct response from Clash.

"get" the horse to back up but rather to "teach" him to back his shoulder off that particular rein pressure. Keep your hand position the same throughout the lesson.

● Since you have worked a lot on hip serpentines, your horse knows the hip motion one-rein cue, and he may confuse this new cue with the one already established. If he continually turns into the rein pressure, even though your hand is in the correct position, try picking up more pressure and bending his head around further. This will unbalance him, and he will likely "fall into the answer" by stepping back to regain his balance.

Photo 85 A–D Once your horse has learned to give his face and shoulder to your new rein cue from a resting position and a walk, you can begin to ask for the same response from the jog. In A, Alisha picks up a relaxed jog, and in B she takes the slack out of the right rein. You can see Clash "brace" slightly against the bit here. This is a normal response when you add speed to a new cue. Clash stops and begins stepping back in C, but she has not fully "given" to the bit pressure with a level head and "soft nose" so Alisha maintains the pressure. Finally, in D her front foot takes that step back, her nose softens to Alisha's hand, and she will get a full release.

● If your horse "walks away with you" and seems to be ignoring the cue, remember that he is just confused. Your job is to hold steady, and fair, pressure until he finds the answer. You are not doing him any favors by releasing on the incorrect response—this only prolongs the lesson.

● Only release your horse when he is "off" the bit. If you let him lean on the bit or raise his head as you give him a release, you are permitting undesirable behavior and will have to deal with the ramifications later.

● The word "Whoa" has not been taught and is being reserved for a later lesson (see Lesson 12, p. 158). Avoid using this verbal cue now.

● Keep your body centered and relaxed. You are teaching a rein cue; you do not want your horse to feel leg pressures or changes in your balance.

● If you do not want your horse to pull on you, then you must not pull on him. Pick up rein pressure and hold steady, don't yank or tug.

● You want your horse to back up his shoulder with deliberate, cadenced steps, so release while he is still moving, not while he is slowing or stopping.

Lesson 15's Benefits

● In an effort to gain control over your horse's shoulders, you have established a basic shoulder response to a one-rein cue. You will build on this response as you begin to use two reins and increase the difficulty of the exercises in the coming lessons. You have begun teaching the "stop," which I discuss further in Lesson 14 (see p. 146). A stop happens during the transition between forward and backward movement: by teaching his shoulder(s) to back up, the stop can be requested by simply offering a release at the point between the transition. In early training, it is more productive to always request a few backing steps when you just want to stop, in order to "overtrain" your horse. That way when you do ask for just a stop, it will seem that much easier to him!

● You have continued to only allow a soft face and relaxed head carriage as you release your horse, and your consistency is already paying off. This will benefit future rides and exercises greatly when your horse does not lean on bit pressure or carry himself out of position.

Green Light

This exercise takes a few training sessions or more. You may find great success early, but in order to "burn" the short-term memory to the long-term memory, you need repetition. Spend several training days working on this lesson. When you do move on in the Countdown and pick up both reins, you will find that your hard work on this basic "give" has aided you greatly.

Moving from the Round Pen to the Riding Arena

There comes a time when the horse needs to come out of the round pen and start to be ridden in a larger area (photo 86). This timing depends on the rider. Are you comfortable with the horse's progress? Does he respond nicely to rein pressure? Does he move forward well from your leg cues? Perhaps you only feel truly comfortable when your horse has learned to stop and back up well (see Lesson 15, p. 138). Most horses are ready for the arena after only a few riding sessions in the round pen and actually benefit from the larger riding area, as the extra space encourages them to move forward. But, this is a personal matter—you are the one who needs to feel at ease.

The first time you take your horse into the larger area, use the Replacement Theory (see p. 23), relax, and put your horse to work on an exercise that he can already do well to focus his mind on you and the requests you are making.

Backing-Up—Part II

Goals

Your first goal is to continue strengthening your *go forward cue* from the horse's back by asking for forward movement repeatedly. Second, you are going to introduce a combination of rein cues when you ask for both the left and right shoulders to move back simultaneously. Third, you want your horse to begin *thinking* "back." This means that even though he is allowed to travel forward, he is very attentive to the rider and ready for his next cue.

Finally, you will reinforce your horse's desire to "get off" the bit pressure. When he feels pressure on the bit, you want him to respond quickly and agreeably by backing his shoulders up and softening his face to find his release.

Check-In

Before you begin this exercise, the following should be true:

▸ You can walk, jog, and lope your horse on cue with an immediate response.

▸ You can remain in the requested gait for a reasonable amount of time without your horse wanting to transition down.

▸ You can perform hip serpentines with a soft rein cue and relaxed steady movement.

▸ You can pick up either the left or right rein and cue that shoulder to take as many steps back as you desire, while the horse keeps his head low, and doesn't lean on the bit pressure.

▸ You can transition from forward movement at the walk and jog into backward movement with a cue from your left or right rein.

▸ You have worked on asking for shoulder movement backward immediately prior to beginning this lesson.

Cues to Use

You will use your left and right shoulder cues to back up, the only difference is you will now use them at the same time (see Lesson 15, p. 138).

Spot, Direction, Motivator, and Release

Spot Right and left shoulders
Direction Back
Motivator Bit pressure
Release Cessation of bit pressure

Teaching Steps

STEP ONE

Begin this lesson after warming your horse up with forward movement under saddle as well as a few hip serpentines. Once his mind and body are relaxed and focused on you, reestablish the one-rein shoulder cues taught in the previous lesson (see p. 138).

Sit on your horse in an open area of the riding arena. Pick up both reins, creating pressure on each side of the

Always enter into rein pressure smoothly and with fairness. When you pick up your reins and smoothly take the slack out of them, your horse will "feel the cue coming." You do not want to startle or aggravate him by "popping" him in the mouth with the bit.

How "Backing-Up" Relates to "Stopping"

A "stop" is the complete cessation of forward movement. The best way to teach your horse to stop is to teach your horse to move backward. In order for your horse to move backward, he must cease moving forward first. A stop occurs at this transition.

In the early stages of a horse's training it is best to teach him to respond to a backing cue before you allow for just a stop. By always asking him for at least a couple of backward steps, your horse learns to prepare for the backward movement, which necessitates a better transition between forward and backward—thus "stopping" better. A proper stop is not a slowing down of the gait; it is when your horse does everything in his power to halt forward movement in preparation for backing up.

You can begin asking for a stop without backward steps when your horse responds well to your cues, and when you do not feel the need to improve his stop. If your horse ever ignores your cues to stop, then backing-up exercises will be your first course of action.

Photo 87 In the two-handed back-up cue, pick up both reins and draw them back, holding your hands shoulder width apart and bringing them to a rest near the horn or pommel of your saddle.

bit, and hold steady with your hands resting a few inches to each side of the saddle horn or pommel (photo 87). The amount of pressure should be just enough so your horse looks to obtain a release from it.

As always, your aim is to release the horse at the right moment. First, you are asking him to take one full step back with either of his front feet. Second, you want him to "give" his nose to the bit pressure by bringing his chin "inside the bit," which means his nose comes in toward his chest in order to avoid leaning or pulling on the bit. Third, you only release your horse when his neckline is level with or lower than his withers. When these three requirements are met, offer a full release by opening your hands and dropping the reins. Follow with some neck rubs and remain still for a minute or so.

"Inside the bit" is a term with negative connotations. I do not want you to "hold" your

horse in a cramped position that is bad for his neck and his mind. Just make sure he is not leaning on the bit, and the way he does this is to bring his nose toward his chest, away from the pressure.

Since you have worked on one-rein shoulder back-ups in the previous lesson, moving to two reins is a small, manageable step for your horse. He should find the answer without increased anxiety or defiance. But, even though this step is small, it is your job to only release him when the requirements are met—you must not do so when he is standing still, leaning on the bit, or raising his head. Ask for only one step at least three dozen times.

STEP TWO

Now you can move on to two steps. Both front feet must take a full step backward. You are still requesting this from a standstill, but are looking for *further*. Increase the number of steps taken before a full release is given, and repeat at least three dozen releases at each step level before moving on.

When your horse leans on the bit, raises his head, or stops his feet, start counting over. This means that if you are looking for five steps back and your horse stops at three steps, begin again at one and get to five before releasing.

This *further* exercise does not have to be completed all at once. Once you have two or more steps, I suggest asking for six to 12 repetitions and then spend a few minutes working on hip serpentines in between sets. Offer a break and begin again. Space your requests out. The horse's reward is a lack of bit pressure and being allowed to stand quietly. Remember, when you ask for movement, and then immediately ask for it again, the horse is spending more time *with* pressure than he is *without* it.

Build your horse up to at least 12 steps backward before moving on. This strengthens his response *further*.

If your horse "falls apart" during this step and stops responding, decrease the number of steps until he can be released more easily. This way, you can either build his responses back up, or end on that good note for the day.

STEP THREE

Once you have had success building the back-up response further, it is time to ask for it to be completed *faster*. For this movement to be performed more quickly, add two new elements: The first is vocal "clucking" to act as a "pre-cue"—a signal to your horse to speed the feet up. This pre-cue is then "backed up" with the real cue where the motivator will be pressure from both of your legs.

Ask your horse to back as before. You should already have achieved a deliberate, cadenced backing motion, but perhaps without speed of any kind. Now ask him to speed up by clucking once every second. The moment he goes *faster*, release him. If your horse doesn't respond, "rock" both your legs simultaneously. This looks like gentle "leg bumping" but with your feet moved forward so they are at or in front of the cinch or girth area. Do not startle him—at first move them slowly without making contact. When he accepts your legs, begin to "bump" him near the cinch, or on his shoulders with your toes. Immediately after he speeds up, release fully and stand quietly.

You are reaffirming that clucking means to speed his feet up. You did this before while teaching forward movement, but now you want him to understand it works for going backward, too. You are also introducing a new leg motivator, which you will need down the road.

In this phase of the lesson the goal is to release your horse during the acceleration portion of the backing maneuver. Ask him to back and when his steps are not quick enough, cluck, give your horse a chance to respond, and if he does not, follow up with leg bumping. At the moment he speeds up, release and stand quietly.

Mix up this exercise with hip serpentines and plan to work on it over a number of days, or even longer, if necessary.

Photos 88 A–C Alisha establishes good forward movement at the walk around the perimeter of the arena (A). She picks up both reins and requests that Clash back up. Clash immediately stops going forward and prepares to back up (B). She takes even, cadenced backward steps, "gives" to the bit, and brings her chin to her chest (C).

STEP FOUR

Eventually, you can achieve a *softer* response with three less demanding cues: One, start to use less rein pressure; two, add a vocal "Whoa" cue; and three, ask your horse to stop with your seat position. At this time you'll work only on the first part—requesting backing up using less rein pressure. I elaborate on the other two later (see p. 158).

Ask your horse for one step back, but this time, don't tighten the reins as much as before. If your horse backs up with a soft face and quick steps, release him. If he is inattentive, add more rein pressure—similar to what you had in Step One—and get the result you want. Then, ask with gradually decreasing pressure, and you'll find he will learn to back up from a much lighter rein cue.

One of the challenges you'll face is the horse may not bring his chin toward his chest as much as before. In order to keep the desired head and neck "shape," just withhold your release until he does. Your goal is to use less rein pressure with each release, but you will have to take a step back periodically and insist with increasing pressure if your horse does not respond correctly.

Remember, whenever he feels pressure, your horse knows to actively look for a release. You have already performed many backing steps with him giving you a soft face as a result of increasing pressure through your legs, voice, and reins. Now he will begin to understand you will only offer a full release when his chin "gives" to bit and moves toward his chest.

Photos 89 A–C Alisha asks Clash to jog five steps while keeping the reins slack (A). She then picks up light, two-handed rein pressure and requests Clash back up. The response is an immediate stop and you can see how Clash is prepared to back as she begins to use her hind end (B). As your horse softens to your hands and begins stepping back with cadenced steps, you can offer your release (C). Avoid releasing your horse while the steps are slowing, stopped, or intermittent. You want to encourage a steady rhythm and reward your horse's good work ethic only.

STEP FIVE

You have now introduced a two-rein request and taken it further, faster, and softer. Your horse should understand how to go backward with quick steps, a soft face, and a level or low head. He knows what "clucking" means and is comfortable with leg bumping. So far, this two-rein cue has only been used from a standstill. It is time to add forward movement.

Ask your horse to walk forward. When you and the horse are ready, smoothly pick up both reins and ask your horse to back up (photos 88 A–C). If your horse stops quickly and begins to back up, release him after three steps backward. If he walks through the request, slows, or halts, continue the rein pressure and begin clucking, followed by leg bumping, in order to motivate him. Get three good steps backward before you release him.

Rest for a few seconds and casually walk off again. Repeat the request from a walk a many times, until you always get an immediate response, with quick backward steps and a soft face. The number of steps can vary—I ask for three to five most of the time, unless the horse is regressing and I feel that asking for more will reinforce my request.

STEP SIX

Move your horse out at a jog. Again, when you are comfortable, pick up both reins and ask your horse to back (photos 89 A–C). You may be met with an immediate "give" and backing response, or you may not! Deal with any problems just as you did when you started to cue your horse to back up from the walk (see Step Five).

Ask your horse to again travel forward at the jog for

three to five steps, followed by another request to back up. Focus on the quality of the back-up and not just the number of steps. By repeating this exercise frequently, the horse will begin to slow down his jog. He'll also anticipate your request and his willingness and ability to back up off both reins will continue to improve.

Work for five to 10 minutes, followed by a few minutes break. Then, mix it up with five to 10 minutes of hip serpentines and another break. Keep alternating these exercises to help your horse stay soft, forward, and build his work ethic.

Rider's Block

● You may be tempted to progress too quickly when it seems your horse understands your rein cues and gives you many good responses. Take your time and know that the more you get your horse to "give" to bit pressure now, the more inclined he will be to respond properly in the future when there is more going on—speeding up, for example.

● When you feel your horse slowing down or "thinking" of stopping while backing, it is best to release him immediately while he is still moving. By releasing him before he stops, you avoid holding the pressure while at the same time struggling to get him moving backward again. This happens when you jump ahead too quickly in the lesson plan or your horse is tired, thus losing concentration. Younger horses have a shorter attention span, and if you spend too long on this lesson, you may well run into this issue. "Too long" can only be defined by you and your horse—it will vary according to the duration of time in the saddle, weather, and the horse's age and energy level. If you spread this lesson out over several days, your horse will learn it with less stress.

● Young horses and others new to training often struggle with going forward. This is an excellent exercise to continue developing your request for forward movement by using leg pressure. Make sure when you ask for forward move-

ment, you get it. If your horse starts to back up when you apply leg pressure (as he may confuse this with the backing cue), continue to pressure him with your legs and voice until you achieve forward. Never release your horse from pressure until he finds the correct answer.

● You want your horse to trust your hands and legs. If you add pressure of any kind too swiftly, you will have "trust issues." As mentioned before, always pick up the reins smoothly and apply your bit pressure fairly. When you "bang" his mouth and cause a "startle" reflex, you are working against yourself—you'll end up with a jumpy, nervous horse that won't trust you. The same goes for your legs. Always begin just "rocking" your legs, followed by "bumping." Then, if you need to add more leg pressure, it will be okay because you have effectively warned your horse that pressure is building.

● You have not asked your horse to stop forward movement and back up from a lope yet. Before you do, you want to be certain that the slower work is thoroughly understood and that both you and your horse are comfortable with the maneuver.

● At this stage you are taking your horse from forward movement to backward movement, and not allowing your horse to merely cease forward movement ("stop"). If you need to stop your horse, ask for at least one or two steps back each time before allowing him to stand still. This keeps your horse responding well to the rein cue. Later in the Countdown you teach your horse to stop—and just "stop"—with the same cue.

Roadblocks

● Some horses have a big "up button." By this, I mean that as you add two-handed rein pressure to ask for backward movement, they tend to rear—lift their front feet off the ground. This is why I suggest working first on one rein at a time (as you did in Lesson 15, p. 138) to give the horse a chance to learn the response you want before being asked to deal with two-handed pressure. In order to deal with this, or other negative responses, keep the pressure level low at first and always show your horse that a release is imminent.

Lesson 14's Benefits

● Backing-up is very important in foundation training. You show the horse how to find a release by backing off bit pressure. Your horse will start to see that no matter how the bit pressure is applied, you require him to soften his face toward his chest and move his feet. This allows you to focus more on his foot placement in future lessons rather than just struggling with a high-headed, hard-mouthed horse.

● Your horse is starting to *think* "back." As you continue to cue him repeatedly, he becomes more attentive to your signals and is willing to "change gear" on a moment's notice. By asking him to stop and back up many times, he will begin to anticipate the request, even when he is moving forward. Your horse is now "prepared to act." He is not necessarily anticipating a back-up request so much as he is anticipating change and is attentive to your cues.

● In Lesson 15 (p. 138) you worked on your horse's response to individual reins. By asking your horse to first "give" laterally, he was more likely to respond well in this lesson, where you asked him to break at the poll and "give" his face straight toward the pressure off a two-handed cue. This progression gave him time to accept and learn the correct response before you upped the ante.

Green Light

This particular lesson is not just a "one time deal"—you will ask your horse to respond to both reins by backing up his shoulders for the rest of his life. You taught your horse what it takes for him to find his release by backing up from standing still, walking. and jogging. When he has proven that he can do so through many good responses, then, and only then, can you move ahead and ask for a "stop" from the lope. Remember that a "stop" is only a backing-up request that is released before an actual backing step is taken by the horse (see p. 146). Backing-up responses taught now directly affect the "stop" response you need in the future.

You will revisit this lesson many times, but the better your horse learns it now, the easier it will be for him down the road. Be mindful that if your horse is still not moving his feet well, "bracing" his face against bit pressure, or raising his head in avoidance or anxiety, it is important you work on Lesson 14 until these issues are gone.

Loping Circles and Straight Lines

Please do not misinterpret it when I recommend "seven to 30" sets or sessions—it isn't an absolute. As with everything in life, "it depends," is maybe the better advice. I have seen many ranch horses follow their buddies out of their corral on the second ride and "follow their nose" down the trail without a problem. I have also come across horses that were not ready to ride in the open after an entire month of "working on it." If you feel unsafe, then stay in the round pen or ask for help.

Goals

In this lesson, you are setting out to accomplish a number of things. First, you want to strengthen your lope departure, as you will now be asking for the lope outside the round pen. Second, you want to strengthen your horse's response to the *hip motion cue* and "follow his nose" as you increase his speed in the arena. Third, you want to eliminate your horse's dependence on the rail to guide his circular movement—that is, you can no longer rely on the round pen to dictate his direction of travel. Fourth, you will introduce the backing-up cue from the *lope*. This is an early stage of teaching a "stop." And finally, you will lope your horse in straight lines.

Check-In

All the responses that you seek in this lesson have been introduced previously, but now you are going to improve them, while increasing the horse's speed and working in a larger enclosed area.

Your horse must be comfortable carrying a rider at the lope. I think it is best to have had at least seven sessions loping easily in the round pen before taking your horse into the arena. Even when you are a top-notch hand, your horse needs to build his confidence with several short loping sessions before you allow him to enter the open space of an arena. But, if you stay in the round pen too long (let's say for more than 30 lope sessions) you are both relying on the round pen and not expanding your comfort zone.

You should also have spent ample time working on hip serpentines at the walk and jog. Your previous work in these slower gaits will pay off now. Your horse will not respond in exactly the same way as the increased speed of the lope makes it more difficult, but the back-up cues will not be "new" and completely unfamiliar, so he'll improve rapidly.

I want to remind you that every time you add speed, your horse will not respond as well as he did at the slower gaits. This is completely normal. If he "gets it" right away, that's a bonus, but prepare yourself for him to struggle a bit.

Do not ask for a back-up from the lope unless you have worked extensively on the response at the standstill, walk, and jog. When you don't already have an "incredible" response—light, quick, soft, collected, and immediate—to the two-rein backing cue, you are not going to achieve the best result at the lope. Take the time now to go back and work on Lesson 14 (see p. 145) until you have met all its requirements.

Teaching Steps
STEP ONE

Warm up your horse in the riding arena by performing one or two 10-minute sessions of hip serpentines

Time Management

When I work a young horse, I like to aim for a one-hour session. With a very young horse that is only being ridden for 10 to 20 minutes, I fill the rest of my time with low-stress handling, such as bathing, hand walking, tying, picking up feet, and so forth. I want to maximize my interaction with the horse. If I do ride a horse for a full hour, I consider the weather and my horse's energy level and attentiveness in order to determine the duration and stress level of the workout. I usually spend 75 percent of my time working on the basics—forward movement, steering, backing-up, and confidence-building exercises—with the remaining time focused on teaching new responses and advanced maneuvers.

Photo 90 By loping on a slack rein and only using them to keep the horse on a circle, he will learn to trust your hands (it is a good confidence-builder, too). That way, when you do pick up the reins, they mean something and evoke a response. Belle lopes along nicely here on the loose rein.

and reconfirming the back-up responses from a standstill, walk, and jog. Be certain that your horse is responsive and relaxed before you begin.

Begin in an area in your riding arena that allows you to make a circle 70 feet in diameter. This should be near one end or corner to give you some "help" holding the shape of the circle: the fence or panels can keep your horse from deviating for at least some of the pattern.

Pick up a jog on the circle. Complete enough circles (three to five) so that your horse has an idea of where he is going. If he struggles to complete a circle at a jog, work on it until he can.

When you're ready, ask for the lope. You want your horse to remain in the lope until you tell him otherwise. If he breaks into the jog on his own, immediately request the lope again. This is your horse's first parameter.

The horse's second parameter is to remain on the path

of the circle. If he takes his nose off it to the right, use your left rein to bring his nose back onto the pattern, and vice versa. When he is loping correctly on the circle, release all rein pressure—you do not want him to lean on or depend on the bit pressure for balance or constant guidance (photo 90). Keep your hands low and the reins slack. (Note: don't let your rope reins "flap," but be certain that there is no pressure on the horse's mouth.)

Ask your horse to complete six circles to begin. Then, take one rein and ask for a small enough turn so that he breaks down into a jog. At the jog, guide him back onto the circle, but this time, travel in the opposite direction. Avoid letting your horse walk, as you want to keep him *thinking* "forward."

Follow the circle a few times in the new direction at the jog to let your horse know what is to be expected. Ask for the lope again, and complete six circles. Bring your horse

Photo 91 Only ask for the back-up from the lope when you feel your horse will want to do it—this sets you up for success. After coming down from the lope, Alisha and Clash transition from forward movement to backward—with cadenced steps and a soft, yielding nose.

down to the jog as you did before. At this point you can allow him to walk, if he chooses to, or turn him again with one rein until he is walking. In your attempt to slow him down, you want your request to be smooth and easy—he is doing well, and you are looking to reward him with a walk. Be sure to rub him on his neck and tell him that he's a good boy. Continue to walk until his breathing returns to normal.

STEP TWO

The more you practice transitioning up to the lope, the easier it becomes. And, the more you remain in the lope before transitioning down to a jog, walk, or resting position, the more confident and comfortable your horse becomes. By continually asking him to remain on the circle pattern, you'll find it growing easier to keep him there.

The next step is to strengthen your horse's response to your cues while increasing the duration of the loping session. In Step One you asked for six circles in each direction. You should keep asking for a few more each new day until you can lope for eight to 10 minutes per side with ease. Loping for this amount of time improves endurance, strength, and balance, as well as relaxes your horse. It may take some time to work up to this point, but that is the goal.

When you are riding a young horse, say in his two-year-old year, be careful not to "overwork" him at the lope. As he matures, his lope work can increase. Conversely, be sure not to short change your loping time. Horses that do not spend time loping for sustained durations miss out on many of its benefits.

Move your circle away from the end of the arena. By so doing, you do not have the fence or panels to help guide the shape of the pattern. Choose an area closer to the middle or on the opposite end of the arena—your end goal is to be able to circle your horse anywhere that you wish, with the same level of success.

STEP THREE

It is only after these first few lope sessions in the riding arena that I want you to ask your horse to back up from the lope. I have reserved this request until now for some very good reasons.

First, you need to have backed up repeatedly from a resting position, walk, and jog. Your horse should know, beyond a shadow of doubt, what the rein cue means and how to respond to it. Second, your horse should perform relaxed loping in a large circle and comfortably maintain the shape of the pattern on his own. Loping sessions do not have to be perfect, but you should be able to relax in the saddle and only apply leg and rein pressure periodically.

Pick up the lope on your circle, and at the time you would normally use one rein to spiral your horse down to a slower gait and switch direction, change your request to a back-up (photo 91). Only ask for the back-up when you feel that the horse will want to. This usually happens after he's loped for a while and wants a break. Since he knows the cue, and is ready for a break at any time, pick up both your reins as you did in Lesson 14 (p. 145), and request the back-up with a soft rein cue.

There is no need to apply great rein pressure. You want to offer this cue to your horse and have it be a positive experience. Allowing your horse to cease moving forward and back up, followed by a rest, is a gift to him. As a result of your earlier teaching, he will most likely plant both his hind feet in the dirt, stopping his forward movement quickly in preparation for the backing response as you apply your rein cue. This is the beginning of an excellent "stop." Ask him to back up a few steps with a "soft nose" and then stand quietly.

In the early stages of this training, I ask for a stop and back-up from the lope a few times per session, at the most. Since you can work on the response at slower speeds, it is best to reserve this cue at the faster gait for when you feel the horse is really listening and wants to stop on his own.

The protective boots you've been using come in handy here, as they prevent your horse from getting "burned" on his hind fetlocks. A horse that knows how to stop really well will "plant" his hind end upon request and begin to back up. By keeping him comfortable, he won't have to think twice about responding to this cue.

STEP FOUR

In Steps One and Two you asked for a circle 70 feet in diameter. Once your horse is comfortable in a circle of that size and is not trying to transition down frequently, you can ask him to lope in a smaller circle—this is more difficult for him.

Ask your horse to complete a 50-foot circle and then guide him back onto the larger one. Continue to first ask for the smaller, followed by the larger circle. Create your own patterns of smaller and larger circles and insist that he stays in the lope.

STEP FIVE

Once you can lope your horse in circles—which means you can guide him with your reins to a much better degree than before—begin to lope him on straight lines. Begin on the perimeter of the riding arena along the fence, which will help you stay straight and give your horse a guide. Then lope straight up the middle of arena, turn him near the end, and again lope up the side of the arena along the fence. Repeat this pattern using both sides of the arena and different lines down the middle.

When loping circles the horse tends to "lean" into the turn; straight lines help your horse lope with his body upright and balanced.

Rider's Block

● Once you start to lope in the open riding arena, you will find speed control becomes an issue—your horse may become lazy and want to "break down." Your job is to insist he stays in the lope. You are not being unreasonable; think of yourself as the "benevolent dictator" who is showing him what you want. You may also be faced with a horse that surges in speed. The only way to deal with this is to work more at the lope. If you ask for the lope every day, he will learn to accept it and relax into its steady rhythm. When you gradually work a young horse up to loping for eight to 10 minutes in each direction, you will end up riding a horse that is willing and confident doing so.

● Your horse will ignore your rein cues from time to time. It usually happens when you come around to part of the circle closest to the "open" end of the arena. Pick up and hold pressure on your rein until the horse stops trying to wander. Do not worry when your horse acts this way! You are riding a young or untrained horse in a large, open area—expect him to think on his own every once in a while.

● Soon, you will teach your horse to respond to new cues

that will help you better control his body "parts." For now, be content with him giving you steady forward movement, following his nose in response to your hip motion cues, and responding willingly to your back-up requests.

● With increased speed, you may find it more difficult to stay "light" with your hands. When you first ask for a back-up from the lope, it is extra important you don't give a sharp, unfair cue. Concentrate on picking up the reins smoothly with a steady pressure (not quickly), until you feel your horse respond to the bit. Once he steps back release him fully as you have in the past. You will need to work hard on keeping your hands, legs, and seat all working independently of one another.

● You may be unsure about how many circles to ride or how much time needs to be spent loping your horse on a daily basis. Start with six circles and add one circle each day until the horse can lope for eight minutes in each direction. As you progress you can use loping in circles as part of your warm-up before moving on to more advanced work. The only way to have a horse that is completely relaxed while responding to your cues at the lope is to spend time doing it.

● Consider the footing in your riding arena. If it has a hard surface it will be uncomfortable and unsafe for your horse, in which case do not ask him for an immediate stop and back-up. If the footing is deep, your horse's joints and muscles can become strained, so you must limit the duration of your riding session. This may mean that your workouts involve less trotting and loping until you can ride on proper footing. Find out how to improve or replace questionable arena footing, and purchase a drag to keep it in good order.

● I still have not dealt with "leads." You may be shocked and thinking, "Loping circles but not asking for a specific lead? This can't be right!" First, establishing forward movement is of utmost importance. Second, you cannot yet con-

trol the parts of the horse's body that you need in order to influence his lead. Third, by teaching only one thing at a time, the horse will find the answer more quickly.

● When your horse speeds up and deviates from the circle, heading toward the gate of the arena, just ignore it. Put him back on the circle and continue loping. If the problem continues, try exiting the arena from a different gate, working at the opposite end of the arena, or working on hip serpentines near the exit. Never rest or tie your horse at or near the gate—this only makes matters worse.

● Watch where you are going to keep the circle's pattern correct. When you focus on your horse's ears, your horse will end up loping a route of his own choosing!

● Always make time for a proper cool-down, walking and bathing your horse until his body temperature and breathing are back to normal.

Lesson 13's Benefits
● Asking your horse to lope outside of the round pen, and in a larger, open area, not only builds his confidence, but also allows him to do what he'd do naturally—that is, move forward over greater distance. A horse that spends too much time in the round pen begins to feel confined and can lose this desire to "move out."

● Your horse is now comfortable traveling on different size circles and straight lines. Plus, you have had the opportunity to reinforce your hip motion and back-up cues at a faster gait.

Green Light
You will lope circles, straight lines, and various patterns with your horse for the rest of his life, and this lesson can be used to warm up, build endurance and strength, and train your horse to control his body and perform new maneuvers. From this point on, your daily training should include loping sessions whenever possible.

MODERN WISDOM

Visualizing Your Requests

Actions always begin in the "thought world." How you *think* affects how you *do* things. Most of us find it hard to hide what we are thinking. We often give away clues with our physical actions. We all have sensed or "picked up" what others are really thinking or feeling, even when it contradicts what they are saying with words. We learn to read body language and interpret other subtle clues that are inadvertently given.

Horses are exceptionally clever at figuring out what you are thinking. I'm not saying that a horse is able to read your mind, but he is aware of small changes in your body language made as your thinking evolves. I'm sure at one time or another you've been on a solid trail horse that you've had for years and just thought "Lope," and before you could give the cue, the horse was already doing it!

Good training requires you clearly visualize what you are requesting from your horse. If you are giving a cue to move a shoulder over, you need to focus on that shoulder and "push it over" with your mind. When you do this, your legs and hands will then give the exact same physical cue every time. You will find greater control comes from thinking and riding this way. Your hand may only have to move a couple of inches in any given direction, and your leg pressure can be so light that an onlooker cannot detect it.

It makes a world of difference when the horse has your undivided attention through focus and visualization. When you let your mind wander, your horse will tend to do the same. When you concentrate and "feel," and are truly visualizing, you'll find he learns faster and easier.

In addition, by keeping your own thoughts on what you are trying to accomplish and visualizing your next move, you will start to be more in tune with what the horse is thinking. As you improve your focus, you will be aware of subtle changes in your horse's body, as well as your own. When you can "feel" what your horse is thinking, you can correct, change, or reward that thought before it gets a chance to play out.

Now, your new "basic training day" can include a little time in the round pen, followed by work in the riding arena, such as hip serpentines; backing up from the walk, jog, and lope; loping circles and straight lines; and the addition of a new lesson or the review of one that needs attention. Lesson 12 (p. 158) deals with advanced stopping and backing-up work. Before moving on to it, I recommend stopping your horse from the lope a handful of times each day for a couple of weeks. This way, you are sure your horse is highly responsive to your rein cue to back up—in all three gaits.

Teaching "Whoa" and Seat Stops

Treat the word "Whoa" with care. You use it to control your horse and it has a response "attached" to it. When you use "Whoa" improperly it loses its clout. I find it amusing when a handler says it 90 times in a row, still hoping that at 91 it will work!

Goals

You are setting out to teach your horse that the word "Whoa" means "Stop forward movement," and that he should begin backing up with a "soft nose" and cadenced steps. You are also going to teach your horse to give you the same response from a change in your riding seat and leg position.

Check-In

This lesson is about teaching your horse to stop and back up from two new cues. In order to teach these new cues, he must be responsive to rein pressure asking his shoulders to back up (see Lesson 14, p. 145). When your horse is still unsure, unresponsive, or plain uncooperative with your rein cues for backing, then good results from this new lesson are unlikely.

When your horse moves forward well and willingly responds to your rein cue for backing from a standstill, walk, jog, and lope, it is the time to go ahead.

Cues to Use

You will introduce two new cues—or "pre-cues." A pre-cue is a signal to the horse that another *cue* and *motivator* is on its way. It is a notice of imminent action. Remember the "clucking" vocal you used earlier in the Countdown? That was also a pre-cue. These are taught by using "association" first, followed by the teaching stage. This lesson will explain both.

The pre-cues taught are saying "Whoa," and changing your seat and leg position (shifting your legs forward and tightening your thighs).

Spot, Direction, Motivator, and Release

"WHOA" CUE

Spots Front feet and nose
Direction Backward
Pre-Cue "Whoa"
Motivator Bit pressure and leg bumping
Release Cessation of bit pressure and leg bumping

"SEAT STOP" CUE

Spot Front feet and nose
Direction Backward
Pre-Cue Change in seat and leg position
Motivator Bit pressure and leg bumping
Release Cessation of bit pressure and leg bumping

Teaching Steps

STEP ONE: INTRODUCING THE "WHOA" VOCAL

The first step in teaching a pre-cue is to begin associating the new signal to an action. In this case, start to use "Whoa" whenever you pick up your reins and request a backing motion. Say it with a low, steady, drawn-out tone, and even repeat it or continue saying it as you back up, whether from a resting position, walk, jog, or lope. Stop saying it as soon as you give the *release*. Continue this association for many training days.

STEP TWO: TEACHING "WHOA" FROM A STANDSTILL

Now that you have consistently said

"Whoa" while backing, your horse has begun to associate the two. Start at a standstill with your reins slack; say "Whoa" as you have before. In your mind, count to two ("One-steamboat, two-steamboats") and if he remains still, pick up the reins and ask him to back up three steps with a "soft nose." Repeat this process.

It's hard to set an exact time on how long to say "Whoa" before you move on with this exercise. When you are working on backing a lot, you can start the next step after just a few days. But, if you are not riding daily, everything takes much longer. It's important that your horse has heard you say "Whoa" many times before you move on.

Eventually, your horse will slowly back up on his own, just from the sound of your voice. He now recognizes that "Whoa" is followed by you picking up the reins and applying bit pressure to his mouth—and he avoids this bit pressure by moving back before it happens. Once he does this, rub him on the neck and let him stand quietly as a reward. He may only take a small step backward at first, but reward the slightest effort.

After small efforts are rewarded, insist that three steps are taken. If he only responds to "Whoa" with a single step back, pick up your reins and ask for all three steps. Repetition is your friend in an exercise such as this, and since this request is quite easy on your horse's body, you can repeat it often.

Practice Step Two until you can say "Whoa" and your horse immediately backs up three cadenced steps. The quality of the back-up should be as established in previous lessons.

STEP THREE: TEACHING "WHOA" FROM THE WALK, JOG, AND LOPE

Most horses do not respond right away to "Whoa" when you add forward movement, so you need to teach the pre-cue at each gait as if your horse is learning it for the first time.

"Whoa" Means "Stop," Right?

By teaching the horse to back up from individual reins; both reins; a change in seat position; and now "Whoa," you are actually teaching your horse to *stop*. These cues all tell the horse to cease forward movement and begin backing up. If you want to really stop, then you quit asking for a back-up *as soon as forward movement has ceased*. So, yes, even though you use "Whoa" to effectively mean "Back up," it can actually result in a stop.

A common derivative of the word "Whoa" is "Ho." When you say "Ho!" sharply, it means "Stop everything you are doing!" This sound is used to tell a horse to quit doing a maneuver—any maneuver, whether it involves forward movement, or not (a turnaround, for example). In contrast, I like to say "Whoooaaa" in a long, drawn-out fashion to "warn" my horse that a stop is coming. This is helpful when loping, as it gives him time to prepare his hindquarters. Most riders will say certain words with their own vocal style, but the importance of reserving specific vocal cues for particular responses still holds true.

Ask for the same response you got in Step Two, but now from the walk. As before, say "Whoa," and count "One-steamboat, two-steamboats," in your head. Then, pick up your reins and give your horse the "answer." When you are both comfortable from the walk, ask your horse to stop forward movement and back up three steps from the jog (photos 92 A & B). As you add more speed do not expect him to respond the same, or maybe at all. Just stay consistent with the exercise and your horse will eventually "get it."

Finally, ask the horse to speed up—this time to a lope—and again say "Whoa." You want your horse to think, "I'd better get moving backward before that bit pressure comes!"

Photos 92 A & B In A Alisha requests a back-up response by vocalizing "Whoa" as she and Clash jog on the rail. Clash has learned to avoid the rein pressure that she knows follows the vocal cue, so in B, she stops and begins to back up. Because her answer is correct, Alisha leaves the reins slack.

"WHOA" QUICK-CHECK

▸ Does the word "Whoa" send your horse backward with a "soft nose" and quick steps from a resting position, walk, jog, and lope?

▸ Can you drop the reins on the horse's neck and achieve the same response at all gaits?

STEP FOUR: INTRODUCING THE "SEAT STOP"

First, it is important to understand what the "seat stop" is. Imagine racing full speed down the length of the arena on a horse that you know is going to screech to a halt at the fence on the far end. How would you brace yourself in preparation? You would most likely put your feet out in front of you a bit—pointing your toes upward—and squeeze with your thighs. Actually, this is the exact seat position you want your horse to respond to with a "stop." For teaching purposes, you will exaggerate your position initially, but in the end this pre-cue will be nothing more than a subtle change in balance.

Just as you began saying "Whoa" *as* you backed your horse, do the same with the change in seat position. By pointing your toes up, moving your legs forward, squeezing with your thighs, and even leaning back a bit, you will "associate" this body position with the stopping and backing request. (Note: do not say "Whoa" at this time since you want to teach each cue separately.) Spend a few days combining the seat position pre-cue with your backing rein cue until you feel your horse recognizes it.

STEP FIVE: TEACHING THE "SEAT STOP" FROM A STANDSTILL

At a standstill with slack reins, ask your horse to back up three steps with a "soft nose" by just changing your seat position. You can be a bit dramatic at this point by leaning back and throwing your legs forward to emphasize that your body position has changed. This helps your horse learn to recognize the pre-cue.

As before, count "One-steamboat, two-steamboats." If your horse has not responded, give him the answer. At the moment you get the response, sit normally in the saddle and remain still. With your seat, you want to differentiate the "backing" position and "stand still" position. Repeat this process.

As you use your seat and legs to cue your horse, he will become increasingly attuned to subtle changes. Further down the road in your training, you will be amazed at how much you can do without using your hands (rein cues) at all.

STEP SIX: TEACHING THE "SEAT STOP" AT THE WALK, JOG, AND LOPE

Repeat the process from the previous steps at the walk. Be consistent until your horse immediately responds to your pre-cue by backing with a soft face. When you and your horse are ready, teach the cue from the jog (photos 93 A–D). Remember, as with teaching "Whoa," when you add speed, your horse may not respond as he did at the halt and walk.

Finally, bring it all together and connect the seat stop with backing up from the lope.

STEP SEVEN: FURTHER, FASTER, SOFTER

Now that your horse is backing well at all gaits from a change in your seat, begin to ask for better speed—still without the use of your rein cues. Begin at the halt, ask your horse to back up, and if the steps are not quick and cadenced, use your toes to bump your horse on the shoulders. If he remains unresponsive, pick up your reins and give him the answer.

The goal is to use your legs as the motivator, telling your horse to "wake up" and speed up his feet. Don't bump all the time or else this action will have no meaning—only use it when necessary. And, as soon as he does pick up the pace, stop using your legs. Soon you will be able to speed up your horse's backing motion without picking up your reins. This gives you freedom to perform other tasks when your horse is involved in more advanced maneuvers in the future. This step also keeps your horse's attention on your legs as he learns to listen to more than your rein cues.

Of course, the real goal is to have a subtle pre-cue. Only exaggerate your seat to teach your horse the "stop" position. In time, allow your "seat stop" to look much more relaxed as you simply (and almost invisibly) release your legs from the sides of the horse, point your toes upward, and squeeze with your thighs.

"SEAT STOP" QUICK-CHECK

▷ Does your "seat stop" send your horse backward with a soft nose and quick steps from a resting position, walk, jog, and lope?

▷ Can you drop your reins and achieve the same response at all gaits?

STEP EIGHT: COMBINE THE PRE-CUES

In an effort to obtain a really strong response to stopping and backing requests, you have now taught your horse to back up from rein cues, a vocal cue ("Whoa"), and a body cue (your seat). If he responds well to each cue *individually*, just imagine what he will do when you combine them!

Ask for a stop and back-up from the lope with a simultaneous "Whoa" and "seat stop." If you faithfully completed the steps in this lesson, you should get a "great" stop and a quick back-up (photo 94). Remember, though, you need to continually reinforce these pre-cues with the proper rein cues when you do not immediately get the response you are seeking.

Rider's Block

● Be sure to wait until you have counted a full two ("One-steamboat, two-steamboats") before picking up your reins. Your horse needs a fair chance to respond.

● Keep your expectations high. Never settle for *slow* backing steps, or accept the horse not softening his nose to the bit when you reinforce the response with your reins. Release him only when he has met all the requirements.

Photos 93 A–D Alisha and Clash travel at a relaxed jog (A). The reins are slack and the rider is focused and fluid. Alisha asks Clash to stop from a change in her seat. Her legs are forward, toes up, thighs tightened, and she is braced as if the horse was sliding to a halt (B). Here the seat stop is exaggerated in order to illustrate the change in body position and to help Clash feel the difference more easily. It can be more subtle in time. Since Alisha was not satisfied with the cadence and tempo of Clash's back-up response, she immediately picks up her reins and bumps Clash's shoulders with her toes to encourage the horse to wake up and "get back" (C & D). As soon as the response is correct, she will drop the reins and release the pressure. Never settle for a lethargic response. Your horse will only give you as much effort as he needs to.

Photo 94 Your horse will quickly learn to give you a great, balanced "stop" off a very subtle request. When working a young filly such as this one, I often request a straight stop after a lope session. She is more than willing to quit loping and already has a good response to a both my "Whoa" and my "seat stop." I allow her to stop and rest as a reward.

Managing the Regression of Cues

Teaching your horse a complete foundation requires many steps. With each step comes a new movement, cue, or both. And, naturally, you will find that as you add the new, your horse may lose his response to what has been previously taught. For example, in the beginning your horse only has to understand one rein cue. As you add more to his "library," he will become confused from time to time. Part of the horse's learning curve is deciphering between the different rein cues. You will help make this happen through repetitive reinforcement, telling him when his response is correct.

Let's say you pick up your right rein to cue your horse to move his right shoulder to the right (see Lesson 5, p. 203), but as you do, your horse moves his shoulders left and *away* from the rein. You must be capable of seeing that the horse is just confusing this request with another (see Lesson 11, p. 165). If you consistently *only release on the correct response*, he'll begin to figure out the difference between them.

Always keep your cues the same and be consistent with your releases. Clear, fair communication helps your horse through periods of confusion.

● "Whoa" does not mean "Stop." It means "Back up." It should sound slow and steady—"Whooaaa"—and be uttered the entire time you are backing. Down the road when you are looking to *just* stop, or you want to quit a maneuver, such as a turnaround (spin), you will use a terser derivative of this word that sounds like, "Ho" (see p. 159).

● Be aware that in some riding disciplines you do not want to teach the "seat stop" as such. The change in your seat position (with your legs forward) will be frowned upon. Knowing your horse's intended career will help you decide if you want to complete this lesson.

Lesson 12's Benefits

● You have just added two cues to your toolbox. Both give you a chance to control your horse without using the reins. They help you learn to be lighter with your hands while improving your horse's attention to details.

Green Light

By keeping the training steps small, success in this lesson is easily measured. Once you finish the last step, you are riding a horse that can stop and back up on either a "Whoa" or a "seat stop," from any gait. This does not mean that regression will not happen; you must continue to practice and improve all responses. I urge you to revisit this lesson each and every time you ride your horse.

"Clockwork"—Part I: Moving the Shoulders Away from Rein Pressure

Goals

In this lesson you will teach the horse a new rein cue to control his shoulders. Previously in the Countdown, you taught him to move his shoulders *back*, but now you will teach him to move them laterally, *away* from rein pressure. (This is the just the beginning! Later you'll teach him to move them *toward* rein pressure, as well as to respond to leg pressure.) The aim here, however, is to isolate the shoulders and establish a lateral response to one rein only.

As you set out to teach this response, continue to insist on soft "gives" to the rein as well as proper shoulder motion with correct footwork (see p. 117). You will work from the ground first, and then from the saddle.

Check-In

Up until this point you have steered your horse by moving his hips over from a rein cue. This elementary *hip motion cue* helped build your foundation of control. You will always have this at your disposal and will need it when you add new responses later.

A finished "bridle" horse, however, is always steered through his *shoulders*. You have already taught your horse to move his shoulders backward—both with one-rein and two-rein cues. The next step is to establish a lateral response whereby the horse moves his shoulders *away* from rein pressure.

All previous lessons in the Countdown are important and should be completed prior to starting this lesson. A confident horse moving forward well from *go forward cues* on the ground and from the leg when ridden will learn this lesson more easily.

Cues to Use

You use one-rein pressure as the cue for your horse to move his shoulder with forward motion laterally—that is, *away* from the cueing rein. With the hand on the side you are moving toward, hold the middle of your reins 2 inches above your horse's mane, just as you did earlier with other one-rein exercises. Reach down the rein with the other hand, pick up the slack in the rein, and hold rein pressure upward. This cueing hand applies varying degrees of pressure as you adjust to ask for less or more shoulder movement. Do not pull the rein toward you or across the horse's mane.

Spot, Direction, Motivator, and Release

Spot The front foot opposite the shoulder you are cueing

Direction Away from rein pressure

Motivator Rein pressure

Release Cessation of rein pressure

Teaching Steps

STEP ONE: STARTING WITH GROUNDWORK

By starting this lesson from the

Your emphasis in the Countdown to Broke is on teaching. Do not get hung up on correctness—that is, rider and horse position. Many times an exaggerated movement or cue is needed to teach a response. In the end, a "finished" horse will be much more responsive when you have worked through each individual lesson and each control point.

Here, your "spot" is the front foot opposite the shoulder you are cueing to move over. You measure accuracy by judging the direction and placement of this opposite front foot.

ground, you gain added control. With both feet planted firmly on the ground, the horse in hand, and your dressage whip as the *go forward cue* and *motivator*, you can concentrate on teaching this cue without the added complications that go along with being in the saddle.

From the ground, your first objective is to reintroduce the go forward cue (see Lesson 21, p. 99). Prepare your horse with his snaffle-bit bridle, protective boots, and saddle, and begin in an open part of the riding arena. Have your dressage whip in hand.

Loop the rope reins over the horse's neck as if you are preparing to mount. Stand on the left side of the horse with your left hand holding the left rein about 6 inches from the slobber strap attached to the bit. Hold the dressage whip in your right hand at your side. Ask your horse to walk around you in a relaxed fashion for a few small circles before letting him stop and face you for a break and head rubs. Switch sides, pick up the opposite rein, and change direction. Repeat on both sides. This initial exercise gets your horse relaxed, moving forward, and reintroduces the whip.

STEP TWO

Again, with body pressure and hind end tapping (if necessary) ask your horse to walk in a small circle around you to the left. Lift your left hand up until you have a light hold on the horse's mouth and take one step toward your horse's left shoulder. Your left hand can move slightly toward his neck. This is the cue for him to move his shoulders *away* from you (and rein pressure). You cause him to move his shoulders over by lifting the left rein and applying pressure to the left side of the mouth. Since forward movement has been established (thus, backward is not an option) and your horse respects you and knows not to step into you (so,

leftward is not an option either) shoulder movement *away* from you—as he steps outside of the small circle he has been walking—will be the result.

Reminder: "forward movement" occurs when your horse moves forward. "Forward motion" implies the horse is moving forward and sideways to some degree (laterally) with correct footwork (see p. 116).

If your horse steps to the right—even a small amount—release the rein pressure by dropping your left hand (maintain a hold on the rein, though). If your horse chooses not to respond, hold constant pressure with the rein until he does. When he does respond, again walk him on the small circle around you.

Remember, for the moment you're only introducing the idea. Do not be overly concerned whether his front left foot crosses correctly in front of his front right foot on the first one or two "gives"—although you will insist on this in Step Three. All you want is for him to walk forward round you, and move his shoulders laterally away from the rein pressure. Ask for at least 12 shoulder motions before you move on to Step Three.

STEP THREE

In order to improve the horse's response and control the shoulder motion away from rein pressure with precision, you need a measurable goal. Imagine the horse's front right foot is placed in the center of a clock face, and he is facing toward noon (photo 95). For this exercise, the size of the clock's face is irrelevant as it's the *direction* (toward one of the hours) that matters. When the horse walks *forward*, his right foot steps toward 12 o'clock; when you ask him to move his shoulders over and *away* from the center position a bit, he steps toward one o'clock. Picture a horse side passing. He would be moving toward three o'clock. At this point, you are just working on the first lateral step toward the one o'clock position. Focus on only the one foot, and the rest of the horse's body will follow.

Photo 95   Imagine that your horse's front right foot is in the center of a clock face, and your horse is facing 12 o'clock. From this center position you can imagine where each hour mark is located. Keep this picture in your mind—it is important to help you gauge success and decide when and where to release your horse.

Back in Step One you needed to reestablish the go forward cue from the ground, which involved possibly several "circles" of movement around you. Now, as the horse settles into the lesson, you can keep the movement around you to a minimum. Use a few walking steps in a small circle to begin each request—"forward movement" helps ensure "forward motion"—and finish by walking the circle again or asking the horse to face you to receive a rest and head rub.

When he responds by stepping toward one o'clock, you can clearly identify and "measure" success so you know exactly when to release him. So, repeat Step Two, but this time, when you are going to the left, watch the horse's front right foot and see where it lands (photos 96 A–D). Offer your release only when the horse is "giving" to the bit (not leaning on it), staying at the walk (not stopping or slowing), and stepping his front right foot toward one o'clock. Repeat this cue two dozen times. Once he consistently achieves this shoulder-away motion from light pressure on the rein, it's time to move on.

STEP FOUR

Starting to the left, ask the horse to move his shoulder away so his right front foot takes *two steps* toward the one o'clock position. Each time he puts the right foot down, imagine it is landing in the middle of a "new" clock face. This means that when your horse successfully takes a second step toward one o'clock, he is taking another step from the middle again.

By holding steady pressure and not offering a release until the horse takes two steps, you build the response *further*. As you ask for more steps in succession, your horse should always be traveling a line aiming at the one o'clock position on a series of clock faces. Initially teaching this exercise from the ground adds a benefit: you can walk toward one o'clock yourself, thereby encouraging the direction of the horse's movement. Your horse will soften his nose and "give" to the bit, so his neck bends toward you— *away* from where he steps. The amount of bend depends on your horse and how much pressure you need to use to evoke the correct response. As long as he is not leaning or pulling on your cueing hand, you can release him when his feet respond correctly. Ask for two lateral steps 12 times, then ask for three lateral steps, and so on.

Continue to build *further* until you can achieve at least 12 steps toward the one o'clock position. You are not looking for quick steps; you are more interested in a correct response with "forward shoulder motion," which means that when the left shoulder moves laterally to the right, the

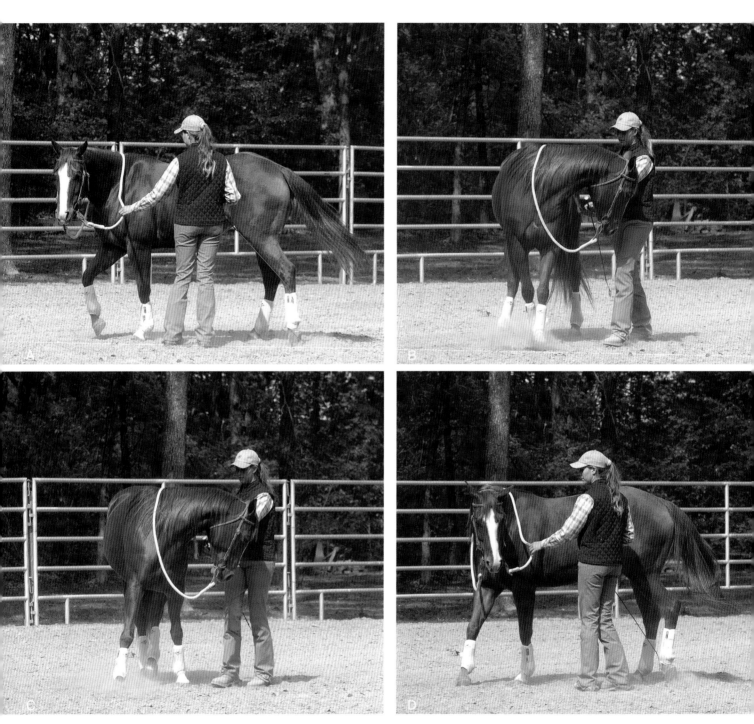

Photos 96 A–D Alisha establishes a slow forward walk with Clash in hand (A). She uses her left rein to maintain a small circle around her, while the dressage whip in her right hand is available for forward-movement cueing. With her left hand on the reins about 6 inches from the slobber strap, Alisha picks up bit pressure and asks for Clash's nose to soften to her hand as the horse's shoulder moves away from her (B). You can see Clash's nose is soft, her neck is level, and her right front foot is stepping toward the one o'clock mark (C). After a correct response and a full release, Alisha asks Clash to again go forward on the circle around her (D). This builds work ethic and promotes proper footwork.

left front foot should *always* pass over *in front* of the *right*. If the horse is stepping *behind* his right foot, use your whip to encourage forward impulsion.

Since you never release your horse when he is leaning on bit pressure, he will turn his nose toward your cueing hand throughout this exercise. In the beginning, as he learns what you are asking for, his neck may bend dramatically as he moves away from you laterally. With more experience, your horse will know that he does not have to bend as much, as long as he responds properly with his feet and "gives" to the bit.

STEP FIVE

Now improve your horse's shoulder motion by asking him to step toward *two o'clock* (photo 97). When you asked the horse to move his shoulder toward one o'clock, you used just as much rein pressure as you needed to make it happen, and as he began to understand, backed off. Now as you ask for more lateral and less forward movement, you may need to apply more rein pressure—hold it *longer* or *increase* it slightly. Since your left hand is positioned only 6 inches from the bit, you can lift the bit upward, as well as toward the horse's neck (this helps to encourage movement *away* from the pressure). As soon as he steps in the two o'clock direction, release the rein pressure and ask him to walk around you in a small circle. By walking the horse forward between requests, you keep his feet moving forward, which helps with the correct foot placement when he moves laterally—*left foot in front of right*.

Just as you did in the Steps Three and Four, ask your horse to perform *one step only*—at least 24 times—and incrementally build your way up to 12 steps in the two o'clock direction. As you ask for successive steps, your horse will, in effect, walk his entire body toward the two o'clock direction, with his neck "counter bent" toward the rein pressure (the horse's nose facing you and *away* from the direction of travel).

Photo 97   Shoulder motion is taught in stages of difficulty. Here Clash's right front foot steps laterally toward the two o'clock mark. Her nose is soft so Alisha will release her once the desired number of steps is taken.

STEP SIX

Ask your horse to step toward the three o'clock position. Begin with one step and work up to 12, as before. If he has *incorrect* foot placement, which happens when the front left steps *behind* the right instead of in front, use your whip and insist he move forward before asking for lateral motion again.

If your horse struggles with the three o'clock position, go back and reestablish two o'clock before trying again.

STEP SEVEN

There are new challenges to absorb when you ask your horse to step toward four o'clock. First, he needs to step *back* with his right foot—in other words it moves laterally but also *backward*. *Forward movement* stops, but *forward motion* is maintained with correct foot placement—that is, the left front continues to pass in front of the right. Second, the horse's right hind remains stationary in order to act like a pivot for the front legs to move around. When he stepped toward three o'clock, his hind end "followed" the rest of his body, but toward four o'clock, he will plant his right hind foot and move his shoulders around it. Picture a reining "turnaround" (spin) where a horse pivots on his right hind and spins to the right. This is a horse stepping toward the four o'clock mark with his right front foot.

Ask your horse to step toward the three o'clock position for a few steps, and as he does, begin "shaping" his steps by walking slightly to your right (clockwise) in a gentle arc around your horse's hind end. Your left hand still maintains rein control and your feet still step into your horse while he turns around his right hind foot. As he starts to move, adjust slightly to your left, closer to your horse's front end to encourage him to step away from pressure. Teach just one step for a while before advancing. Repeat Steps Three and Four with this new position. In the end, you will be able to "step" your horse around his hind end—also known as a "turn on the haunches" (photos 98 A–E).

This is not an easy lesson to teach. Your horse will most likely find stepping toward the one and two o'clock positions quite easy, while the three and four o'clock positions will take him longer. Thus, it is beneficial to remain at the easier level (one and two o'clock) until both you and your horse are really ready to advance.

STEP EIGHT

Now that your horse has successfully managed to get to one o'clock—and all the way to four o'clock—with numerous steps, it is time to check your work. Pick a random clock position and a number of steps in your head, and ask your horse to perform. You might begin with five steps in the two o'clock direction. Then, ask for six steps to four o'clock. By alternating requests, both you and your horse will learn how pressure and handler body position (since you must walk in the correct direction, too) change depending on the destination.

STEP NINE

Repeat the entire groundwork series (Steps One through Eight) from the horse's right side. You only worked from one side—the left—at first to help your horse understand the lesson better and grasp it more quickly. Now, after switching sides you will find he does not understand even the first clock position! This is normal, and it is your job to take the proper amount of time to bring the right side to the same level as the left. Do not rush this work!

Remember that an imaginary clock face is attached to each front foot and that the foot is always in the center of it. Now that you have changed sides and the *left front* moves first, the directions will be toward 11, 10, nine, and eight o'clock.

STEP TEN: MOVING TO SADDLE WORK

After you have completed Steps One to Nine in the groundwork section, it's time to mount up and transfer these new skills to the saddle. You no longer use the dressage whip as your motivator to ask for forward movement, but your legs and vocals (as established in prior lessons), instead.

Note: you are isolating the shoulders and teaching them to respond to only one rein. The motivating pressure and cue for the shoulder motion are both generated from that one rein only. Avoid using leg pressure or the opposing rein to "help" in any way. The horse's response to cues in the end is always much stronger when you have taught a solid foundation from individual cues.

Begin on your horse in the riding arena, and ask him to walk forward a few strides. Hold your rope reins in the middle with your right hand, about 2 inches above the mane, reach down and pick up rein pressure with your left hand to cue your horse to move his shoulders over (to the right, *away* from rein pressure) and move his right front foot to the one o'clock clock position (photo 99). *Do not* pull back on the rein; *lift it* up and hold it directly in front of your saddle horn or pommel. The rein can touch the side of the horse's neck, but should not cross over the mane.

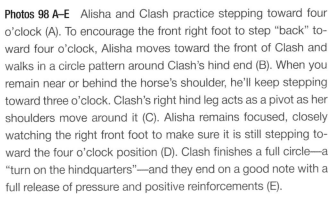

Photos 98 A–E   Alisha and Clash practice stepping toward four o'clock (A). To encourage the front right foot to step "back" toward four o'clock, Alisha moves toward the front of Clash and walks in a circle pattern around Clash's hind end (B). When you remain near or behind the horse's shoulder, he'll keep stepping toward three o'clock. Clash's right hind leg acts as a pivot as her shoulders move around it (C). Alisha remains focused, closely watching the right front foot to make sure it is still stepping toward the four o'clock position (D). Clash finishes a full circle—a "turn on the hindquarters"—and they end on a good note with a full release of pressure and positive reinforcements (E).

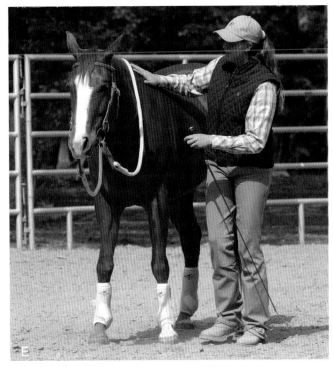

Photo 99 Once mounted, you ask the horse to move the shoulders with a rein cue. Here, Alisha has Clash step toward the one o'clock mark with a left rein cue. Since Clash was taught this motion on the ground first, she "falls on" the correct response much more quickly than if it was newly introduced.

Photos 100 A & B In A, Alisha's cue is incorrect, creating rein pressure across the horse's neck. This effort is not consistent with the shoulder cue that was practiced on the ground, and you can see from Clash's stance that she is confused. It is important to keep the cues as similar as you can—escalating pressure does not mean changing the way a request is made. Your rein should create pressure up and slightly toward the neck as you visualize "pushing" the shoulder over, shown by Alisha in B. As a result, Clash willingly steps toward one o'clock with her right front foot.

When you apply this rein pressure, your horse will "counter bend" to some degree. This is a result of one-sided bit pressure and the horse's desire to "give" to it. As he bends his neck, the rein will "appear" to cross over the mane. That's okay. This can happen with motion *away* from rein pressure. Make sure that your cueing hand applies the bit pressure upward and angled a bit toward the neck of the horse (photos 100 A & B). Remember, pressure is pressure; your horse is looking to avoid it and find his release.

By repeating shoulder motions, you are building muscle memory. Since you need your horse's "automatic responses" to be correct, insist on the right footwork from the start, and then, when you add speed later, you are less likely to have a problem.

As soon as you see and feel your horse move his shoulders *away* from the side with the rein pressure, open your hands and offer a full release. As before, never release while your horse's head is above level height or when he is leaning on the bit.

In between shoulder-motion requests, ask your horse to "follow his nose"—that is, travel straight or in arcing patterns—by using your *hip motion cue* (see Lesson 16, p. 131). This allows you to steer your horse around the arena and helps him to decipher between the two cues that you are using—shoulder away motion versus hip away motion. Remember, the shoulder motion cue is a *lift up* of the rein, whereas the hip motion cue is a *draw back of the rein* toward the horse's hip. When you draw your rein toward

Photos 101 A & B   As I walk a circle in A, I ask Belle to take a step toward two o'clock by lifting my left hand and creating upward pressure on the left side of the bit. Belle responds in B with a nice step in the desired direction. Note Belle's soft nose and neck bend in both photos, and also that I am not putting any pressure on the right side of the bit with my right hand.

the horse's hip, guiding him in the direction you want to go, be certain to only release him when he responds properly. Then, pick up your shoulder cue and ask for a step toward one o'clock again. As you go back and forth, your horse will begin to recognize your different rein cues and learn how to respond accordingly.

Ask your horse to move his shoulder to the right, stepping toward the one o'clock mark, a couple dozen times.

STEP ELEVEN

Continuing at the walk, only release your horse when his right front takes *two steps* toward one o'clock. Work on two steps a dozen times, then three steps a dozen times, and so forth, until you can achieve 12 good steps in that direc-

tion. The most important thing is to release *only* when your horse is taking "good" steps. If you release him as he is slowing down, raising his head, leaning on the bit, or using incorrect footwork, you slow the learning process.

As he takes multiple steps in the one o'clock direction, you'll travel an angled path across the arena. His nose should look left a bit and be soft to your hand. If your horse "roots" his nose or leans on the bit, withhold your release until he "gives."

STEP TWELVE

While walking forward, ask your horse to step toward two o'clock (photos 101 A & B). You need to add more rein pressure. As soon as he takes the proper step, release and allow

Photos 102 A & B Alisha asks Clash to step toward three o'clock. Alisha's position isn't ideal—her upper body could be quieter (straighter) and her cueing hand should be lifting up, above the saddle horn, rather than off the corner of the saddle swell. Nevertheless, Clash's footwork is good, as you see her left front foot passing in front of her right front foot in A, and a good sideways step toward three o'clock with her right foot in B.

him to walk forward on a slack rein. Begin by asking for one good step two-dozen times. Then, ask for two steps. Work on two steps a dozen times followed by three steps, and so forth, until you can achieve twelve good steps in a row.

When you apply firm rein pressure, your horse will bend his neck toward your hand. Only release him when he is "giving" to your hand. The height of his neck will likely be higher than ideal in the early stages of this exercise, but as long as he is not bracing or leaning on the pressure, or showing signs of avoidance behavior, it's acceptable at this stage. Your end goal is of course a level neck line and a "soft face"; however, now it's more important to focus on correct footwork and proper "giving" to the bit.

STEP THIRTEEN

Walk your horse forward, pick up your rein cue, and ask him to move his shoulders toward the three o'clock mark—just one step at this point. You may have to pick up a bit

more pressure or hold your cue until the horse finds the right answer. Continue asking for *further* steps as you did with earlier positions (photos 102 A & B).

Your horse is moving to the right, and his hips will likely be slower than the shoulders. This is all right—you are not performing a side-pass. You are isolating the shoulders for teaching purposes and should not be concerned yet with the nose and hips being in complete alignment.

You are teaching your horse to "give" his shoulders, but be aware, at this stage his "shape" will not resemble that of a finished bridle horse.

STEP FOURTEEN

With your clock face in mind, think about the different angles of various lateral movements to the right. A half-pass, a move that is forward and sideways, angles halfway between one and two o'clock on the clock face. A side-pass angles toward three o'clock, and a turnaround or spin requires the horse take his right front foot and place it toward the four o'clock mark. Think of a back-up as a shoulder motion toward the six o'clock position, while walking straight forward is toward noon. All these different angles of shoulder motion are obtained by varying amounts of rein pressure.

You introduced the four o'clock foot position from the ground (see Step Seven, p. 169), and you have built up to it methodically from his back. Walk forward, pick up your rein, and ask for a step toward three o'clock. As he steps in this direction, increase your rein pressure and hold steady—you are looking for his right front foot to take a step toward the four o'clock position. The only way he can do this is to step over toward three o'clock, but also back a bit.

Your horse will try to figure out how to avoid the added rein pressure. He might respond in a variety of ways— speeding up his feet, walking forward, raising his head, or some other evasion—but only give a release when he takes his right front foot and puts it toward four o'clock.

Practice getting one step many times. Once the horse begins to understand the request, you can ask for that one step from a standstill, making sure that the left front always passes in front of the right. When it does not, ride forward again, and give it another go. You teach your horse the step from a standstill because a "finished" turnaround maneuver begins and ends at a standstill.

When you ask for two steps toward four o'clock, your horse will begin to plant his right hind foot (as he did in the groundwork series) and his hind end will remain stationary as his shoulders move around it. This action is the beginning of your turnaround—also called a "turn on the haunches" (see photos 103 A–H, p. 176). Build the response slowly, asking for many repetitions at each step level before asking for more. In time, you can use less rein pressure, allowing your horse to perform the motion with a "straighter" body since he will not need to counter bend as before.

STEP FIFTEEN

Now mix up your requests and ask for the four foot positions to the right in different order, with a different number of steps for each. This exercise underlines the importance of varying rein pressures and correct responses.

As you mix up the different clock positions, start to cue with the lightest rein pressure possible (*softer*). Your ultimate goal, as with all the work in the Countdown, is to get your horse working off the smallest amount of pressure possible.

STEP SIXTEEN

Switch sides and repeat Steps One through Fifteen, now moving the horse's shoulders to the left with your right rein. Focus on the horse's left front foot landing on your imaginary clock's 11, 10, nine, and eight o'clock positions (photos 103 A–H).

Rider's Block

● If you really struggle with the three or four o'clock positions, ask for an assistant on the ground to help. He can tell you whether your horse's foot is stepping toward the correct time, thus letting you know exactly when you should release.

● You must encourage correct footwork. Repetition is the only way to build the horse's muscle memory, so he can eventually give you an "automatic response."

● This lesson *cannot* be taught in a one-day session— not by any means. The groundwork alone may take four days—or longer. The saddle work may also take a while— it depends on your horse and the quality of your releases.

● As I mentioned, your horse is going to be confused by the cues for hip motion versus those for shoulder motion. For a while, it will feel as if you have lost your steering. This is normal. Just remember, *only* release your horse when he gives you the response you want.

● Your horse's legs cross over a lot in this lesson. As always, it is prudent to put good protective boots on all four legs. I recommend also using "bell boots" or "overreach boots" that cover the coronet band.

Photos 103 A–H Alisha and Clash work on the beginnings of a turnaround (spin) to the left. Alisha lifts her right hand to give the cue for Clash to step with her left front foot leftward and back toward eight o'clock. Throughout, Clash's right front foot steps in front of her left front foot, her neck stays level, and her nose soft to the bit.

Intermittent Breaks

Taking breaks from work is good for both of you. Whenever your horse is performing an exercise well and you are at a good place to stop the lesson, take the opportunity to just sit quietly on your horse and relax. At an appropriate time in your training session, you can even dismount and tie your horse up for a short break before continuing. You will be amazed at how mental and physical rest positively affects performance.

● When you are working on achieving a set number of steps—say, eight in the three o'clock direction—and you feel your horse's left front foot is about to step behind his right front, which is *incorrect*, stop the motion altogether or walk forward and release him *before* he makes the mistake. You need to adjust your expectations from time to time, which does not mean that your goals change or that you look for less of a response, just that when your horse becomes confused, you recognize it and make the work easy to understand again until he begins to respond better.

Lesson 11's Benefits

● First, you teach your horse to move his shoulders over in a precise manner in response to a specific rein cue. This is a key building block in his education. Second, you insist on *proper footwork* by only releasing him when he moves over correctly. Third, your horse learns to "soften his face" even more since you never release while he leans or pulls on the bit. Fourth, your horse's confidence level increases dramatically. And finally, your own ability to recognize a precise foot placement improves.

Green Light

Before you move on, take the time to teach this lesson carefully with much repetition and cueing for every possible response. In the next lesson you ask the horse to move his shoulders laterally with speed (*faster*). If you horse does not understand this exercise at the walk and standstill, you will find it difficult to go on with the Countdown.

Shoulder Serpentines and Circles

Goals

You want to strengthen the *shoulder motion cue* taught in Lesson 11 (p. 165), where the horse's shoulder moves laterally *away* from rein pressure, by practicing it at a walk and standstill, and adding the jog and lope. You will request it in both directions, alternating from one rein to the other. You are aiming for an accurate response from the lightest possible rein cue (a lighter rein cue allows your horse to remain aligned, with his neck only bending slightly toward the rein pressure) while he still offers you a soft face as he "gives" to the bit.

Check-In

The horse's response to a shoulder motion cue must be automatic—to both the right and the left—before you add speed and alternating cues. It is best to warm up by reviewing the work in Lesson 11. This way, the correct response is fresh in your horse's mind before you increase difficulty.

Teaching Steps

STEP ONE

Ride your horse forward at a walk with your reins completely slack. Pick up one rein and cue your horse to step toward two or 10 o'clock—depending on the direction you start with—as you did in Lesson 11 (photos 104 A & B). If your horse "gives" his face softly to the bit—bending his neck slightly toward the rein—and correctly steps in the right direction, *release* him after six steps. (The number of steps is a guide-

line and should be adjusted depending on the response you get.) Should he lean on the bit, require added rein pressure, or take steps anywhere but toward the two or 10 o'clock direction, keep cueing him with the rein until he does it right. This rein pressure is your *motivator* as well as your *cue*.

Once your horse "gives" and you have a chance to release him, allow him to walk a few steps with slack reins. Next, pick up the opposite rein and ask for the same response in the other direction. Alternate this request from side to side. The pattern you ride will look like a series of large arcs, similar to the hip serpentine exercise (see Lesson 16, p. 131). As you repeat the maneuver, your horse will become progressively softer and easier to guide.

Work for 10 minutes, followed by a break, and then 10 minutes performing hip serpentines to remind your horse that he is not supposed to always move *away* from rein pressure, and that he needs to recognize the difference between rein cues. Left rein pressure, resulting in the horse "following his nose" round to the left, is used to move the hips to the right, as well as to move the left shoulder laterally to the right. Since the two cues— hip and shoulder—are different, it will take repetition and correct releases to teach your horse how to respond. Expect your horse to confuse these two cues at first, and only release when he gives you the correct answer.

After a break, repeat Step One— shoulder motion to two or 10 o'clock

Photos 104 A & B Here, I ask Belle to step toward two o'clock, and she responds, crossing her left front foot in front of her right. Steering a horse with shoulder motion feels a lot different than hip motion. Instead of having the hind end swing around when you cue the horse with your rein, as I am here, the front end engages and makes the effort to move for you. It helps to visualize the shoulder moving toward the requested mark. This helps you stay consistent the next time you make the same request. If you think the same, your body will most likely act the same.

for 10 minutes, a break, and 10 minutes of hip serpentines. Repeat these sessions until your horse responds well to both exercises.

STEP ONE QUICK-CHECK

▶ Does your horse move away from pressure toward two and 11 o'clock consistently with a "soft face" and willing steps?

▶ Will your horse take at least six steps without a missed step or break in motion?

▶ Can you perform hip serpentines without your horse confusing the hip and shoulder cues?

▶ Is your horse more relaxed than when you began?

STEP TWO

While at the walk with slack reins, pick up one rein and cue your horse to move his shoulder toward the three or nine o'clock position. Start by asking for only two steps. Since you worked on two and 10 o'clock in the previous step, it can take a minute for your horse to get his *release*. You might have to increase pressure and hold it steady. As soon as he responds correctly, release, and let him walk forward a few steps. Now, pick up the opposite rein and request a movement toward the three or nine o'clock mark.

Begin building your response *further* by asking for three, four, five, and then six shoulder-motion steps. Be sure your horse walks forward between requests to encourage correct foot placement. If he stops, add legs and vocals to get his feet moving again, and *only* release him while he is in motion.

Continue building this response and see how subtle your cue can be (*softer*). Mix up the number of steps you ask for in a 10-minute session and follow with a break. Work 10 minutes at a time, with breaks, until you come to a point where you can finish the day on a good note.

STEP TWO QUICK-CHECK

▶ Does your horse consistently move away from pressure toward the three and nine o'clock marks with a "soft face" and willing steps?

Photo 105 Here we do a quarter-turn on the hindquarters: Belle is crossing over with her right front foot before stepping toward the four o'clock mark with her left front foot while pivoting on a stationary left hind foot. My right rein gives the upward cue, while my left rein remains slack.

▶ Will your horse take at least six steps in the requested direction without a missed step or break in motion?

▶ Is your horse more relaxed than when you began?

STEP THREE

From a standstill ask your horse to take two steps toward four or eight o'clock. As before, when you ask for more shoulder motion, you may need to use more pressure or hold the pressure longer. Once he takes two good steps, *release* and sit quietly on his back. Wait for five seconds (or longer) and ask again. Repeat on the same side a couple dozen times, offering breaks after every response. Switch sides and repeat the process.

After he's made two good steps numerous times on both sides, he is ready for more consecutive steps. So,

from a resting position, ask your horse to pivot on his hind end—cueing the shoulder to move toward the four or eight o'clock mark—one-quarter of a circle, or about three or four (photo 105). Immediately upon completion, ask him to walk forward. After a number of repetitions, ask your horse to stop and back up three steps (cue with both your reins). Release your horse on a good back-up response.

After a short break, pick up the opposite rein and pivot your horse around his hind end one-quarter circle in the other direction. Again, immediately ask your horse to walk forward after the request, back up three steps, and release him. Repeat this routine until you find that your cues can be soft, your horse is relaxed, and you are seeing consistent results.

Note: at this time, it is best to not ask for more steps than is necessary to complete one quarter of a circle.

STEP THREE QUICK-CHECK

▶ Does your horse consistently move away from pressure toward the four and eight o'clock marks with a "soft face" and willing steps?

▶ Does he pivot one quarter of a circle without a missed step or break in movement?

▶ Is your horse more relaxed than when you began?

▶ Is your rein cue becoming light and only offsetting the horse's nose a few inches?

STEP FOUR

Repeat Step One at the jog (photo 106).

STEP FIVE

Repeat Step Three at the jog.

STEP SIX

Choose an area in your riding arena where you can travel in a circle that is 70 feet in diameter. "Hold" this circle at

Photo 106 Expect your horse to lose some responsiveness as you add speed. Remember, even at the jog, the teaching method remains the same: hold the cue or motivator until the desired response is given. Make sure to only use one rein during this exercise in order to isolate the control point—the shoulder—as I am here.

Photo 107 With your inside rein you can now control your horse's front end without moving his hip or taking his nose out of position. Here, my inside rein guides Belle back onto the circle pattern. I keep her body "shaped" (bent) to the circle, while asking her to respond to the rein cue.

the jog with only your "inside" rein (the rein closest to the center of the circle).

Grasp the middle of the rope reins with the hand to the outside of the circle. If your horse *drifts in* toward the middle of the circle, cue the *inside shoulder* with the *inside* rein to move back on the circle track. If he *drifts out*, use the same *inside* rein to move his *inside hip* over and ask him to follow his nose back in to the circle. Your "outside" rein, the one furthest from the center of the circle, remains completely slack (photo 107).

This exercise helps the horse understand the difference between the two cues—shoulder and hip—even though they both come from the same rein, and also helps strengthen your *go forward cue.*

Jog these circles for five minutes, rest and sit quietly, then switch directions. Resting your horse between sustained exercises allows him to catch his breath, relax, and realize that when given the opportunity to rest, he should take advantage of it.

STEP SEVEN

Perform Step Six at the lope. Expect your horse to lose

some of his responsiveness to the rein cues as you add more speed. If the problem is minor, keep at it, only releasing your horse when he is on the correct circle pattern. If you have great difficulty getting him to respond, take a step back and work on Step Six again—or go back even further—to reestablish your shoulder motion and hip motion cues.

You want your horse to perform circles with minimal guidance and with a steady cadence. He may require constant cueing in the beginning, but whenever he decides to travel his own path, put him back on the circle. Your horse may also try to speed up or slow down. Insist that he remain at the lope and, in time, he will relax and not surge forward or "stall out" because when he slows down you always "hassle" him with leg bumping and vocal cues. This builds his work ethic. In Lesson 8 (p. 189), I'll take this further.

Rider's Block

● Your goal throughout this training program is to keep your horse free and clear of pressure when his behavior is what you want. So, when you ask your horse to travel in a circle at the jog or lope and he does, be sure to keep pressure off his mouth. By doing this, his neck will stay level, and he'll become much more trusting and responsive to the bit when you do need to use rein pressure.

● These are *one-rein exercises* and the cues should only come from *one* side of the horse at a time. Do not try to "help" your horse by using your second rein. Remember, this is a teaching process—performing a jog or lope circle is not your goal, as most horses can already do this. You are trying to build a *foundation of cues* that will be used to shape your horse's behavior and bring it to a much higher level. Later on, you will use the second rein, but for the time being, both you and your horse need to isolate each cue and learn it fully.

● Give your horse a chance to "work off less." This means that your cues should never be any firmer than they need to be. If, at any point your horse is not responding, pick up rein pressure. A subsequent request should then again be light, giving your horse a chance to "work off less."

Roadblocks

● If you have a "dull" horse, it may take more time to get him soft and working off light cues. Your approach to training should not change; however, use the amount of pressure necessary to obtain the requested response. As he improves, he'll work off a more subtle cue. Conversely, you may have a "sensitive" horse that does not require much pressure at all. This is where the teaching principle, "As much as necessary, as little as possible," comes into play. (Thanks to Ray Hunt for popularizing this great concept!)

● If your horse loses his desire to move forward, use an appropriate amount of pressure to make it happen—*every* time. By not insisting on forward movement whenever you ask, you can create a new problem. When the horse's feet are not moving, your ability to teach him ends, as well.

Lesson 10's Benefits

● In Lesson 11 (p. 165) you began to show your horse how to respond to the new shoulder motion cue. In this lesson you've added speed, changes in direction, and various patterns. All of these teach your horse how to find his release from pressure in different situations.

● As you progress to working your horse in a faster gait, you will find that he becomes softer at the slower ones.

Green Light

Never settle for "good enough"—this will likely only cause miscommunication as you add and combine more cues in the coming lessons. Make sure to work on this lesson until you can achieve a great response off a light cue. When your horse shows a poor response, whether now or later, revisit the exercise in question and teach it again. A cue is only truly "taught" when your horse responds 100 percent of the time.

Collection

A highly collected horse—that is, a horse in self-carriage—is beautiful to watch, and even more incredible to ride. *Collection* in a horse is mental as well as physical, and must be built up slowly with each exercise. A collected horse rounds his back and brings his hind end forward, up and under the bulk of his own weight, with the hocks not extending out behind him, but rather remaining under his barrel and reaching forward with each stride. At the same time, the horse's front end is light and elevated, in preparation for a change or continuation of movement (photo 108).

A collected horse can carry his head at different elevations and neck shapes, depending on the breed and type of competition involved. As long as the elevation of the head and shape of the neck is healthy for the horse and does not require the rider to hold the position through rein pressure, your horse can be collected.

Collection and Nose-Softening—Part I

Goals

Now you will show your horse how to collect himself. You are looking for a rounded back, engaged hind end, level neckline, break at the poll, and a "soft nose." Collection is taught using the combination of two previously learned responses: the horse "giving" you his nose and engaging his hips with forward movement.

Check-In

Throughout the Countdown you have set yourself up for success by always insisting that your horse "gets off" bit pressure. This means that he is never allowed to lean or pull on the reins. He has learned to stay away from bit pressure by softening his nose, as he understands that a release will not come when he doesn't.

You have had ample time to teach your horse to be responsive to your legs and vocals. You will now ask him for two things: one, keep his nose soft to the bit—meaning that he cannot lean or pull against it—and two, respond to your leg bumping by engaging his hindquarters. The result will be his hind end taking a small step forward, while his front feet do not move forward at all. The nose will "give" to the bit—moving in the direction of the horse's chest—as much or as little as you ask for it.

This is just the beginning of "collection." The goal is not to ask for a high level of "compression" of the body or self-carriage, but rather to begin the process of teaching him to

respect both the rein and leg pressure simultaneously, giving you the ability to shape the horse's neck and face while encouraging a stronger, more balanced movement.

Cues to Use

While there are no new cues taught here, there is a new combination of them: you ask your horse to "give" his nose with the same rein cue you use for backing-up, while at the same time your body tells the horse to move forward with leg bumping. Since he cannot move forward—out of his respect for the bit—his only option is to move his hind end forward and compress his body, even if the slightest amount.

Spot, Direction, Motivator, and Release

Spot Nose and hind feet
Direction Nose—toward chest; hind feet—toward front feet
Motivator Nose—bit pressure; hind feet—legs and vocals
Release A complete removal of any pressure

Teaching Steps
STEP ONE
Warm up your horse by walking, jogging, and loping various patterns and reviewing exercises from previous lessons. This lesson is best taught when your horse is relaxed and attentive. Since you will "trap" the front end with your reins while asking for the hind end to move forward, you

Note: the horse's hind feet should not move backward, only forward. His front feet must stay still.

Photos 109 A & B I ask Belle's front end to remain behind the bit pressure—not leaning on it—while also asking for forward movement with my legs. At first, she is not quite sure what to do to find her release. I have to pick up more rein pressure to keep her from walking forward (A). As Belle begins to understand my request, her hind end starts to "walk itself" up under her body (B). I am waiting for her nose to "give" to the bit pressure, at which point I'll give her a full release. She is learning that to get away from both motivators—leg bumping and bit pressure—she must bring her nose and tail closer together, or "ball up."

want your horse to respond to both the bit and leg before you begin.

At a standstill in your arena, gently pick up both reins and take the slack out until you can "feel" your horse's mouth with both hands. At the same time, begin bumping your legs gently as if asking him to move forward. As you hold your hands steady—still feeling the mouth—and use your legs, the horse will need to figure out what you are after. If he steps forward, increase the bit pressure. If he steps backward, increase your leg pressure. If he softens his nose and "gives" to your hands, release all pressure and let him relax. You are looking for the slightest try at this point. It may only be a small response, with the nose "giving" an inch or so, but reward the effort.

If you miss the release point, your horse will take longer to understand the request, so remain attentive and ready to offer the immediate removal of pressure. Your horse may sidestep, back up, or walk through the bit as he tries to find the answer. As soon as he sees the release comes while he softens his nose and remains still, he will begin to "get it."

STEP TWO

Once you can release on the first small "give," sit quietly and reward your horse with a neck rub. Pick up your reins and ask for the same response. At this time, be content with a "soft nose"—one that is not leaning or pulling on the bit—and your horse remaining still.

After a dozen small "gives" go back to jogging shoulder or hip serpentines for 10 minutes (see Lesson 16, p. 131, and Lesson 10, p. 179). After a break, ask for another dozen "gives." Once you are sure your horse knows to soften his nose to the bit and understands that he shouldn't back up, sidestep, or walk forward, Step Three will be easier.

STEP THREE

Now hold rein pressure and wait for your horse to take a small step under his body with his hind end (photos 109 A & B). As before, he is going to feel the rein pressure as well as your leg bumping and begin to look for a response. You previously released him when he "gave" his nose so he should respond with that first—but you want more this time. As soon as he starts to move either hind foot forward—even a tiny step—offer a full release.

You are teaching the horse to move his hind end and front end closer together, while staying off the bit. This frame or position is known as "balling up," "collecting," "the wheel," "sucking up," or "being in frame"—and I am sure there is more lingo that applies.

Continue working on this response until your horse consistently brings his hind end and front end closer together, while remaining off the bit. See just how light you can be with your hands and legs while "balling up" your horse.

Rider's Block

● Let your horse know that rein pressure is coming! When you pick up heavy rope reins, he should feel the cue is on its way, and once you reach the point of contact, keep your movement smooth and fair—never do it with quick, unexpected force. You are attempting to build trust. Your horse will not trust your hands if you are unfair, and you'll notice signs of *avoidance behavior* (see p. 78).

● Your horse may become confused with this request and offer you a back-up instead. This is actually a good sign; it means that he is trying to find the answer. *Think* "forward," as this affects your balance. Keep pushing him forward with your legs, as you ask for a soft nose with your reins, and only release him on the right answer.

● A "hard-mouthed" horse is one that has not experienced fair and timely releases—if he has ever been truly released from pressure at all. If you apply a lot of rein pressure and "muscle" a response, you just teach him this is the cue, and of course, it is what will most likely be necessary the next time. So, always pick up the rein pressure giving him enough room to respond on his own: when you hold or "muscle" his nose too close to his chest, there is nowhere for your horse to go to escape the pressure.

● This is a form of "trap"—a situation causing constriction, claustrophobia, and restrictive movement. If your horse gets upset during this lesson, mix it up with some moving exercises and keep your teaching steps small. Work on getting many small "gives" over a number of days, weeks, months, and even years! *Never* jump straight to the difficult steps, such as holding a collected position for a long time.

● Carefully watch your horse's response as you do not want to miss your release point. The more consistent you are at releasing the moment he responds well, the quicker he will learn.

● Never release your horse when his neck is higher than level. If his head is not low and relaxed, it may be because you are: applying pressure unfairly; not releasing at the appropriate time; using too much or holding pressure too long; or asking for too much too soon.

Roadblocks

● You may have a horse that is not "trap friendly." This means he is not comfortable when his flight option is taken away, or he just hates being constricted. This type of horse can be more difficult to teach, but by showing fairness and building his confidence, you can prove to him that it's worth the effort—with repetition, consistency, and predictability,

Improving One Thing

As you set out to train your horse, each day remember to *always improve at least one thing*. It may be getting a response from a *softer* cue or taught *further* or *faster*, or it may be a confidence-building exercise. You can choose something easy...it does not have to be a difficult lesson, but make sure that your time on the horse's back is productive!

full well-timed releases work! Your horse learns that "giving" is the best and easiest option.

● Horses that do not naturally "give" to pressure (lack sensitivity), or those with poor conformation that makes it difficult for them to bring their hind end underneath their body and "round" their back, can be harder to teach collection. But even if a horse's body is not capable of a high level of collection—like a well-bred dressage or reining horse—you can still teach him to "give" to pressure and respond well to your cues. Making him into a "picture-perfect" performance horse does not have to be your goal—teaching him to "give" to pressure as you build a skill set and develop his confidence should be.

Lesson 9's Benefits

● You are increasing the level of communication between you and your horse. Slowly but surely he is learning to deci-pher your cues as you teach new ones and combine established ones.

● The ability to pick up the reins and soften your horse's nose is an important measure toward building a "bridle" horse. By introducing the concept in this fair and easily understood manner, the next phase in his training will not seem like a vast leap.

Green Light

Before moving ahead, be sure that you can perform this exercise from a standstill and with a light cue. Spread this out over a number of days—I like to use it as one of my cooling-down exercises.

Collection and Nose-Softening—Part II

Goals

You want to encourage early stages of collection and a "soft nose" with both reins, while the horse is moving forward and responding to *shoulder motion cues*. You want your horse to accept and "give" to both sides of the bit as he travels.

This new exercise will introduce a new "feel" to your horse: he has not yet been asked to go forward with both reins picked up. Your aim is to show him how to respond from the additional control you now have over his nose and neck.

Check-In

In Lesson 9 you taught your horse how to collect himself while at a standstill. That exercise taught the horse to respond to two simultaneous cues—the rein cue to keep his nose in and the *go forward cue* to move his hind feet forward.

With understanding that combination, your horse is now ready to learn how to find his release as you ask for a "soft nose" and early stages of "collection" while in motion and performing shoulder serpentines and circles. If your horse is not yet light and willing when doing one-rein shoulder serpentines (see Lesson 10, p. 179) or collecting himself easily at the standstill (see Lesson 9, p. 185), it is best to wait until he is. These prerequisites are important.

Cues to Use

While there are no new cues in this lesson, you now ask the horse to respond to both simultaneous cues *and* a new "feel." Use your legs and vocals to ask for forward movement, and one rein to move his shoulders over and the other to "give" so his nose looks toward the direction his shoulders are going (photo 110).

Teaching Steps

STEP ONE: SHOULDER SERPENTINES AT A JOG

Begin by practicing some shoulder serpentines at the jog with one rein for 10 minutes. If this exercise goes well, move ahead with Step One. If not, spend as many 10-minute sessions—interspersed with breaks—as necessary to get the correct response.

Ask for a jog to the left. Pick up both reins lightly and with the *outside* rein ask the horse to step left (toward 10 o'clock). Your *inside* rein applies just enough bit pressure to keep his nose from looking away from the turn. At this stage of training, you want his nose to be a few inches "off" straight, as he bends his body and looks into his turn.

Your "outside" rein is the rein furthest from the center of a circle, arc, or direction of turn. The "inside" rein is the one closest to the center of the circle, arc or turn.

Only ask for a couple of steps at first, and as soon as you get them—with his neck bent into the turn

You may have had great success in the past with one-rein shoulder serpentines, but this does not guarantee that you will today! Never assume a horse remembers anything from one day to the next. Check his responses and use previous lessons as warm-up exercises before trying to advance to something new.

Photo 110 Here my right hand cues Belle's right shoulder laterally away from the rein, while my left hand supports her nose and neck shape with a steady rein pressure. I'm asking Belle to move leftward with a "soft nose" with her shoulders leading the way. The support rein is helping her look into the turn and keep both shoulders upright and balanced.

Photos 111 A–E I begin in a relaxed jog with slack reins, then pick up the reins evenly with my left hand as the inside support rein (holding Belle's nose just slightly inside the turn) and my right hand as the active teaching rein cueing the shoulder to the left (A).

slightly, his nose softened to the bit pressure, and his head kept level with his withers—offer a full release as you continue at the jog. He will be *bending* and *looking* into the turn. Let him travel a number of steps without any pressure on the reins (photos A–C).

Next, pick up the reins and cue the horse to turn to the right in the same fashion (photos D & E). Only look for two good steps. This is all new for your horse as he has not felt both sides of his mouth pressured while he is moving.

As you pick up the reins and cue your horse to turn, your horse might react in a variety of ways. One, he may transition down to a walk—immediately push him back up to the jog. Two, he may raise his head when he feels rein pressure—ask with less pressure and continue to cue until he responds appropriately. Three, he might move his hip

over, as he mistakes your inside rein cue for a hip motion cue—use less pressure with this rein and add a bit more to your outside rein. Remember, the inside rein is simply "shaping" and positioning your horse's neck and face.

How much "face" do you want from your horse? At first you look for only a small "give," holding the correct position—looking toward his turn a few inches—and tucking his chin toward his chest the slightest amount. Just because your horse "gives" to the bit well does not mean that you should encourage a dramatic overbending of his neck—not by any means. The amount of *vertical flexion* (nose moving toward the chest) you ask for depends on your horse and the discipline you ride. True, a good horse will respond to this cue, but a good horseman does not ask for a position that is unhealthy or uncomfortable for his horse.

Photos 111 A–E cont.   I am looking for two responses simultane- ously: first, Belle should move left through her shoulders, and second, she should soften her nose to the bit pressure (B). Since I get the desired response, I offer a full release (C). Here the release does not necessarily look full, as Belle holds her nose in, but there is no pressure coming from my hands. Now I pick up my reins and cue her shoulders toward the right—my left rein is my active teaching rein while the inside right rein is my support rein (D). I again offer a full release once Belle moves softly through the cue (E).

In training circles, you will hear references to "giving face," "chin tucking," "softening his nose," or "being inside of the vertical." All refer to the shape a horse's head and neck make as you ask him to bring his nose toward his chest. This shape does not necessarily mean that the horse is correctly "collected," although this can be the case (see p. 184). A horse that "holds" this position does not have to "give" to the bit either. In riding disciplines where contact is normal, horses can learn to lean on the bit and rely on it for leverage and guidance. This is not particular to one discipline, as trail riders, ropers, hunt seat riders, dressage riders, and many others can all fall into this habit. The common goal, whether English or Western, or even in harness, is to have a horse that always "gives" to the bit while carrying himself "better."

At the jog, continue to pick up both reins and cue the horse to turn in this way, alternating from left to right. The pattern will resemble a serpentine, but you are not concerned with the pattern as much as you are good movement and proper "gives." Keep your horse jogging for a full 10 minutes. Take a break, and repeat. Each 10-minute session, add a step to the right or left. You might spend an entire training session working on this exercise alone—two to four 10-minute workouts. Work on Step One a number of times over a number of days before moving on to Step Two.

STEP TWO: LOPE CIRCLES

You can now add the second rein while loping circles. In Lesson 10 (p. 179) you began using a *shoulder motion cue* to help steer your horse in a circle. Now you will pick up both reins and ask for a "soft nose" while the horse bends and looks into his turn.

Begin by jogging a circle approximately 70 feet in diameter. Complete one or two circles to show your horse where he needs to travel. Ask for a lope departure with leg bumping and vocal cues.

As long as your horse is on the circle pattern, leave him alone. If he transitions down on his own, use appropriate leg pressure and vocals to move him back up to the lope. And if he drifts toward the center of the circle, lightly pick up both reins. Your *inside rein* actively cues the *inside shoulder* to move back toward the circle's path, and your *outside rein* holds steady pressure while both reins "soften" the horse's nose. As soon as he is back on track, release all rein pressure and continue loping.

When your horse "fades out" of the circle or turns his nose away from the center, again pick up both reins lightly. Use your *outside rein* to cue the *outside shoulder* back toward the circle. Your *inside rein* holds the horse's nose so he's "looking in" toward the center, and both reins together are used to "soften" it. As soon as your horse is back on the circle pattern, release all rein pressure and continue loping.

If you feel your horse is not responding well, immediately go back to shoulder serpentines at the jog (see Step One, p. 189). This "step back" will review his release and response to your cues. Then attempt the lope circles again. Repeat this process, remembering to always end on a good note. And if that means ending at the jog, that is fine.

You are cueing your horse differently as he advances in the Countdown, which is your goal; however, never think it is wrong to deal with a problem by "reworking" a basic response with a basic cue. For example, if your horse lets his left shoulder—a control point—drift toward the center of the circle while loping counterclockwise, you might want to reestablish what the inside rein means by reviewing Lesson 11 (p. 165). This way you can "isolate the control point" and deal directly with the left shoulder by itself and gain control over it again.

Rider's Block

● This exercise asks for your horse to soften his nose, while he moves his shoulders. You are not asking him to curl up with his nose tucked toward his chest—you want him to "give" to the bit at the same time he is responding to another cue. This is the beginning of asking a horse to "hold" a head and neck position. He should never rely on bit pressure to carry himself. "Self-carriage" is what you are looking for—your horse should be balanced and collected without restraint of any kind.

● You isolate each control point—shoulders, hips, and the nose—in the Countdown to Broke. You have one or more cues to use to control each point. Isolating them helps you adjust to failure (and success) during an exercise. When you see a shoulder moving out of the circle, bring it back in; the nose looks in the wrong direction, shape the neck with your reins; if your pressure is too strong on one side and not enough on the other, adjust your hands. Time spent working hard on individual parts, gives you the ability to solve more complex problems on the fly!

Lesson 8's Benefits

● You have shown your horse how he needs to respond to two reins when moving forward. You can bend his nose in the direction of travel, whether straight or turning, as well have him soften it to your hands.

● Use shoulder serpentines daily. They are a wonderful way to warm up—they gain your horse's attention (actively seeking a response), soften his face ("giving" to bit pressure), and flex him laterally (bending and "giving" while being turned), while improving shoulder control and motion. It is also an exercise that does not deplete all energy, leaving more "fuel in the tank" for new lessons.

Green Light

Perfecting lope circles and gaining impeccable shoulder

Being Open-Minded

In the horse community, *everyone* is always trying to learn more, amateurs and professionals alike. When you ask questions—and you should ask as many as you can—horse people love to share their own knowledge and experience. I encourage you to pose lots of questions whenever you can in a sincere manner, so you are not misinterpreted as merely "challenging" a horseman's practices.

There are many styles and methods of horsemanship that work. Each variation can teach you something new and is worth investigating. Be open to new ideas and different disciplines, and try to see how their "style" can help you with yours.

control with a "soft nose" is an ongoing process. You will spend a lot of time reviewing these exercises as you progress with your horse. Before you move on in the Countdown, you should be able to perform both Step One and Step Two with a very soft rein cue.

As I've said many times, you always want your horse to respond from the lightest cue possible. As you move to the lope, you may need to use more pressure. However, your next request should not be as firm. This way, your horse has a choice to respond to the softer cue—or not. If he does, you can release him. If not, increase pressure and cue him until he does. By always giving him a choice, in time, he will learn to "respond from less." Without this choice, he will always need a strong cue.

Cueing Hip Motion in Response to Leg Pressure

Goals

You will teach your horse to move his hip over in response to a leg cue (in place of the rein cue taught earlier, see Lesson 23, p. 89). This cue is taught with the horse at a standstill. The end result is a horse that "turns on the forehand" (his hind end pivots around his front end, which remains stationary) without the use of rein pressure.

Check-In

In order to teach this leg cue you must have confirmed hip motion from a rein cue, as you did back in Lesson 23. Since that time, you have only used your legs to speed up your horse's feet. Since *basic* forward and backward movement is so important to establish with a young or untrained horse, it's best to wait until now to introduce this new leg cue.

Cues to Use

Your new *hip motion cue* comes from your leg. Say you want to move to the *right*—you cue the *left hip* by sliding your *left leg* back and resting your heel or spur on your horse's barrel a few inches behind the front cinch, but in front of the rear cinch. Your calf muscle should be resting on the horse's side. Eventually, when the cue is better understood, your calf position alone will be enough to move the hip over. The opposite cue moves the right hip over to the left.

Spot, Direction, Motivator, and Release

Spot Hip

Direction Away from leg pressure

Motivator Leg pressure

Release   A complete removal of leg pressure

Teaching Steps

STEP ONE: GETTING USED TO SPURS

Warm up with some shoulder serpentines and lope circles (see Lesson 10, p. 179). After you have moved your horse out for a while and he is relaxed, dismount and put on your spurs.

Work on shoulder serpentines again, this time using your legs very gently and carefully to ask your horse to move forward. Given all your previous work, your horse should not overreact, but he may need some time growing comfortable with the new sound—Western spurs make a metallic "jingle"—and feel of the spurs. Work in 10-minute sessions as you have in prior lessons.

End your workout on a quiet note and put your horse away for the day.

STEP TWO: MOVE THE HIP WITH REIN AND LEG PRESSURE

During your next riding session, repeat Step One. At the end of the day's work, if your horse is relaxed and accepting of this new "appendage," offer him a break in an open part of the arena. Pick up your right rein and ask him to move his hip to the left two steps, as you taught him in Lesson 23. Once you get two steps with a "soft nose," release your horse from rein pressure and sit quietly. If he walks forward, increase the pressure until he stops. Repeat this six times, or until you have six in a row that are perfect. Switch sides and repeat the process. Next, combine your leg cue with the rein and complete a dozen responses from the right, then a dozen times from the left (photos 112 A–C). Repeat.

Remember you do not want your horse to step forward or backward. Make sure to release fully and rest him between cues. This is a good step to use as a cool-down after your workout and should be done in a relaxed manner.

STEP THREE: MOVE THE HIP WITH LEG PRESSURE ONLY

Immediately after Step Two, during the same training session or the following day, ask your horse to move his hip with your leg cue *only*. Let's say you want him to move *right*. Slide your left leg back as described in Cues to Use (p. 194) and apply steady pressure with your spur. In your head count, "One-steamboat, two-steamboats," and if there is no response, pick up your left rein and move the hip over two steps without walking forward. Follow this with a full release of rein and leg pressure.

If your horse moves his hip before you finish your two-count, release your leg and reward your horse with a rest and a neck rub. After a short break slide your left leg back again and repeat your request. At this time you are looking for the smallest attempt at understanding the cue. When one step is taken, reward your horse for trying by releasing your leg.

Work on getting one good step from your leg cue alone, until you can ask for a single step 10 times in a row without a mistake. Then switch sides and move in the opposite direction (photo 113). Use this one-step response and lesson as a "cool-down" exercise for the next three riding days—at the end of your workout, spend 10 to 15 minutes on it.

STEP FOUR: TAKING IT FURTHER

In Step Three, you established one good hip-motion step using your leg cue only, and you practiced it for three days.

Introducing Spurs

Using spurs is, of course, your choice. I like to do so around this time, before I begin adding leg cues other than "leg bumping" for forward movement. The reason why spurs help you train is simple: not only do you have a better motivator from your leg, but you can cue your horse more precisely. I find that using spurs too early—while you are still building your horse's confidence—can be too much for him to handle. I do not want to frighten or accidentally "jam" a green horse with a spur, causing him to react out of fear or discomfort. Once he has had ample time under saddle and is used to your legs, then introducing spurs is a logical and useful step.

I prefer spurs with a wide band (more than 1 inch), a 2-inch shank, and a medium-sized soft rowel with soft or flat points. Note: the smaller the rowel on your spurs, the sharper the pressure. And a long shank can be hard to control and should not be used by inexperienced trainers.

Never kick a horse with spurs. Spurs are not meant to inflict pain. Just like any other training tool, they are meant to be used as a cueing aid and motivator. They are meant to be used for soft "bumps," holding pressure steady, or a gentle rolling action where the rowel spins against the horse's skin. Over time, some horses can become very relaxed with the "riding experience," and "going forward" becomes a problem. The soft heel of your boot is more of an annoyance than it is a motivator, and in this case, spurs can help speed up the learning process. As with other motivators, begin softly and only increase pressure gradually if needed.

When I was a guide in the high country, I did not use spurs. I was leading pack horses and loaded down with equipment. I couldn't "manage" my legs easily—with equipment under my fenders—and a mistake in those circumstances could have been dangerous. However, when training performance horses in an arena, I have found spurs helpful and, in my case, necessary. If spurs do not appeal to you, you can certainly train your horse without them. Some responses may be more difficult to teach, but in time, results will be the same.

Photos 112 A–C Belle and I practice turning on the forehand with the one-rein hip motion cue (A). Once she responds correctly to the rein cue only, I add spur pressure to her barrel at the same time as the rein cue (B). We are moving to the left, so my leg cue is applied to the same side as the rein—in this case, the right—slightly back from where it hangs down naturally near the cinch. After two good hip steps to the left (notice Belle's hind legs crossing as they pivot around her front end), I will release my rein and spur pressure and sit quietly as a reward (C).

Photo 113 My reins are slack as my right spur cues Belle just in front of the rear cinch. She responds correctly, moving her hip to the left.

MODERN WISDOM

"Advanced" Means "Concurrent"

As you moved through the Countdown, you have taken your horse through a series of lessons that isolate the five control points (see p. 14) and teach him to respond to various cues. One of the reasons why a solid foundation is so important is that you will need to use these cues simultaneously as maneuvers increase in difficulty. Advanced maneuvers require you control more than one part of your horse at a time.

Advanced control of your horse's body shape and way of going also requires the rider's ability to consistently and completely influence the five control points. When you perform a particular maneuver and one of your control points is "out of position," you need to be able to "put it back in place," while at the same time, managing the other control points. This is multi-tasking in the saddle!

On Day Four, ask for two good steps. Day Five, ask for three good steps, and so forth. By increasing the number of steps by one each day, you will soon be able to perform a complete circle with your horse pivoting the entire way around his front legs (a full "turn on the forehand").

When you can perform a complete turn on the forehand, ask for the same maneuver with less pressure. Cue for hip motion by just sliding your leg back with your calf muscle against the horse. Your spur can be ready to apply pressure if needed, but give your horse a chance to move without it. If he doesn't give the correct response after a two-count, add your spur, and even rein pressure, until he "gets it."

Rider's Block

● Be careful not to apply sudden or strong spur pressure when you teach this new leg cue. If you need more pressure, apply a small amount with your spur, but then back it up with your rein cue. When you rely on heavy spur pressure only, you can wind up with a disgruntled horse that hates your leg.

● If your horse confuses your new leg cue with the *go forward* request, pick up your rein and move the horse's hip to help him find the answer. This stops him from moving forward as he moves his hip around and pivots on his front foot.

Lesson 7's Benefits

● By gaining control over your horse's hips with a leg cue you are freeing up your hands to cue your horse's shoulders and nose. This ability allows you to begin shaping your horse's body for various maneuvers and skills.

Green Light

In Lesson 6 (p. 198), you will ask for hip motion from your leg together with forward movement, so be sure this leg cue is understood at the halt.

Once you can complete a full turn on the forehand in both directions with your leg cue only (and with slack reins), you can move ahead. I recommend at least several days of practice at this level to be certain that the horse's response stays strong when your request gets more challenging.

Hips In

Goals

You will teach your horse to move his hip away from leg pressure. This lesson is an extension of Lesson 7 (p. 194), but you will now ask for hip motion from a walk and jog. You will also require your horse hold his position as he travels forward.

Check-In

In the previous lesson you introduced a leg cue to ask your horse to move his hip over. You also introduced spurs. Before you move ahead with Lesson 6, your *hip motion cue* must be well established at the standstill.

Cues to Use

This lesson combines a few cues. Your newly taught *hip motion cue* from your leg; your *shoulder motion cue* with your reins; early collecting and softening of the nose; and your *go forward cue*.

By using these cues simultaneously, you are going to perform a maneuver called "hips in"—also called "haunches-in," "traverse," or "three-tracking." The result is your horse will travel on one track straight forward with his shoulders, while his hind end will travel on another track, to the inside (closer to the center of the arena). This means that when you travel down the rail and ask your horse to move his hips in to the left, his outside (right) legs pass and cross in front of his inside (left) legs—his right hind leg lines up directly behind his left front leg, and if you were to stand in front of him as he comes toward you, you'd only see three legs. Hence, the terms "three tracks" and "three-tracking."

Teaching Steps

STEP ONE

Warm up with some shoulder serpentines, lope circles, stopping, and backing up before you review Lesson 7. When your horse is relaxed, attentive, and responding well to your leg, immediately move to Step Two, as the leg cue and hip motion response should be fresh in your horse's mind.

STEP TWO

Your aim is to have the horse take one good step in toward the center of the arena with his hips, while keeping his shoulders walking straight along the fence or panels. You will utilize the long straight lengths of the arena for this step.

Walk your horse to the right, about 2 feet away from the arena fence. Slide your left leg back a few inches and lay your calf muscle against the horse's barrel—your "soft" hip motion cue—asking him to move his hip over (photos 114 A–D). Have your spur ready to make contact if needed. Your horse naturally wants to remain aligned, as it's easier for him, so you need to "hold" the right shoulder—using your right rein to cue leftward—from drifting into alignment with the hindquarters moving in. Note: "straight" is just the perfection of left and right, so if your horse moves a shoulder over, put it back on the same path you started with.

Photos 114 A–D   Belle and I begin at a relaxed walk down the rail to the right (A). I apply my left leg while using my right rein to keep her nose looking straight and shoulders from drifting in-ward (B). My leg uses the amount of pressure needed to move her hips inward, and I use the rail to eliminate movement left at this time (C). After the desired number of steps is completed, I offer a full release of leg pressure and continue walking down the rail (D).

Photo 115 Once Belle yields her hindquarters at a walk, we go back to the rail and I ask for the same response at the jog. Do not expect your horse to do well at first. Both the hip and shoulder responses will "fall apart" with speed. You need to teach the correct body position all over again.

If your horse moves his hips over to the right, even a very slight amount, release all leg and rein pressure and allow your horse to continue walking forward. If your horse is unresponsive, add your spur and rest it on your horse's right side in the same way you did in Lesson 7. If he responds, offer a full release. If still unresponsive, "energize" your spur with vibration and jiggling. If he still doesn't "get it," it's time to revisit Lesson 7 and repeat all the teaching steps outlined there.

Once your horse "gives" to the leg cue, allow him to walk a number of steps forward. Repeat this request a few dozen times in each direction. Note: right now you are look-ing for one step over toward the inside; you are not expecting your horse to hold the "hips in" position.

STEP THREE

Repeat Step One at the walk but withhold your release until the horse has moved off your leg two steps down the rail in the "hips in" position. Your horse is now "three-tracking." You may have to add more pressure on your inside rein to prevent the inside shoulder from shifting over to "match" the hindquarters. This increase in rein pressure also keeps your horse's nose straight or slightly to the inside.

Practice requesting two steps—one step shifting the hips and one step traveling forward—dozens of times in each direction. If at any time your horse becomes unresponsive, rest your spur against his side.

Keep the teaching steps small. Only ask for one additional step (*further*) at the walk on each new training day; it won't take long before you can three-track your way down the length of the arena. When you can consistently three-track more than 12 steps in a row, ask for "hips in" off the rail and away from the arena's fence, which helped "hold" your straight line. If you have trouble, focus on an object in the distance and walk toward it.

STEP FOUR

Once you have built up to at least 20 correct "hips in" responses, and you can perform the maneuver away from the fence with a "soft nose" and in a straight line, you can repeat the same exercise while at a relaxed jog (photo 115). Go back to working next to the fence, and begin again asking for one step only. Any time you find your horse unresponsive, work on the exercise at the walk before moving back to the jog.

STEP FIVE

At a walk, choose a straight line down the center of the arena. Keep your horse's front end straight, and ask your horse to perform "hips in" to the left for three steps, followed by "hips in" to the right for three steps (photos 116 A–D). Practice various numbers of steps in different parts of the arena.

Photos 116 A–D Belle and I begin walking in a straight line in the middle of the arena (A). I apply my right-leg hip motion cue to request "hips in" to the left (B). Note: it helps to focus on something at the other end of the arena, such as a tree, to keep your path straight. Belle responds well, so I release her from rein and leg pressures, allowing her to walk straight again (C). I signal for her to move her hips in to the right with my left leg while holding her front end straight with my rein cues (D).

Rider's Block

● Use your spur as a teaching tool and be careful to never startle or unfairly jab your horse. He is learning to move his hip over from a particular leg cue (one that is placed farther back than a shoulder movement cue, see Lesson 3, p. 215) and eventually you want the response to come from just your calf. The spur acts as an additional motivator when you need it.

● If you decide to not wear spurs you may have to revisit Lesson 7 (p. 194) several times or take more "steps back" and back up your leg cue with the reins. The response will be just as strong in the end, but may take more time to teach.

● Your reins should *not* be in constant contact with your horse's mouth. Cue your horse with bit pressure to soften his nose, followed by a release. Use the reins to move a shoulder back to the straight line you want to maintain, and then offer a release. Keep your horse "between your reins," but never allow your horse to lean or pull on your hands.

● Your horse should move away from your leg to the point that the inside front and outside hind foot are on the same track. If your horse bends even more than this, you can allow it, or just use less leg pressure.

● If your horse speeds up when you use your leg, pick up both reins and ask him to stop and back up a few steps with a "soft nose." This leg cue can be confused with a go forward cue.

Lesson 6's Benefits

● You are now controlling your horse's hip motion with your legs and not your hands. This gives you more options for cueing when you take into account that these two control points—the left and right hips—no longer require the use of the reins.

● "Three-tracking" teaches your horse to bend his spine—the front end and hind end are on different tracks or paths of travel. This shape sets your horse up for proper lead departures and more advanced maneuvers down the road.

Green Light

This lesson is a very important building block. You need it to be well understood before you begin Lesson 4 (p. 211). Before trying that lesson, answer these questions:

▶ Can you pivot one full circle on a front leg without picking up your reins? In both directions?

▶ Can you "three-track" your horse down the fence for 20 steps without using more than a light leg or rein pressure? Can you do this down the center of the arena?

▶ Can you switch "hips in" from side to side, asking for a few steps one way and then a few steps the other, with the horse's front end remaining straight?

▶ Can you perform all the above while jogging?

Continue to practice "three-tracking" at a walk and jog, along the fence and in the open, for many days, even as you advance to the next lesson. The more time you practice this response now, the more successful you will be when you teach "leads."

"Clockwork"—Part II: Moving the Shoulders Toward Rein Pressure

Goals

You will teach your horse to move his shoulder over in response to an inside rein cue. You want your horse to *think* "shoulders" when you pick up your reins and direct his movement to precise locations on the imaginary clock face you used in Lesson 11 (p. 165).

Check-In

Your horse must fully understand how to move his hip from your leg cue only. When your horse still requires you to use the reins, it will be more difficult teaching him to *think* "shoulders." So, hold off starting this new lesson until the response to the leg cue is automatic. When you first taught your horse to move his hip in response to a leg cue, you used your rein cue to give him the "answer." As soon as the leg cue is better understood, your leg itself acts as a motivator when your horse is inattentive or unresponsive. By increasing leg pressure and adding vocals, you can avoid using your reins altogether. If he doesn't give you the proper response, you can always pick up a rein, but try to avoid this from now on.

Guiding your horse's direction of travel through hip motion is only a teaching step, and is not how you want your horse to respond in the end—you want the horse to steer through his *front end*. You do need control over your horse's hips but not from your reins, as they are busy controlling other parts of the horse.

By using your reins to control your horse's nose and shoulders only, he will not have to "second guess" where to put his weight. When you pick up your reins and your horse already knows his front end is going to move, he can confidently put his weight on his hind end and be ready to respond. When a horse is unsure whether a rein cue signals a front or hind end move, there is a delay and possible incorrect response.

When you perform "hips in" (see Lesson 6, p. 198) your horse moves—engages—his hips, stepping over from your leg cue, and at the same time your hands instruct the horse to soften his nose and remain traveling straight. This keeps the shoulders aligned as they respond to your rein cues and elevated as the hind end takes weight. "Collection" is not only encouraged by this maneuver, but maintained, as it requires weight to be balanced on an engaged hind end.

Conversely, when you practiced hip serpentines (see Lesson 16, p. 131) your horse was more likely to drop his inside shoulder, thus putting excessive weight on his front end. This makes the horse lose impulsion from his hind end—something key to collection. This basic hip exercise had a purpose early in the Countdown, but it should be abandoned once more advanced movements are being taught.

Lesson 5 allows you to strengthen shoulder control, as both reins will be able to move the shoulders to any spot on your imaginary clock face.

Photos 117 A & B In A you can see a one-rein shoulder motion cue as it draws the rein toward the right side of the saddle horn or pommel. This cue asks the horse to move his right shoulder. (The left rein on the left side of the saddle horn moves the left shoulder.) The angle of the rein is different from the hip motion cue you used earlier in the Countdown, which you see in B. There the rein is drawn toward the horse's hip.

Cues to Use

This new shoulder motion response is cued by a rein. Pick up the slack in the rein on one side and hold steady pressure a few inches or more to the outside of the saddle horn or pommel, in the *direction* of your own shoulder (photos 117 A & B).

This cue resembles the one-rein back-up cue you learned in Lesson 15 (p. 138), but it is angled slightly more away from the saddle horn or pommel. That cue is also a shoulder motion request, but as you may recall, it is performed to the six o'clock position on the imaginary clock face (see p. 167). This new cue asks the horse to step two to five o'clock from the right rein, and 11 to seven o'clock with the left rein.

Spot, Direction, Motivator, and Release

Spot Front foot

Direction Toward an "inside" location on the imaginary clock face

Motivator Bit pressure

Release Cessation of all bit pressure

Teaching Steps

STEP ONE

Begin by reviewing Step One, Lesson 15 (p. 138). Once you've completed this step again, your horse will be *thinking* "shoulders" when you pick up your rein, making the following steps much easier. Note that Step One from Lesson 15 may require some work as your horse has learned to depend on two reins now, but take the time to get it right before you move on.

STEP TWO

Your horse is now consistently stepping toward the six o'clock position from either the left or right rein. Focus on your right rein only. From a standstill, pick up your right rein and hold steady pressure a few inches to the right of where you held your rein for the back-up cue (the six o'clock response). Do not use vocals, legs, or your left hand at this time.

You want your horse to step toward the *five o'clock position* (see photo 95, p. 167). Since you were just asking for six o'clock, your horse will most likely back up. Your rein cue *is* different. Continue to hold rein pressure. At the moment that you see the right foot take that step toward five o'clock, release all rein pressure and sit quiet. If your horse feels the difference in your rein cue and mistakes it for a hip motion cue, hold pressure until the right foot takes that step. This could be a result of moving your hand too far away from the horn.

Aim for a one-step response. Then sit quietly and reward your horse with a neck rub before asking again. Don't pick up your reins too quickly between requests— allow your horse to be rewarded with a real break. Work on Step Two until you get an immediate response two dozen times in a row without a mistake.

Photo 118 I ask Belle to pick up her left front foot and place it on seven o'clock. I do not pick up rein pressure and visualize the shoulder moving away from my hand, but rather picture the shoulder moving toward it. I release as soon as the left shoulder motion occurs.

STEP THREE

At the standstill, pick up your right rein and ask your horse to move his right front foot toward the *four o'clock position* by moving your right hand away from the saddle horn or pommel another inch. Because you only release on this precise step, your horse will learn how to "read" the rein cues even when they differ only slightly. Repeat this request until you can achieve two dozen one-step responses without a mistake.

STEP FOUR

Repeat Steps One, Two, and Three using your left rein (photo 118). Step Two will be toward seven o'clock and Step Three toward eight o'clock.

STEP FIVE

Practice one-step shoulder responses to your one-rein cue to four, five, six, seven, and eight o'clock at the end of your riding session for a number of days.

STEP SIX

At a walk in the riding arena, hold the middle of the reins with your left hand a couple of inches above the horse's mane. With your right hand pick up the rein and cue the horse as you would for a one o'clock response. The difference now is that your horse is moving forward. As your horse softens his nose to your hand and steps toward the one o'clock position, release the rein pressure and continue walking forward.

Now hold the middle of the reins with your right hand and use your left hand to cue the left shoulder in the same way toward the 11 o'clock position. Ask for a good step with a "soft nose" one dozen times in each direction. Then, asking for two steps toward the one o'clock and 11 o'clock positions. Work in sets of 12, and continue adding one step with each set until you can perform gentle arcs and circles. (This is the same as shoulder serpentines—see Lesson 10, p. 179—but using the inside rein as opposed to the outside rein.)

STEP SEVEN

While still at the walk, make your arcs and circles tighter. This gets your horse's feet stepping toward the 10 and two o'clock positions in each direction. In order to step around more with the shoulders, use slightly more pressure with your rein until the horse understands the cue. This is not a big stretch for him, as you have asked him to follow his nose for many rides now. Continue practicing until the horse is very soft to your hands, has a level neckline, and is stepping toward the correct clock mark every time. Remember to walk in a relaxed fashion between requests, rewarding correct responses.

STEP EIGHT

At a walk hold the reins with your left hand a couple of inches above the horse's mane. With your right hand, cue the horse as you would for a four o'clock step as you pick up more pressure. You want your horse to begin by giving his nose and stepping around with his shoulders. The release point will come when the horse stops his right hind foot and steps toward the four o'clock mark. Release after one good step.

This request tells you whether your horse is *thinking* "shoulders" yet. If he softens, and immediately starts to step around with his front end, you can release him. However, if he moves his hip to the left and follows his nose around to the right, you must hold your rein pressure until the hind end stops moving and the front end takes a shoulder step. Never release while the hind end is moving, as this encourages hip motion on a shoulder cue.

Get a dozen good responses before repeating the same request on the left side.

STEP NINE

Repeat Step Eight, but his time, look for *two* good steps with a "soft nose," a level neckline, and a motionless hind end. Once you have two steps or more, the inside hind foot will begin to act as a pivot. This will look similar to the "reverse arc circles" that you did from both the ground and saddle in Lesson 11 (p. 165). The difference here is the horse is looking into his turn and is being cued from the inside rein.

Continue this step over several days, adding one extra step as your horse is ready. If you ask for too much too soon, you may have a hind end that moves around rather than acting as a pivot on the correct inside foot.

When your horse pivots on his outside hind foot, whether you are asking with the inside or outside rein, you need to take a step back and correct this problem immediately. Some horses fix it themselves when speed is added, but some will not. It is best to only release when your horse's footwork is correct.

STEP TEN

From Step One until now may have taken anywhere from five to 15 days. The amount of time it takes is not important. What *is* important is that your horse understands the new inside rein cue and is *thinking* "shoulders." Once your horse is responding well, you can ask for some speed.

At a jog in the riding arena, hold your reins in the middle with your left hand a couple of inches above the horse's mane. With your right hand, pick up the right rein and ask your horse to step his shoulders to the right in a gentle arc, just as you have in the steps prior. Ask for a few steps to begin with, only releasing the horse when his nose is soft, the neckline level, and you feel his front end guiding your direction. Change hands, allow your horse to jog a few steps without being cued and pick up on the left side. Work on various size arcs and circles and request different numbers of steps. Never release your horse if you feel his hind end moving—except to move enough for the horse to follow his nose (photos 119 A–D).

Work in 10-minute sessions as you build the shoulder response. Also use this as a warm-up, cool-down, or softening exercise on a daily basis.

STEP ELEVEN

Jog a straight line. Pick up both reins and ask your horse to stop and back up three steps with a "soft nose" and quick footwork. Pick up your right rein and ask your horse to pivot on his hind right foot one quarter of a circle. Immediately release the reins and ask him to jog off. After a dozen steps or more, ask for the same response, but this time to the left.

Continue working on quarter circles, until they are perfect. Later, you can ask for half circles and full turnarounds (spins).

Getting to where you can ask for a medium-speed, multiple-circle turnaround might take you 10 to 12 months. Your horse could most likely perform fast circles earlier than this, but in order to build a solid foundation with correct footwork in the pattern and a willing attitude, it's best to wait (see sidebar, p. 116).

STEP TWELVE

Practice shoulder serpentines at a jog, now using both your inside and outside rein to shape your horse's neck, soften his nose, and control each shoulder. The "shoulder response" should be improved and there should be less confusion in your horse's mind about which end—front or back—to elevate and move.

Pay attention to all the control points—nose, right shoulder, left shoulder, right hip, and left hip—and adjust your rein and leg pressure to keep your horse bent into your turns and moving forward. You can now "lift" an inside shoulder that has "dropped." This means that when your horse leans into a turn, and the inside shoulder is lower than your outside shoulder, you can use your inside rein to "pick up" that shoulder and ask it to engage.

Rider's Block

● When you begin teaching this new inside rein cue, your horse will offer you hip motion in response to the pressure. As you go through this lesson, you will learn how to *only* release on the correct shoulder motion and teach your horse the difference in the new cue. He may still offer hip motion from time to time, as moving his hips is less work and has found him a release in the past. It is very important on your part to watch and feel which end of your horse is responding to your inside rein cue. If you are not getting the proper response, withhold your release.

● If your horse is crossing his outside front foot *behind* the inside front foot, you need to establish forward motion again. Go back to easy positions on the clock face at a walk (see Step Six, p. 206). This encourages the correct crossing-over pattern. As you build the response back up, your horse is more apt to place his feet correctly.

● Do not be tempted to use both reins as you teach this new cue. Even though the second rein can "help" you get the response you are after, your horse is then responding to that second rein—this lesson is meant to teach your horse how to respond to the *inside rein only*. Only once this cue is

Photos 119 A–D I begin at a relaxed jog with loose reins (A). I pick up my left rein and cue Belle to move her shoulder so the left front foot goes first, allowing the rest of the feet to follow (B). When jogging forward the left front foot will reach close to 10 or 11 o'clock. I "feel" Belle change: she gives to the bit, picks up her shoulders as she turns, and remains moving forward (C). I reward her good effort with a full release of pressure and allow her to move freely (D).

Lesson 5 Goes Further, Faster, and Softer

FURTHER

First, you need the horse to recognize and respond to your new shoulder cue. If your horse doesn't understand what the new rein cue means, practicing it with multiple steps or more difficult positions on the clock face is pointless.

Next, follow the lesson plan and work on gentle arcs and circles. The more releases your horse finds, the stronger the shoulder response will be. Then, as you ask for more difficult shoulder motions, such as a turnaround, keep the number of steps minimal. In this lesson you start with quarter circles. By focusing on *quality* instead of *quantity* of steps, your horse will practice correct footwork and learn accuracy.

In time you can begin asking for half circles, full circles, and multiple circles turning on the hind end. Again, proper footwork and a timely response are your main focus. You are building "muscle memory" to ensure accurate footwork once speed is requested at a later date.

FASTER

Gradually ask for faster gaits as your horse's response improves. It is important to understand that when you ask for more difficult steps, such as a turnaround where your horse steps to the four or seven o'clock marks,

you need to hold off asking for speed until your horse is ready.

If your horse is doing well you may be tempted to ask for more. This can be a mistake. Especially if you plan to show your horse in an event that requires quick and precise shoulder control, you want to build "muscle memory" before you ask for speed.

You may need to wait months before asking for any additional speed. As long as your horse is in a steady rhythm and responding with the correct footwork, focus on building the *further* portion of the exercise first. After 10 to 12 months you will most likely be able to ask for a medium-speed turnaround with multiple circles.

Remember, asking your horse to turnaround, or spin, is not all that difficult. Asking for a *proper* turnaround with an elevated front end, properly shaped neck and face, correct front-end footwork, a stationary hind-end pivot, and an agreeable attitude from your horse—all done on a subtle cue—is very difficult. Take the time necessary to build the right foundation.

SOFTER

With each lesson step you have worked toward gaining a correct response on a light rein cue. Only use more pressure when needed, and continually ask with less pressure, always giving your horse a chance to "work off less."

successfully taught and practiced should you begin combining the two cues simultaneously, as you do in Step Twelve (p. 158).

Lesson 5's Benefits

● Since shoulder response requires effort, when you can control your horse's shoulders impeccably well, you are the leader. This means your horse will "give" you his nose and hips also.

● Since you have isolated each shoulder with both your inside and outside rein, you now have the ability to shape a more complex maneuver, such as a "rollback" or "canter pirouette." You can also correct a poor maneuver, such as a "dropped shoulder" during a lope circle or half-pass.

● Now that the horse's shoulders are cued by the inside and outside rein, you can use just your legs to move the horse's hips. And your horse will not second guess which

Diversity of Styles

There is a wide variety of riding and driving styles around the globe. Each style is unique and has its place in the equine community. Your horse is unaware of which style you prefer to ride, whether it is English, Western, or another.

Regardless of your riding style, you want your horse to be respectful, confident, and skilled, and the Count-down to Broke works for any riding discipline. Which one you focus on after the foundation has been laid depends on your personal aims, but *nothing* is possible until your horse responds to your cues and gives you control over his body.

end to put his weight on when you pick up the reins, as the rein cues are always going to ask for front-end control.

Green Light

This basic lesson cannot be taught in a day, or even a week. As you teach, re-teach, remind, practice, and strengthen shoulder control, you will revisit it.

But for now, in order to move on, you need to have followed all the steps and established good control over your horse's shoulders—he should know what you are asking and how to respond. The response does not have to be perfect, but you do want your horse to find the answer when you need it. If you struggle with a good response at any time, simply start working your way back through the lesson's steps to find what your horse needs to review.

When you can perform one-rein serpentines on a light cue and quarter-circle turnarounds without your horse "offering" his hip, it's a good time to move ahead. Always include shoulder exercises in your workout, as a warm-up or cool-down exercise, to continue to improve the response.

Lope Leads

Goals

Now you will teach your horse a *one-leg cue* that results in him loping off on a requested lead. Your left leg cues your horse for a right lead, and vice versa. Your aim is to only use your leg to cue your horse for the lope departure, from this point on. You are also setting out to establish a departure where your horse immediately responds to your leg and engages his hind end.

Check-In

You have all the tools needed to teach your horse how to depart and remain in a requested lead. Your hands control your horse's nose and shoulders while your legs move the hips to the left or right. These skills help you shape the horse's body for the correct lead departure.

Your earlier lope work has your horse moving forward off your leg pressure as well as growing more comfortable traveling in this gait. It is time to cue your horse for a specific lead each time you lope off.

Cues to Use

To ask for a departure on the left lead, slide your right leg back and apply spur pressure on the horse's barrel a few inches behind the front cinch, but in front of the rear cinch. Your right calf muscle rests on his side and your left leg is not in contact with the horse at all. You do the opposite for the right lead departure.

The lope departure may include a vocal "smooch," "kiss," or "whistle" as needed to entice an immediate response.

Spot, Direction, Motivator, and Release

LEFT LEAD
Spot Left hind foot
Direction Reaching forward and driving the horse into a left-lead lope
Motivator Right leg and spur pressure
Release Cessation of leg pressure and allowing the horse to travel forward at the lope

RIGHT LEAD
Spot Right hind foot
Direction Reaching forward and driving the horse into a right-lead lope
Motivator Left leg and spur pressure
Release Cessation of leg pressure and allowing the horse to travel forward at the lope

Teaching Steps
STEP ONE

At a standstill, practice turning your horse on the forehand in both directions with only your leg cues—this response was taught in Lesson 7 (p. 194). Since you need his hips to respond well in this exercise, it is best to double-check your teaching and remind your horse what the leg cue means before you move on.

Now practice "three-tracking" (as you did in Lesson 6—p. 198) at the walk along the fence as well as down the middle of the arena. Keep your horse's front end straight and his nose soft, and ask him to give a "hips in" from the left to the right. Practice

When you ride a clockwise circle, the "true lead" is the horse's right lead, and on a counterclockwise circle, it is the left lead. The "counter lead" is when your horse lopes with the opposite lead than the direction he is traveling. The "requested lead" is the lead that you cue for—which can be either the "true" or the "counter lead."

Photo 120 I now have all the cues I need to "shape" Belle and confidently ask her to pick up the correct lope lead. As we walk down the rail to the left, I keep her front end straight, her nose a couple inches to the left, and her hips shifted over onto the inside track—"hips in" or the three-tracking position—as I prepare to ask for the lope.

this hip motion and body shape until your horse is responding well to your cues.

The best way to ask your horse to pick up the requested lead is to set him up physically so that response is most likely to happen. A "hips in" or "three-tracking" body shape puts your horse in the ideal position (photo 120).

STEP TWO

Next, you have to establish a *great* lope departure. The best place to work on the departure is in the round pen. The curve of its panels keeps your horse traveling in a circle without your needing to worry about much else.

What Is a Lead?

While your horse is loping, he is said to either be on the left or right lead. To understand how a lead is determined, it is best to begin with the question, "What is the lope?"

A lope has three beats. This means the horse's legs hit the ground three times during a full stride. On a circle, the three "beats" are: the outside hind foot lands on the ground; the inside hind and outside front feet land at the same time; and the inside front foot lands.

When your horse is on his "right lead" as he should be when circling to the right (his "true" lead) the right hind and left front feet land simultaneously. When your horse is on his "left lead" on a circle left, the left hind and right front feet land at the same time.

Ask for the right lead first. This direction encourages the "true lead" as well as the "requested lead" that you are working on (see sidebar, above). As you walk the perimeter of the round pen clockwise, lightly pick up your reins and ask your horse to look into the circle a couple of inches. Slide your left leg back onto the horse's barrel. You should feel him shift his hips in onto the inside track (closer to the middle of the circle). Then, apply your spur and use a vocal cue to ask for the lope.

If the lope departure happens and he's on the requested lead, immediately take your leg away and allow him to lope freely for five circles before walking again. If it does not happen, keep your spur on the horse's side and use vocal encouragement—you must not release the cue/motivator until he lopes. Increasing intensity of your vocal cues can make a big difference, and use a saddle string or open-handed slap on the horse's rump if needed. Since you have spent many days loping, the answer will not be hard for your horse to find.

"Five circles" is of little significance other than you want to reward your horse with free movement, while at the same time you do not want to lope for too long because you want to practice the departure again.

When he lopes off on the *left* lead—the counter lead, and not the lead you requested—stop your horse using both reins, back up three steps with a "soft nose," and begin again. This is also how to correct a horse that picks up a different lead in front than he does in the back, which is called a "disunited" or "cross-canter" (see p. 214). When you "shape" your horse in the ideal position, but he does not lope off on the lead you requested, he most likely "realigned" himself while you weren't looking.

Request at least three departures before you change direction and repeat the process, now traveling counter-clockwise and asking for the left lead.

STEP THREE

Once you have achieved a few good departures on both leads in the round pen, work on Step Two in the larger riding arena. Begin in either direction and ask your horse to pick up the true lead.

Always request the same number of departures on each lead. Train both sides equally, but expect to find that getting the requested lead is more difficult on one side than the other.

STEP FOUR

Walking in a straight line down the rail, ask your horse to "three-track" for a few steps and then request a lope departure (photos 121 A & B). Once you begin loping correctly, practice steering your horse into a large circle or keep him along the fence.

Rider's Block

● Once you start this lesson, avoid using two legs for cueing. Your new *one-leg cue* is what you now use for all departures.

Photos 121 A & B Belle and I stay straight along the rail, then I ask her to shift her hip over "one track" by using my leg cue (A). She is now ready for my lope departure request. With a loud cluck and leg pressure from only my right leg, I request the left lead. This is her "true lead," as we are moving in an arc to the left (B).

Trail Work

Every horse needs his confidence built up. He needs to experience new surroundings and situations in order for him to learn to always be relaxed and willing. One of the best ways to increase the horse's experience level is to spend time riding on the trail.

Ranchers and outfitters know the importance of logging time on the trail. They will ask a young horse that has been started at the ranch to pack a light load into the high country. This is a safe, practical, and productive way of building the horse's experience level.

By asking a young horse to follow a more experienced horse, you keep his mind relaxed while promoting steady forward movement. As your horse gains trail experience, you can begin leading the group in short sessions. This helps your horse develop his confidence even further, as leading the trail is more stressful.

● Should your horse feel your spur and offer you a "hips in" motion, stick with the cue until you achieve the lope. He might be confusing the cues for the hip motion with the lope departure, but it will not be long before he understands the difference. Your job is to *only* release him on the correct response.

● When your horse refuses to lope, use hind-end tapping and vocals to make it happen. If you let your horse ignore one *go forward* request, you will struggle with every subsequent request.

● If your horse repeatedly picks up the wrong lead, as some do, stick with it until he gets it right—then immediately reward him. Not all horses are gifted with lead departures so this lesson may take patience.

● Until you have worked on cueing leads for some time, don't ask for anything but the true lead. This means that when you want a left lead, only do so when you are circling left or in a straight line. A counter lead is more difficult and I cover it in Lesson 2 (p. 221). For the time being, avoid this more difficult request until the basics are taught.

Roadblocks

● Some horses pick up different leads with their front and back legs. This is coined as "cross-firing," "cross-cantering," or a "disunited canter." There is usually no problem recognizing this movement as it feels as if the tires are coming off your ride! This is a mistake, so stop your horse, and begin again. (Note: "cross-firing" actually means that the hind legs come into contact with the front legs, but in Western circles, it is commonly used as mentioned earlier.)

Lesson 4's Benefits

● All advanced maneuvers at the lope are going to depend on correct lead departures. This is a fundamental response that you need to control your horse's movement and balance at the lope.

Green Light

When you can request 50 left-lead and 50 right-lead departures without a mistake, your horse is beginning to "know" his leads and you can move forward in the Countdown. You can spread out this exercise over a number of days and even weeks. The better your horse understands how to lope in response to your leg cue, the easier the remaining lessons will be.

Cueing Shoulder Motion in Response to Leg Pressure

Goals

You want to teach your horse to move his shoulders *away* from a leg cue while at a standstill, walk, jog, and lope. You want to achieve the same quality of response as you did with your reins. You are setting out to steer your horse by cueing his shoulders with your legs, as well as teaching him to perform a turnaround (spin).

Check-In

In preceding lessons you taught your horse to "give" or move his shoulders in response to your reins. You also spent time practicing shoulder control through serpentines, circles, and turn-arounds. At the point you feel your horse is responding well with his shoulders, add this new leg cue. It requests shoulder motion from your horse, just as your rein cues have. This cue is not meant to replace the reins entirely, but to improve your ability to control your horse with your legs only.

Cues to Use

You are introducing a new cue: leg and/ or spur pressure near the front cinch, where your leg naturally hangs down (photo 122). You have already taught a *hip motion cue* with your leg, by sliding your leg back from the cinch a few inches and applying pressure there. This new leg cue does not require you to move your leg forward or backward.

Not only is this new leg pressure used to cue your horse to move his shoulders, you can increasingly strengthen it as an effective motivator.

Spot, Direction, Motivator, and Release

Spot Front shoulder (cueing side)
Direction Away from leg cue
Motivator Leg and/or spur pressure
Release A full removal of all leg and/ or spur pressure

Teaching Steps

STEP ONE

From a standstill pick up both reins and ask the horse's shoulders to move to the left around his hind end one quarter of a circle. Repeat six times with a 10-second break between each maneuver.

Use both reins to ask for a "soft nose" and correct footwork as you step your horse toward four o'clock on your imaginary clock face.

Photo 122 The leg cue for shoulder movement is pressure applied on the horse's barrel where your leg hangs down naturally, close to the cinch or girth.

Photos 123 A & B In A, Belle and I begin at a standstill. Then in B I ask for shoulder motion with both a rein cue and my new leg cue—leg and spur pressure near the front cinch or girth. This helps Belle begin to associate the two cues.

Next, ask for the same counterclockwise quarter-circle turnaround, but this time *add* your new leg cue to the rein cue (photos 123 A & B). Since you want your horse to move *away* from your leg, use your right leg. *Leg* pressure should be steady and firm, while *spur* pressure should be steady and light. After the quarter circle is complete, release both rein and leg pressures. Repeat 12 times with a 10-second break between movements.

By asking for shoulder motion with both rein and leg cues, your horse will begin to associate the response. Keep him from walking forward or backward while you do this.

STEP TWO
From a standstill, apply your right leg *and* light spur pressure to the horse's side as you did in Step One, but this time *without* using the rein cue, again asking for a leftward shoulder motion. Count to two ("One-steamboat, two-steamboats") in your head. If your horse takes even one tiny step from just your leg cue, release leg pressure and offer much praise (photos 124 A–C). If he does not respond by the count of two, pick up both reins as you did in Step One and cue him with rein pressure to complete

the quarter-circle turn on his hind end, followed by a full release and a break.

Once you can consistently achieve a one-step response from just your leg cue to the left, begin again, this time asking with your left leg for lateral shoulder motion to the right. Complete at least two dozen successful requests.

STEP THREE
You now need to spend time practicing the new cue and teaching the response *further*. In Step Two you asked for one-step responses in both directions. Now, apply your leg and spur and when one step has been taken, continue to hold pressure and only release when a *second step* is achieved. When this does not happen, apply more leg pressure and jiggle your spur. Note: do not apply hard or bouncing spur action; just hold the cue with enough pressure to evoke the correct response. If your horse walks forward or backward, pick up your reins, put him back where you started, and follow with a full release. At any time your horse regresses or becomes overly confused, use your reins to help him find the answer.

Photos 124 A–C Leaving my reins slack, I request the shoulder motion to the left with my right leg and spur (A). Belle responds well, crossing her right front foot in front of her left and keeping her hind end stationary (B). I offer her a full release and make sure to assure her that she is doing a good job (C).

Remember—the more times you release pressure for a correct response, the faster your horse will learn!

Ask for two dozen two-step responses before moving on. Work on both sides equally. Now, you can add a third step. Again, ask for two dozen correct steps in a row, and then add a fourth, and so on.

STEP FOUR

After teaching Step One through Step Three, use this relaxing exercise to cool down at the end of your training sessions. Mix up your requests by asking for different numbers of steps and for turns to both the left and right.

The more you repeat this request, the more the correct response will be burned into the horse's memory. And, by spreading the lesson out over many days, you can achieve this while keeping your horse interested and happy.

Work on the turnaround from a halt without using rein cues until you can get one full circle—with just your leg—in both directions for a few days straight (photo 125). The horse's steps around can be slow, but should be in steady rhythm and with correct footwork. His head should remain level with his withers or lower and he should not show any signs of protest.

STEP FIVE

Once you and your horse are comfortable at the standstill, you can begin to use the new leg cue at a walk (*faster*). You want to steer your horse through his shoulders, with your leg cue only.

Begin walking your horse around the arena to the right with the reins completely slack. With your left leg, apply the new leg cue. After working on the above steps, your horse will most likely step away from your leg with his shoulders to the one or two o'clock position. As soon as you see or feel him do this for one or two steps, release your leg pressure and allow the horse to continue walking forward.

both legs to insist he *go forward*, then immediately go back and ask for the shoulder response.

After you get your first shoulder motion off your leg cue to the right, reverse direction and request your horse move to the left away from your right leg. Work on one or two steps in both directions for a while with gentle turns and arcs around the arena. Ask for more steps and longer turns in slow increments. Look for two dozen good responses in a row in both the right and left direction before you ask for an additional step.

Work on building the response *further* until you can perform serpentines and large circles at the walk without mistakes. Once you reach this point, ask for movement with your leg only, and keep your spur off the horse unless he doesn't respond (*softer*). Practice the cue at this level for several days at least before moving on to Step Six.

STEP SIX

Repeat Step Five while asking your horse to remain at the jog. Expect your horse to "fall apart" and not respond well at first. Remain patient and consistent with your cues, and return to your work at the walk if your horse gets frustrated.

You will graduate to performing serpentines and circles at the jog in time. This may take a few days or even weeks. It depends entirely on how well the steps in this lesson are taught, frequency of training rides, and of course your horse. Avoid rushing this step and work at this level until you and your horse are both performing the request and response extremely well.

STEP SEVEN

An important consideration is whether your horse can decipher between your *shoulder motion* and *hip motion* leg cues without fail. You will now test your horse's response to both.

At a standstill, ask your horse to move his shoulder over one quarter of a circle to the right with your *left-leg shoulder-motion cue*. Release on the correct response. Now ask your horse to move his hip around his forehand one quarter

Photo 125 By following the steps in the Countdown, your horse will learn how to respond to your leg cue without help from the reins. Here I demonstrate the ultimate test: Belle steps over willingly and with correct footwork without a bridle or reins.

When your horse does not correctly respond immediately, hold and increase the firmness of your leg cue until he does. If he continues to be inattentive, you can even tap him on the left shoulder with the toe of your boot to say, "Hey, wake up…I'm talking to you!" Then continue to hold the leg cue until he takes one or two steps to the right. If he tries to slow down or stop when you ask him to step to the right, use of a circle with your *left-leg hip-motion cue* (see Lesson 7, p. 194). Release on the correct response. With both legs ask your horse to walk forward three steps, and using both legs ask your horse to stop and back up three steps. Release all leg pressures and halt.

Repeat the same requests, but change direction and use your right leg to cue the horse. By changing up your requests from hip motion to shoulder motion, you help your horse clarify the difference in your leg placement, reducing confusion and gaining a more immediate response.

Mix it up and ask for different numbers of steps in different patterns as a way to cool down your horse at the end of a riding session. By continually reviewing these small "gives," your horse is reminded of what the cues all mean and how to find his release. And, by only using your legs to cue the horse, he learns to be more aware of your seat and legs at all times.

STEP EIGHT

When your horse can perform all the steps in this lesson up to now and you have practiced the responses many times, ask for shoulder motion in response to your leg cue while loping.

In the beginning add your leg while you use your reins to guide the horse. For example, if you are loping a large circle in a clockwise direction and your horse drifts into the circle, use your right rein and leg to cue the horse's shoulders back out onto the circle pattern. Or, if your horse is fading out of the clockwise circle, use your left rein and leg to guide his shoulders back into the circle. It is important to keep your shoulder motion leg cue in the proper position on the horse's side when loping. Remember, if your leg slides back, you will be cueing your horse's hip to move over.

With repetition and a lot of practice, your horse will respond to your leg pressure alone at the lope (photo 126).

Rider's Block

● When you ask for motion of any kind with a leg cue you want a reaction, but not an *overreaction*. Your horse should understand the cue and how he can get his release.

Photo 126   You will soon be able to control your horse without the use of reins at all. Belle and I practice lope circles without a bridle or reins. I use my shoulder motion leg cues to keep her on the correct pattern.

If he is intimidated or confused, you may get an overreaction. To avoid this, apply spur pressure in a fair manner. Use just enough to obtain the correct response and *always* work toward using less. Never startle or punish your horse with your spurs. Fair warning: just as horses become "bit sour" and learn to hate bit pressure, they can become "leg sour," too.

● Your horse will demonstrate what a learning curve really looks like with this lesson! You will find that he "learns" the movement one day, and then the next, acts as if he has never been taught it at all. When this happens, take a step back and build on what he *does* respond to. In time, your horse will respond to all of your cues, (almost!) all of the time.

When your horse performs a turnaround with incorrect footwork, go back to working on them with the use of your reins. In a turnaround, the quality and correctness of the foot pattern should always supersede introducing a new or lighter cue.

Lesson 3's Benefits

You now have a leg cue for moving both the horse's hips and shoulders. The ability to direct your horse's motion through your legs frees up your hands to "shape" your horse's neck and nose as you work on more complex maneuvers.

Also, when combined with a rein cue, this new leg cue allows you to ask for a response more softly. The more you can relay a message to your horse without uncomfortable pressures, the more compliant he will become.

Green Light

This lesson is the prerequisite for many advanced maneuvers in various disciplines that are not within the scope of this book. Spend time isolating the shoulders and teaching them to respond to your leg cue only. You can and will want to combine leg and rein cues later, but in order to have a perfect response, teach the cues separately.

Once you can perform serpentines at the jog with just your legs cueing the horse, you can move on to the next lesson. Continue to teach this lesson until you have completed all the steps as you spend time on the final two lessons in the Countdown.

Perfecting Leads

Goals

First, you want to practice loping in different directions with the horse staying on the requested lead. Second, you want your horse to pick up the requested lead even when he is not in the ideal departure position. Third, you want to improve the overall balance and alignment of your horse's body while he is loping.

Check-In

As discussed in Lesson 4 (p. 211), when your horse travels in a circle to the right—clockwise—his "true lead" is his right lead while his "counter lead" is his left lead. The same holds true for circles to the left—counter-clockwise. The true lead feels natural to the rider. The counter lead does not feel as natural in the beginning. One of your goals with this exercise is to bring the horse into greater balance on both his "true" and "counter" leads in both directions.

Until now, you have only requested a lope departure into the true lead by "three-tracking" (see Lesson 6, p. 198). You will now work on your horse picking up the lead you ask for, even when he is better positioned for the other lead—that is, when he is bent left you can get the right lead, and vice versa.

Before you begin working on counter leads and counter lead departures, you must teach your horse to pick up the true lead every time— review Lesson 4 if necessary.

Balancing Act

A horse naturally picks up the most comfortable lope lead when left alone in the field. This is usually his "true lead." However, in this situation, he does not keep his shoulders evenly balanced, and the inside shoulder tends to lean into his turns. You want your horse to keep his shoulders "lifted," balanced, and ready for a lead change—that is, *aligned*. "Alignment" does not mean perfectly straight. It means "balanced and ready." He can be balanced and ready through a turn or in lateral movement. The best way to achieve this is teach your horse to anticipate a lead change. When he thinks a change is coming soon, he will learn to prepare himself.

To recap: when your horse lopes a circle on his "true lead," two things happen—one, he drops the inside shoulder and leans slightly into the middle of the circle; and so two, he is not ready for a lead change. Your aim is to improve his balance and prepare his mind *and* body for a change of lead by:

1. Loping left, right, and straight on both sides equally.

2. Asking for a change of lead, to improve *readiness*.

When you are first counter loping, avoid making sharp turns. Your horse is performing a new and difficult movement. If you ask him to change direction too quickly he will most likely break out of the gait or make a "flying" lead change (switch from left to right, or right to left) on his own.

Teaching Steps

STEP ONE

In the arena, ask your horse to lope a dozen true-lead circles in a clockwise direction. The circles should be large (60 feet in diameter or greater). Then, transition down to the walk for a full circle, change direction, and lope a dozen circles on his left lead. If your horse is relaxed and willing, move ahead to Step Two. If he is not, repeat the circles in both directions. Note: you do not want to deplete your horse's energy too much.

STEP TWO

Walk your horse on the perimeter of the arena in a clockwise direction. As you turn the corner at one end of the short side so the length of the arena is ahead of you, ask him to depart on his left lead, the *counter* lead. Lope down the rail and as you approach the opposite short end, steer your horse through the corners in a gentle arc with your reins (photo 127). You want to avoid sharp turns!

This counter lead is going to feel awkward to both of you. Your job is to keep your horse loping on his left lead and give him time to adjust to the feel of it. After each gentle arc on the short side, there is a long, straight portion of the arena to relax him a little bit before asking him to turn again.

If your horse breaks gait, set him back up to pick up the left lead on the straight line and begin again. If your horse changes leads on his own in the corner, stop, back up three steps, and immediately ask again for a counter lead lope departure. Continue loping until you feel your horse relax. Note: encourage forward movement with leg bumping (one leg only) if you feel him trying to break gait.

Counter lope for at least five minutes, then transition down to a walk, change direction, and walk the perimeter in a counterclockwise pattern. Let your horse catch his breath before repeating the exercise in the new direction.

STEP TWO QUICK-CHECK

▶ Can you pick up the requested lead with an immediate response?

Photo 127   By asking for straight lines and gentle turns, your horse has a chance to grow comfortable in his "counter" lead. Here, Belle is on her left lead as she lopes the perimeter of the riding arena in a clockwise direction.

▶ Can you keep your horse in a lope without constant encouragement or breaking of gait?

▶ Is your horse relaxing as he turns corners while on his counter lead?

STEP THREE

Walking clockwise around the perimeter of the arena, pick up the left lead on a straight line and begin loping. As you reach the corner on the short side and guide your horse in a gentle arc around the end, hold the arc and continue counter loping on a large circle. After one-and-a-half circles, return to the perimeter. Repeat this circle pattern at the opposite end of the arena.

After numerous circles, slow to the walk and let your horse have a break. Then walk the perimeter in a counter-clockwise direction and repeat the exercise on the horse's right lead.

By asking the horse to travel in a circle on his counter lead, you increase the level of difficulty. By doing so in a gradual way, your horse will be less likely to break gait or grow anxious.

STEP FOUR

Walk clockwise on the perimeter of the arena and depart on the horse's left lead. As you head into the corner of the short side, begin loping a large circle on the counter lead as you did in Step Three. This time, instead of breaking the pattern after one circle, complete six circles, then return to the perimeter, lope off down the long straight side, and repeat the same request on the opposite end of the arena.

After you have completed two circle sessions at each end, break down to a walk and allow your horse to relax and catch his breath. Then, repeat the same exercise in a counterclockwise direction. You have now increased the difficulty of the exercise by requesting that your horse remain on his counter lead for a longer duration of time.

STEP FIVE

At one end of the arena begin loping a large circle clockwise, but this time on your right lead—your true lead. After a few circles, pass directly through the center of the arena and change direction on a figure-eight pattern (while maintaining the lope), and circle your horse on his counter lead at the opposite end (photo 128). Remain on the counter lead for a few circles before again passing through the middle of the arena, changing direction, and circling a few more times on his true lead.

If your horse changes his lead on his own as you change direction, stop him, and immediately get back onto the requested lead. Continue with this exercise until you have loped circles at both ends of the arena a few times each.

Walk and after your horse has had a break, reverse and repeat the same exercise on his left lead.

STEP SIX

Beginning with your right lead in either direction, create your own pattern. Remain at the lope and in the requested right lead while riding circles, figure eights, and straight lines. Avoid sharp changes of direction. Any time you feel your horse anticipating a change of direction, circle him until he relaxes again. Take a walk break, pick up your left lead, and repeat the exercise, working both sides equally.

STEP SEVEN

You will now request a left lead departure while gently bending the horse's body to the right. Your horse is "out of position" and you are testing the lope departure cue. If your horse "knows," his leads he should always depart on the one you request.

Walk a large circle in a clockwise direction. Slide your right leg back and request the left lead departure. *Do not three-track first as you have before.* Allow your horse to walk with only minimal guidance from the reins while he "feels" the lope departure cue. He is learning to prepare his body for the requested lead and will position his own hip where it needs to be.

After the left-lead departure, continue loping on the same circle you just walked. After a few circles, transition down and walk one circle. Repeat the counter lead departure and circles a few times. Then, change the route and begin the same exercise in the counterclockwise direction.

If your horse picks up the wrong lead, stop, back up three steps, and ask again. Never allow your horse to continue loping if it is not the lead you requested.

Rider's Block

● As you ask your horse to counter lope he may want to break down from the gait. This is quite normal at first, so use your one-leg lope cue to encourage him to go forward through the first number of circles.

Photo 128 Belle lopes in a large clockwise circle on her left (counter) lead before we go through the middle of the arena, change direction, and lope several circles on her true lead. This figure eight exercise helps develop her balance and a better response to my lead requests.

● You want your horse to be introduced to counter loping in a way that he can find success. In order to keep him comfortable and in the requested lead, keep the pace relaxed and avoid sharp turns.

● Your horse may surge in speed or act defiantly the first few times you counter lope or change direction into it. This is because the counter lead is more difficult for him than his true lead. Be patient, keep him in the gait, and let him get used to it.

● Short lope sessions can actually work against you when on an anxious or green horse. You want to make sure to lope long enough so your horse becomes relaxed and "accepting." If your horse remains a bit concerned by counter loping, end your day with time circling on his true lead. As with all lope work, you want to end on a relaxed note.

Lesson 2's Benefits

● The lope work in this lesson improves your horse's overall balance. The difference before and after can be quite dramatic. Your horse learns to not "settle into" a circle pattern and is ready to react to a change of direction at any time. Counter loping forces the horse to elevate his shoulders and use his hind legs to drive the gait.

● By asking for a lead departure with increased difficulty, you improve the horse's response to that cue. Each time you release pressure on the correct answer; he is more inclined to respond correctly in the future. You do not want to leave it to chance that your horse picks up the requested lead in the show pen!

● You will also find that your horse learns to rate his own speed while loping. Counter loping is hard work, and the faster he lopes, the more difficult it is. The result: your horse slows down.

Green Light

In order to move ahead with "flying" lead changes (switching leads while remaining at the lope), you want your horse to be attentive, responsive, willing, and balanced. This exercise prepares the horse for Lesson 1 (p. 226), where the Countdown ends with you asking for a lead change on the fly.

Until you can lope on both the true and counter leads comfortably and your horse picks up the requested lead all the time, do not proceed to Lesson 1. It is not that he couldn't perform a flying lead change…maybe you already know he can. But to set him up for the best chance of success, I recommend you complete and confirm this lesson first.

Flying Lead Changes

Flying lead changes can cause anxiety and anticipation—the request is a high-energy maneuver. As a general guideline, begin by only asking for a small number of lead changes on each training day. As your horse grows more skilled and comfortable, start to ask for six to 12 changes per riding session. In time, your horse's confidence and ability will be such that you can ask for more.

Goals

You want to teach your horse to perform a *flying lead change*. This is a loping maneuver where your horse changes leads without transitioning down, but remains in the lope as he switches the orientation of his footfalls. Your aim is for your horse to respond agreeably with a smooth transition. You want him relaxed and confident when you make your request.

Check-In

By preparing your horse with the previous lessons in the Countdown, teaching him to change leads while loping is a natural progression in his training. He may or may not be a "natural lead changer," but what you *can* control is whether or not he is prepared for the request. The following checklist tells you whether your horse is ready for flying lead changes:

▶ You can move your horse's hips with a leg cue at a standstill, walk, and jog, which means you can turn your horse on the forehand *without reins* as well as perform "hips in."

▶ Your horse is relaxed, comfortable, and confident at the lope. You have worked through any problems with him raising his head, surging in speed, breaking down to a slower gait, as well as any confidence issues stemming from having a rider on his back.

▶ Your horse is balanced while on both his true and counter leads. He has experience and is now comfortable with exercises that work on both.

▶ Your horse *always* picks up the requested lead, whether he is looking left, right, or straight ahead.

▶ Your horse trusts your legs and is not overreactive to a spur being used as a cue.

Cues to Use

You will use both your left-lead departure and right-lead departure leg cues during this exercise to ask your horse to change leads while remaining in the lope. When he is loping on his left lead and you want to change to the right, make sure your right leg is off his side before applying your left-leg lope departure cue. The opposite is true for a flying lead change from the right to the left.

Spot, Direction, Motivator, and Release

FLYING LEAD CHANGE FROM LEFT LEAD TO RIGHT LEAD

Spot Horse's left hip

Direction Away from the left leg and to the right

Motivator Leg and/or spur pressure

Release A removal of leg and spur pressure

FLYING LEAD CHANGE FROM RIGHT LEAD TO LEFT LEAD

Spot Horse's right hip

Direction Away from the right leg and to the left

Motivator Leg and/or spur pressure

Release A removal of leg and spur pressure

Teaching Steps

STEP ONE

Start by walking the perimeter of the riding arena in a clockwise direction. At the beginning of the long side of the arena, use your right leg departure cue to ask for a left lead lope (your counter lead). Keep your horse in the lope for a couple minutes or until you feel your horse relax.

As you round the second corner of the short side of the arena and begin loping the long side in a straight line, take your right leg off your horse and use your left leg to cue the horse for the right lead (your true lead). Lay your leg on the horse with steady firmness. If wearing spurs, pressure should be steady but light.

Wait for your horse to sense your leg cues and change leads from his left to his right. As soon as you feel the change happen, remove your leg and spur pressure and continue loping the perimeter of the arena. After one more pass around the arena, transition down and allow him to walk (photos 129 A–C).

If your horse does not change leads, continue to hold your left leg and spur on his side until he does. You are asking him to change from the counter lead, his more difficult lead, to his true lead, which is more comfortable for him. You are also asking for the change to occur on a straight line. These two facts should help ensure the change happens without too much confusion.

The lead change may happen immediately or take a while for the horse to "get it." Either way, your job is to hold the cue with your left leg and wait for the correct response. If he breaks gait and starts to jog, use your left leg to encourage him to pick up the new lead and begin loping again immediately.

The first few times will not necessarily look pretty. Your horse is being asked to perform a difficult maneuver

Level of Difficulty

There are five situations in which you can request a flying lead change, which I list below. They range from the easiest to the most difficult. Knowing this will help you set your horse up for success during your early requests.

1 Changing leads while loping a straight line.

2 Changing from a counter lead to a true lead while on a large circle.

3 Changing from a counter lead to a true lead while on a small circle.

4 Changing from a true lead to a counter lead on a large circle.

5 Changing from a true lead to a counter lead on a small circle.

at speed and needs a few good releases before he catches on. Practice this clockwise pattern until you can achieve two correct changes. Then, go counterclockwise around the arena and repeat Step One, beginning on the right lead.

STEP TWO

Lope your horse on his right lead in a figure-eight pattern. The circles in either direction should be large—at least 60 feet in diameter. Remain on the right lead so one circle is on his true lead while the other his counter lead. Complete the pattern a few times or until your horse is relaxed.

Again pick up your right lead on a circle to the left, so you are counter loping, and look to the center of the arena where you will cross over, change direction, and complete the second half of the figure-eight pattern. Think of your

Photos 129 A–C Missy is loping a straight line down the middle of the arena on her left lead (A). My right leg is lightly resting on her side to help her feel the change that is about to happen. Once Missy is aligned, I take my right leg off her side and apply my left leg (B). Even though Missy has not been asked to perform a flying change before, she knows her leads and has "counter loped" a fair bit, so she swaps leads without hesitation (C). I release my leg and start a circle to the right. Her confidence with this request will improve with repetition.

figure eight taking on the shape of two tear drops, with a long straight section across the middle of the arena. Once your horse is on this straight line and heading to the second circle at the far end of the arena, take your left leg off and apply your right-leg lope departure cue with steady firmness. (Again, any spur pressure should be steady but light.)

Wait for your horse to shift his hips over and switch his lead from the right to the left. As he changes, remove leg pressure and allow him to lope as you begin counter loping the second half of the figure-eight pattern. Ride the pattern a few times without asking for a flying lead change before taking a break.

You need your horse to listen to your lead requests and not decide on his own which lead is correct. So, do not always change leads when you change direction. Even though you need to be on the "correct" lead in a show ring, train your horse to not associate a specific direction with a certain lead.

Softer Lead Changes

As you practice flying lead changes, your horse will become more understanding and willing to respond to your leg cue. Through repetition, he will feel you shift your seat and respond to that and your leg pressure without the use of your spur. Always have spurs available, but as you practice this lesson, you do not need to apply this motivator unless your horse fails to react.

Your horse may surge in speed, kick out, break down to a jog, pin his ears, swish his tail, or remain on the right lead as you head down the straight line connecting the two ends of your figure eight. Your job is to hold steady pressure and guide his movement on the same pattern until you feel the change happen.

If your horse breaks down to a jog or walk, continue to hold your left-lead lope departure cue until he picks it up. If he begins the new circle still on the right lead, continue to hold the left lead cue until he changes. It may happen halfway through the circle or it may happen on the second straight portion of the figure-eight pattern. If you have to hold the cue for two entire circles before he switches, then that is what you have to do.

If your horse is "cross-firing" (see "disunited canter" on p. 214) where he changes his lead in front but not behind, continue to ask for the full lead change for several strides. If it does not happen after one or two strides, bring him down to a jog or walk and immediately pick up the lope on the lead you want.

Once you get two good changes from the horse's right to left lead, begin Step Two again, this time changing from left to right. When you have had success twice on this new side, work on something else or quit for the day, and wait until the next session to ask for another flying lead change.

Practice Step Two until you can get two good changes from both leads on any given day.

STEP THREE

Begin counter loping in a large clockwise circle on your left lead. Focus on keeping a perfect circle pattern and ask your horse to travel with a "soft nose," looking a few inches into the circle.

After about four or five minutes of continuous counter loping, ask your horse to change from his left lead to his right. Take your right leg off his side and apply your left lead lope cue. Your horse is more comfortable on his true lead so will most likely welcome this request.

As soon as your horse changes to the right lead, release your leg pressure and allow him to continue loping for a couple of circles before you transition down to a walk and offer him a break. If he does not change, hold your cue until he does, as you continue on the large circle pattern.

Repeat the same circling exercise with the opposite lead. You want to teach your horse how to change leads equally on both sides.

STEP FOUR

As your horse grows more comfortable, request a change that is more difficult. Repeat Step Two, but lope a smaller circle at either end of your figure eight—around 50 feet in diameter.

STEP FIVE

Lope a large circle in a clockwise pattern on the right lead (your true lead). Ask your horse to change from his true lead to his counter lead by sliding your right leg back. This change is more difficult because your horse is "shaped" toward a clockwise circle.

As before, only release your horse when the correct change happens. Counter lope a few circles before transitioning down. Practice in both directions.

Rider's Block

● When you ask your horse to change his lead on the fly, he may pick up speed and grow anxious. If this behavior continues, ask him to transition down to the jog after he's taken several correct strides. This will help him by promising a more relaxed gait after the high energy maneuver.

● If you always take a break under the shady tree in your riding arena, your horse will soon always want to stop there. If you always ask for high energy maneuvers in the center of your arena, he will soon always grow overly anxious in that area. To avoid this, refrain from performing flying lead changes in the center—instead, practice them everywhere but there.

● A "simple" lead change is when you lope on one lead, transition down to a jog, and then pick up the opposite lead as you lope off. In the beginning, your horse may perform a simple lead change as you request a flying change. You want to avoid this from happening. When your horse jogs between lead requests, his back hollows out and his body elongates. A flying lead change, on the other hand, requires "elevation" and energy. That said, it is okay, if necessary at first, to transition to a walk or halt before asking for the opposite lead. When you ask for a lope departure from a standstill or walk, you can shape your horse better and engage his hind end.

● Pain is a deterrent to learning. If your horse already knows to move his hip over from a leg cue, then you do not need to continue to use the spur. Your horse may become preoccupied with pain from the spur and show signs of displeasure. Remember, you just want enough pressure to motivate him, but no more than that.

● Your horse benefits from working on hip motion exercises on a continual basis. This keeps his responses immediate and light. A good hip motion response helps him understand that you want him to shift his hind end over as you request a flying lead change. Correct flying lead changes take place in the hind end first; the front end follows.

● Even when your horse has never "cross-fired" before (see "disunited canter," p. 214), he may now as the difficulty of the exercise increases. Hold your leg cue until the *full change* happens. If it does not, stop your horse and pick up the new lead from the walk.

● During a show you often have to perform a flying lead as you change direction—from one true lead to another true lead. This type of lead change should only be practiced minimally, as you do not want your horse to ever think he can change leads until you have requested it.

● When working on circles or figure-eight patterns, your horse may anticipate a change in direction as you approach the middle of the arena. If this happens, continue to circle him—or otherwise break the pattern—until you feel him relax.

Roadblocks

● If your horse has difficulty with a solid three-beat lope as described on p. 212 and does not know how to engage his hind end well with a "light" front end, flying lead changes are very difficult to teach. Some horses "trope"—that is, they travel in a shuffling gait halfway between a trot and a lope. The hind end skips along with a cadenced head bob. To fix this problem, speed up the lope until you get a correct, solid three-beats.

Lesson 1's Benefits

● Teaching your horse to perform flying lead changes is fun, useful, and it is a maneuver required in many performance classes in various disciplines. You are perfecting your horse's ability to respond to your lead cues, while remaining at the faster lope gait. This lesson teaches you horse to become even more attentive to your legs, as well as learn to be ready for a lead change. This keeps his front end "light" and encourages hind-end impulsion and overall body balance. You are on your way.

Final Check-In

You've done it. In completing each lesson's objectives, your horse now has a solid foundation of conditioned responses and behavioral patterns. This foundation allows you to further his education and pursue pattern, rail, speed, ranch, or recreational disciplines with confidence. Great job!

The Countdown to Broke is not just about completing a lesson plan; it is about reaching *objectives*. Now that you better understand the teaching process, it is easier for you to create objectives of your own, or adjust parts of this program to suit your own style or discipline better.

As far as being truly "broke," your horse still has a ways to go. All do. Trust and respect can be quickly established, but for both to be *perfect*, more time is needed. As far as your horse having an "infinite" skill set, well, all you can do is keep working on it. If you ever get there, let me know!

You will find these exercises become easier for you with each horse you train. Round-pen work can be exhausting, until you learn how to become efficient with your steps and body position. Groundwork with the dressage whip can feel a bit clumsy, until you've repeated the lessons a few times. Small progressions with only minute changes feel senseless at times. But, I promise your efforts will pay off with a horse that now knows his stuff.

Index

Page numbers in *italic* indicate illustrations or photographs.